The Christian Codependence Recovery Workbook:
From Surviving to Significance
by Stephanie Tucker

Published by:
Spirit of Life Recovery Resources
18652 Florida Street, Suite 200
Huntington Beach, CA 92648

All monies from the sale of this book will help accomplish our mission. Spirit of Life Recovery supports people struggling with emotional and spiritual challenges, including addiction and codependence. Spirit of Life Recovery is a 501(c)(3) non-profit Christian Ministry— Fed tax #27-3278002. To learn more, visit www.spiritoflife-covery.com.

Unless otherwise indicated, all Scripture quotations are taken from the Holy Bible, New Living Translation, copyright 1996, 2004. Used by permission of Tyndale House Publishers, Inc., Wheaton, Illinois 60189. All rights reserved.

Scriptures marked (MSG) taken from The Message. Copyright © 1993, 1994, 1995, 1996, 2000, 2001, 2002. Used by permission of NavPress Publishing Group.

The stories and examples may or may not be based on actual clinical situations; however, where applicable, names have been changed to protect privacy.

This book is not necessarily intended to diagnose or treat your individual issues. If you are in a serious or life-threatening situation, please get professional help immediately. This book is by no means intended to replace the need for professional and/or medical treatment.

For grammar, editorial or any other issues pertaining to the quality of the production

The Christian Codependence Recovery Workbook:
From Surviving to Significance

THIRD REVISION

Written by Stephanie Tucker

Acknowledgements

Thank you to my best friend, partner, mentor and husband, Dr. Robert Tucker. Your passionate pursuit towards helping people encounter freedom through the blood of Jesus Christ is evident in all you do. You have been a guiding influence in my understanding of the nature of addiction and the reality of spiritual warfare. How blessed I am to share, learn, grow, love and experience the fullness of a relationship designed God's way with you.

A special thanks to the students who participated in our first workshop training when this workbook came to fruition. Your encouragement, testimonies and absolute commitment to God's solution inspired me. May God bless and prosper your faithfulness.

Chris G.
Dawn S.
"3Bob"
Heather R.
Juliet V.
Kenny G.
Mike L.
Mike B.
M'Liss S.
Patrick S.
Randall O.
Roxanna G.
Tia D.
Theresa G.
Tracy C.

Dedication

To the men and women who suffer from the soul sickness of codependence. May you learn, understand and be set free through the true Healer. There is a life of passion, purpose and fulfillment awaiting you.

To my precious Bob - without you as my God-given husband, this book would have never been written. You are my rock and my covering. You dealt with the pressures and challenges that came about while working on this project whilemanaging ministry and two little girls. Thank you for loving me through it.

To my beautiful girls, Arianna and Isabella - you are my precious gifts from God who teach me even more deeply the love of our Father in Heaven. I count you as the more important fruit in my life that I will ever have the honor to bear.

And most important, to my Lord and Savior, Jesus Christ. For all You've given me, rescued me from and delivered me out of, Your grace is always sufficient. This is written through You and for You, may You be glorified in it.

Preface

by Stephanie Tucker, MDAAC, RAS, M.Min.

I know so well what it's like to be skeptical. I studied every book, theology, church and belief system imaginable in a desperate quest for life's meaning. With so much information, so many conflicting truths and so much of a disconnect between the Bible and psychology, it seemed sifting to find answers was merely impossible.

The answers to what? To life. To relationships. To love. I wanted to know why my life didn't work. I wanted to know how the Bible, if it really spoke truth, would help me. I found it frustrating that somehow a Bible scripture was meant to apply to me personally, when on the inside, I was so messed up and simply could not make its claims real in my life.

While I certainly won't say I have all the answers, I know that there came a point in my life when I cried out for help. All my "responsible" choices, efforts, attempts to "figure it out" and obsession to "hold it together" left me utterly confused, helpless, hopeless and filled with despair. At my lowest point, I asked Jesus Christ to reveal Himself to me, no matter what the cost might be.

What I found in my state of brokenness is the place I believe every human being that ever existed so deeply desires - a sweet, intimate place of resting in the love, care, guidance, nurturing, protection and kindness of my Lord and Savior. Oh, I knew His theology before. I knew what the Bible taught *about* Him. I just didn't know *Him*. He wasn't a real Person up until the moment that I truly came into a relationship with Him based on His love and grace towards me. And through that relationship, He freed me from my dysfunctional and warped way of thinking, feeling and living. Those changes didn't happen overnight, but they did happen.

What I learned about the soul sickness called "codependence" is something I could never understand had I not experienced it myself. I know the deep pain of codependence. But I also know its deceitfulness. It is a mask that covers people, families, churches and societies, all in the name of "doing good." However it looks on the outside, I know how it kills and destroys life within.

Through my own journey, God prepared me to be able understand, identify, expose and help people, through the direction of the Holy Spirit, overcome the chains and bondage linked to the lifestyle of "survival." I am humbled and honored to be able to dedicate my life both personally and professionally to the arena of Christ-centered codependence recovery. As the Director of Codependence Treatment at New Life Spirit Recovery and Workshop Facilitator at Spirit of Life Recovery, I've been able to participate in the lives of thousands of men and women courageous enough to say "there must be more." And through that willing heart, God has planted a new seed that has led them into a journey of healing, hope and wholeness in Christ Jesus.

If you are skeptical, just as I was, I encourage you to simply open your heart and ask God to reveal truth to you. Wherever your own journey takes you, may His love set you free.

We have improved this edition even more! We've also added a group leaders guide. I personally hold both workshops and training sessions on a regular basis. To learn more, please visit my blog at www.christiancodependence.org.

In His unlimited and matchless grace,

Stephanie Tucker, D. Min., CATC, RAS
Director of Codependence and Family Programs
New Life Spirit Recovery
Director of Codependence and Healing Ministires
Spirit of Life Recovery

www.christiancodependence.org
www.spiritofliferecovery.com
www.newlifespiritrecovery.com

Foreward

Perhaps the most painful experience a sincere leader, pastor, counselor or loved one could endure would be to sit by and watch the destructive behaviors of addiction operating within a family unit with little or no hope of a healthy solution. In truth, no one seeks a solution to a problem they don't believe exists. Alcoholic and addict behaviors are more easily identified, labeled and understood. On the other hand, codependent behaviors typically present themselves as "good acts" being done to benefit others. In most, if not all cases, this is far from true.

This book has the ability to take the reader on a journey of revealing deep conflicts within the soul. With Jesus Christ at the center, this workbook assists the reader in:

- exposing lies
- disclosing truth
- disposing dysfunctional strongholds
- receiving His true healing

I am fortunate to be in a position that allows me to experience firsthand the results of this Christ-centered solution.

Many that struggle with addiction also struggle with codependence. I would like to encourage ministry leaders, Christian treatment facilities, church recovery groups and anyone interested in helping others through the recovery process to add this book to your curriculum.

Dr. Robert T. Tucker
Director of New Life Spirit Recovery
President of the Association of Christian Drug & Alcohol Counselors

Table of Contents

1

Facing Codependence

Workbook Keys

- DEFINE CODEPENDENCE
- ATTRIBUTES OF CODEPENDENCE
- CODEPENDENCE & RELATIONSHIPS
- STEPS TO RECOVERY

And may you have the power to understand, as all God's people should, how wide, how long, how high, and how deep his love is. May you experience the love of Christ, though it is too great to fully understand. Then you will be made complete with all the fullness of life and power that comes from God. (Ephesians 3:18–19).

Our Window of Life

We all grew up with families and experiences that helped us develop our sense of identity and set rules for life that remained with us throughout adulthood. Somewhat like a picture window, these experiences gave us unique insights into what the world was all about, how families function and what to value in our lives. While growing up with these unique windows of perspective, we knew only what we were taught and automatically assumed it was right. Messages and belief systems began to be imprinted upon us, teaching us about ourselves, what to expect from people, how to live our lives, what roles to play and how to care about the people around us. We also developed our concept of God or our lack of belief in Him.

As we approached adulthood, we lived our lives based on those acquired beliefs. We thought, felt and behaved accordingly. What we did seemed to simply be a by-product of who we had become, whether it was right or wrong. Or so we thought.

Some of us have reached a point where we realize that the foundational ways we think, feel, act and live in our relationships are causing us pain. We may continue to believe that other people are responsible for that pain. Or we may be exceedingly harsh on ourselves. We may attempt to fixate on the current events of our lives, not understanding that the issues of today are often influenced by deeper things. In reality, our struggle in relationships and our chronic inability to resolve the problems we face need to be addressed at that foundational level.

Why a Recovery Approach?

Whether or not you identify with being "codependent," rest assured, the purpose of this workbook and the process it outlines has little to do with merely giving you a label. We use this term to describe and identify struggles and behaviors we share. Being able to do so is a gift. By realizing we aren't alone, we can reach out and share in our journey of healing. However, we must never confuse this with allowing the label of codependence to define who we are—it does not.

This workbook is written to encourage those who not only seek to overcome codependent behaviors but who also want to view life and live it from an entirely new perspective. Each chapter is designed to bring a new challenge and an opportunity for growth. Hopefully, this intensive process will help you come to grips with the issues in your life you may not have completely understood. This requires two phases:

- We must see and understand the things in our lives that haven't been working and learn the reasons why.
- We must embrace the authentic design of our lives through the "window of perspective" of a Father who created us for significance, pleasure, passion and the fullness of Himself in us.

Application Points:

Write out your story of what brought you to the point where you are today. Include this information:

1. Beginning with your earliest experience, write your life story of past events and situations that have influenced you, homing in on the painful dynamics that may have affected you. Ask God to show you things you need to see. Visualize yourself walking hand-in-hand with Him, allowing Him to guide you through your past.
2. Describe the current events that led you to realize you need help right now.

I spend money uncontrolably.

The Window of Codependence

Historically, the term *codependency* or *codependence* was used to refer to the significant other of an active alcoholic. That's because it became apparent that just as the alcoholic suffer from distinct symptoms, the dependent family member also share in a unique pattern of behavior. Namely, these are tools of compensation and ultra-controlling behaviors used in an attempt to resolve the alcoholic's problem.

The definition, as we understand it today, applies to much broader situations,

• Growing up poor, moving so much because we were so far behind in rent.
• changing schools.
• Getting beat up.
• Liking my aunt Barbara to come and visit.
Spending the summer with my aunt Judy.
Babysitting my cousin Ann.
My father drinking & falling to sleep with cigarettes.
My brother being a drug dealer.
My brother fondling me as a child.
His friends laying on top of me.
Borrowing clothes to wear to school.
Our house catching on fire twice.

although codependence is most obvious in the addiction cycle. For our purposes, we are going to define codependence as a set of learned coping skills used to function in an environment that is imbalanced and dysfunctional. It is a counterfeit method of expressing love and engaging in healthy, spiritually based relationships. Codependence manifests itself in a variety of behaviors, but the driving factor of a codependent is an internal brokenness.

Definition

In truth, codependence can develop or exist wherever relationships (past or current) are love deficient. It also occurs when we look for something from the outside to fill an "inner void." Since that inner void can be filled only by God, a codependent unknowingly attempts to put a person, situation or thing in God's place. Before we get overwhelmed by that definition, recognize that by default all human beings do this. Therefore, it would be technically correct to say that all people are at some point codependent.

Using things to fill that inner void!

Caregiver Role

Often as codependents we develop a caregiver role to balance a relationship or family system that was imbalanced because of a person who was physically, mentally or emotionally unavailable. The need to overly focus on the needs of this person caused a disruption and misunderstanding of the purpose of relationship. As we focused more on that other person's needs, we may have focused less on our own. Since the person we cared for was unable to give back in the relationship (emotionally, spiritually, financially, physically) we learned to become a compensator and sometimes even a "rescuer." In the process, our own needs were neglected or malnourished, resulting in our spiritual, mental and emotional growth being stunted.

Externally Referenced

Over time, we became very sensitive to the needs and expectations of the people and circumstances surrounding us. As we became accustomed to meeting and accommodating other people's needs, we began to use people or outside circumstances as a reference point for everything in our own life. Our life consisted of our efforts to "read" people through unspoken expressions or by "analyzing" their irrational behavior. By fixating on how to read our environment, we became externally referenced. It drove us to levels of insanity because that reference point often had no logical or rational perspective driving it.

Still, we believed something "on the outside" had the answer to what we needed "on the inside." We ultimately came to believe that our own sense of happiness and fulfillment rested on our ability to help, care for and please the people in our lives. Our inability to do this had the potential to completely crush our sense of worth.

In more advanced levels of codependence, we became so enmeshed with the people in our lives that we were unable to identify our own feelings, thinking and acting. This way of living caused us to disconnect with our true selves, our authentic identities and our true needs. We became a catalyst to the needs of those around us and in some ways our sense of "self" was entirely dissolved. Unable to identify this pattern or the reasons behind it, we were caught in a vicious cycle of attempting to help, fix, change and please others, while at the same time feeling empty, angry, disappointed and disconnected.

Where Is Codependence Developed?

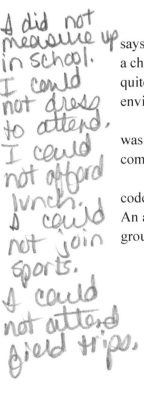

The seed of shame has at some point taken root in the codependent's life. Shame says, "I don't measure up; something is wrong with me." Sometimes shame is imposed on a child in very subtle ways, such as living in a strict Christian home where the child doesn't quite measure up. Sometimes it is imposed in brutal ways from a very chaotic and abusive environment.

The codependent was also most likely not properly given or modeled love. If love was absent or seen as something needing to be earned, the codependent would develop compensation behaviors in adulthood.

Families of origin aren't the only place where a person may be exposed to codependence. Sometimes outside events and relationships can also usher in these behaviors. An abusive marriage, rejection at school or a dysfunctional friendship can all be breeding grounds for codependent tendencies.

Attributes of Codependence

- Believing a relationship with a significant other will fill the ultimate need for love.
- Depending on relationships with emotionally unavailable people to meet own needs.
- Bound in relationships by performance (what I do) rather than core value and worth (who I am).
- Obsession with other people's problems and needs.
- Overly caring for other people to the neglect of self-needs. Feeling victimized and "used" as a result.
- Inability to say NO.
- Tolerating mistreatment or abuse from people, while justifying their behavior and trying to defend them.
- Avoiding conflict with other people to the point of being unable to speak true feelings or ask for valid needs, oftentimes countered by fits of anger or rage (passive-aggression).
- Covering up for irresponsible people in life by lying or "filling in the gaps" to "help" them.
- Doing for others what they should be doing for themselves.
- Attempting to protect a person from emotional pain or the consequences of unhealthy behaviors, such as using drugs and alcohol. Unaware that doing so enables the problem rather than solving it.

Handwritten margin note: I did not measure up in school. I could not dress to attend. I could not afford lunch. I could not join sports. I could not attend field trips.

- Directly or indirectly attempting to fix, manage or control another person's problems, even if meant in a loving way.
- Trying to please people in life by going out of the way to be helpful, thoughtful or caring and then becoming angry or discouraged if the desired response does not come. (Motives were to get the person to respond, rather than to try to bless them.)
- Migrating toward people who need help, yet having a difficult time receiving help from others.
- Being willing to compromise personal belief systems or morals to please another person or to have emotional needs met.
- Worrying about other people's feelings so much that it has a direct effect on one's own feelings. Being bound to another person's emotions. (Happy when they are happy, upset when they are upset.)
- Losing one's own interests and identity in close relationships. Believing that the people in one's life are a direct reflection of oneself.
- Fear of being alone or withdrawing out of fear of close relationships.

The Codependent Personality

As codependents, we often entered into relationships with an external package of loving acts, sacrifice, strength and stability. While some aspects of this truly represented our character, often others covered an inward brokenness. If we were honest, we could admit that deep down we were empty inside, disconnected emotionally and in need of connection to others. We unknowingly attracted broken people into our lives who could initially give us the validation of "feeling needed." But sadly, since we often brought unhealthy people into our lives, these people had little or nothing to offer in return. Thus the cyclical effort to earn love from unavailable people resulted in inner anger, emptiness and a disconnect.

For example, Dana spent most of her life jumping from one relationship to the next. The initial stages of the relationship were filled with passion and excitement. However, as the relationship progressed, she found herself entangled. While at first she appeared to be ultra-loving and caring, Dana was desperately trying to find worthiness by being overly responsible in the relationships. Emotionally, she didn't know how to separate herself from the other person and therefore focused on whatever her partner needed.

Since she often drew addicted or emotionally unavailable men into her life, the relationships would eventually spiral into the depths of insanity. Often these same men she "helped" in so many ways abused, misused and took advantage of her. She would leave a relationship feeling sickened by the compromise of her own morals at the expense of the other person's needs or desires. She usually claimed to be a victim and reasoned that "men are jerks." Even when she swore "never again," she would end up in a similar relationship, and the cycle would be repeated.

Understanding the Behaviorally/Chemically Addicted Personality

To understand a codependent, it's helpful to form an idea of the type of person the codependent attracts. Behaviorally/chemically addictive personalities (BCAP) do not necessarily refer to people who are actively using drugs or alcohol. In fact, addictions come in many forms including anger, rage, sex, religion, and more. Just the same, people who are chemically addicted can, for the most part, possess attributes of codependence. Thus, substance abuse is not what defines these personalities.

Instead, assessing the manifestation of what we will refer to in this chapter as the BCAP can be done through other distinguishing features. These personalities are usually in a survival mode. However, unlike the codependent, they use aggressive, controlling and manipulative methods to get their needs met. Just the same, BCAPs can be charming and sometimes quite sensitive, which can make their pattern of behavior even more confusing. While codependents see their role in relationships as "giving," BCAPs normally see relationships as a means of fulfilling personal needs or interests. They can grow accustomed to being the center of attention and thus feel a deep sense of entitlement.

BCAPs have a genuine need for love, but they are unable to express or support emotional and spiritual connections. They may be able to bond with someone to a degree and even be a "romantic" at first, but eventually this wears off. Often, as negative patterns continue, they can be increasingly hostile and self-centered, making love in their relationships almost impossible.

How Does an Addicted Personality Develop?

As horrible as the behavior may sound, like the codependent, these personalities are usually quite broken inside. While they learn different ways to cope and survive, the codependents and addicts are typically the by-product of the same dysfunctional family system.

Some BCAPs develop in extremely chaotic, abusive and negligent homes. They are required to physically, mentally and emotionally survive without leadership and often "check out" at a very young age. Other BCAPs can be bred in an environment where a parent(s) has not dealt with his or her own codependency issues and has consequently overly "loved" and overly "nurtured" the child through controlling tactics. This parent unknowingly prevented the child from maturing, creating a pattern of learned dependency. Because this type of parent often managed and hovered over the child, the child resented these controlling tactics. While on one hand the child may have rebelled, on the other hand, that same child learned how to manipulate the parent's emotional weaknesses.

For example, Jeff, an active alcoholic, still lived with his mother although he was well into his forties. He occasionally left the nest while involved in an outside relationship, but often those situations were temporary. Although Jeff was an adult, the relationship with his mother remained that of the parent-child dynamic. Jeff's mom took care of his meals, his laundry and all other necessities. In return, Jeff was his mother's friend and companion. He mastered the art of being charming toward her to get whatever he needed. In return, he gave her emotional security.

Jeff's mom wanted the best for him, including that he quit drinking, but she honestly thought her "love" was enough to make him stop. She didn't even mention his drinking or do anything to directly confront him. While others warned her about his alcoholism, she felt it was truly her job to take care of him.

Jeff didn't have any life skills and didn't know how to function outside that family system. He was accustomed to a mother who bailed him out. He denied his alcoholism and used his mother's emotional vulnerabilities to manipulate her and get whatever he needed.

The Cycle of Enablement *powerful*

Why are codependent personalities and BCAPs attracted to each other? It should be obvious. As codependents, we feel affirmation by excessively helping, managing and fixing the people who "need" us. Somehow, we believe our needs will be met through this person as we are able to display acts of "kindness" and "service." We often believe we can rescue a person through efforts to love him or her. Because our need to be loved and accepted is so deep, our attachment to the addicted personality is in fact an addiction itself. What we often don't understand is that it stems from our own brokenness, even though it displays itself as genuine love. The BCAP could not possibly offer the codependent love in return any more than the codependent can offer the BCAP authentic love.

The BCAP needs a codependent in his or her life. The codependent feeds the BCAP's needs on a regular basis and allows him or her to be irresponsible, neglectful and unavailable without experiencing any consequences. The BCAP knows the codependent is seeking his or her love and emotional response and will take advantage and manipulate that at any and all costs. As the addiction or negative behavior increases, the need to have the codependent also increases. The codependent becomes the necessary link to make the BCAP's life "function." If the BCAP had to face the brutal consequences of this kind of behavior without the codependent's intervention, life would not be able to continue as it is.

Table 1: The Cycle of Enablement

Typical Codependent Behavior	Typical Behaviorally/Chemically Addicted Personality (BCAP)
The "love" of the codependent's life is the BCAP. This love controls and influences his/her own thoughts, feelings and behaviors.	The "love" of the BCAP's life is substance (e.g. alcohol, drugs), self-needs or other behavioral problems—this is what controls his/her own thoughts, feelings, and behaviors.
The codependent is dependent on the BCAP and unable to function without the relationship.	The BCAP is dependent on the substance or other behavioral strongholds and unable to function without them.
The codependent is excessively loyal to the BCAP despite the BCAP's disrespect and irresponsibility. The codependent feels a personal responsibility to "help" the BCAP.	The BCAP is avoidant and unfaithful because the addiction or self-needs claim first place in his or her life.
The codependent has the "job" of protecting the BCAP's feelings and therefore is unable to directly ask for his or her own needs to be met.	The BCAP demands the codependent meet his or her personal needs. While appearing strong, the addict is actually emotionally weak, causing others to "walk on eggshells."
The codependent plays the role of the caregiver—needing the BCAP personality to be sick in order to continue in this role. The codependent neglects self in the process.	The BCAP feels entitled and accustomed to be being taken care of. The BCAP needs the codependent in order to continue to live with his or her behaviors.
The codependent becomes a "rescuer" and finds significance in "saving" the BCAP from poor choices, emotional problems or spiritual needs.	The BCAP needs to be kept from the consequences of irresponsibility to remain in his or her behavior pattern.
The codependent is overly responsible to meet his or her own validation and need to be needed.	Because of the irresponsible behavior of the BCAP (emotional, physical, spiritual or other), the BCAP needs someone to blame or to "fill in the gaps."
The codependent suffers from a lack of identity and changes to please others, losing his or her own identity in the process.	The BCAP tells people "who they are" to maintain a sense of control or sometimes ignores and invalidates others altogether.

Typical Codependent Behavior	Typical Behaviorally/Chemically Addicted Personality (BCAP)
The codependent has low self-esteem and self-worth—believing the love of the BCAP will fix him or her.	The BCAP has low self-esteem and self-worth—believing the substance will fix him or her.
The codependent has poor personal boundaries and is easily led to compromise core values and beliefs to earn the love of the BCAP.	The BCAP has no respect for boundaries and will push them to get his or her own needs met at any cost in order to remain in that behavior.

Sadly, this cycle can last a lifetime with neither party being able to identify the underlying driving issues. Whether or not the addictive/enabling cycle applies to us, it's important to know we can participate in this cycle anytime we end up being in imbalanced relationships where we begin to compensate for another person. While the fruits of it might not appear this extreme, often they are similar since codependence revolves around a person who is emotionally, spiritually or physically unavailable. Here are some examples:

- A spouse who chronically works
- A family member with an anger issue
- A child who has emotional problems
- A mother who is overly involved in church activities
- A boss who is aggressive and controlling

If we can recognize this cycle at any level, it's important that we truly understand how and why we may participate. Through our own recovery process, we can alter the harmful ways we have engaged in this behavior. Breaking the cycle of enablement does not always come easy, however. If one person does recover, the other party may initially resent it. Still, the truth is that when the cycle is disrupted, the relationship has a much better chance of eventually becoming healthy. The disruption may allow both parties to eventually find a pathway of recovery. In time, a healing can occur.

Before we go any further, remember that true change occurs at a heart level. That's why if we simply went out and tried to stop or change our external behavior, we would fail. But if we are courageous enough to deal with our own situation, we will enter into a season where we cease striving to make the relationship work and instead make a commitment to deal with our own personal issues and needs. That doesn't mean the relationship will end, but it does mean that our perspective will be altered.

What Is Recovery?

Definition → Recovery is simply bringing something back to its original purpose. The key here is to understand that our ultimate purpose is to be in a relationship with God first and then to have healthy and whole relationships with others. In recovery, we address the "whys" and "hows" of damaging behavior. This is done only to lead us to a genuine solution.

In the prior examples, both Dana and Jeff needed recovery solutions that would enable them to see their problems. It wasn't until Jeff's mother passed away that he was forced to deal with his deep and skewed dependency on both alcohol and his relationship with his mother. When Dana endured enough pain and suffering from a recent break-up, she finally came to understand that something must not be right inside herself.

In recovery, Dana and Jeff needed to do this:

- Understand and identify the problem of their behaviors
- Learn the "why" of their behavior, tracing it to a root level
- Understand what God intended for their lives both personally and in relationships
- Overcome the negative effects of shame
- Embrace the authentic purpose and identity for which they were created

While the codependent and BCAP have different issues, the recovery is very similar. Like a person recovering from any form of addiction, a codependent's recovery is multi-layered. As we deal with one set of issues, we discover more at deeper levels. Therefore, recovery is by no means something that can be performed quickly. It's something that must be worked toward for an entire lifetime.

The steps of recovery introduced in this workbook include these:

1. Identifying our belief systems, emotional strongholds and relationship patterns learned from childhood or other influencing circumstances.

2. Understanding and personally experiencing the love of God; learning to differentiate true love from the counterfeit version of codependence.

3. Learning to surrender our will to the care and provision of God Almighty. This means ending our own efforts to change outcomes in people and circumstances.

4. Seeing things as they really are no matter how painful that may be. God leads us out of our painful past by giving us new belief systems based on His truth.

5. Understanding our true needs and properly grieving and letting go of things that were lost.

6. Removing shame and the effects of negative experiences by learning how to give and receive forgiveness properly. Forgiveness brings ultimate freedom.

7. Understanding that who we are in God's eyes holds much value and allows us to let go of the need to "do things" in order to gain acceptance by God and others.

8. Reconnecting with our true self, the person God made us to be. Finding our authentic identity, purpose and God's plan for our lives.

9. Setting and adhering to healthy boundaries to protect and guide us in healthy ways.

10. Accepting God's promises in our lives despite our circumstances or what other people say or do.

11. Day by day, minute by minute, learning to be internally referenced by the Holy Spirit residing within us, no longer being bound by the external reference of what other people think or feel. Simply put, learning how to "walk in the Spirit."

12. Serving other people by serving Jesus first. Being obedient to whatever and however God chooses to use us in other people's lives. Learning how to not accept the failure or receive the victory for what happens to another person. Truly understanding that God (not me!) is in control.

A Prayer about Codependence

Father God,

      I am reading this book because I recognize that something isn't working in my life. I often feel detached, broken and empty, all the while seemingly being engaged and in a role of "helping" others or holding things together. It's so confusing. It seems I'm doing the right thing, yet at the same time, something is fundamentally wrong in my life and relationships. Please, Lord, help me. Show me truth, but offer it under the power and kindness of Your love toward me. Give me the wisdom and strength to find recovery, and offer me hope that it will lead me into Your abiding joy and peace.

In Jesus's name, amen.

Application Points:

What characteristics describing codependence from this lesson apply to you?

felling, not good enough, rejected - Feeling passed away by friends.

What is your understanding of codependence?

Using coping skills to survive in a situation that is dysfunctional.

Do you identify with the cycle of enablement? How?

Yes! I enabled Paula & Lee to say & do things that were not of the Lord.

In your family of origin, were you in a compensation role?

Yes

In your current family, are you in a compensation role?

What do you hope to gain from recovery?

I want to be free of needing friends to feel accepted. I want to be in control financially

What are you willing to do for recovery to occur in your life?

Read & study this book & pray!

Describe specifics in your life story, not necessarily your current circumstances, that reflect the need to enter into recovery. Be very specific.

Never feeling like I had enough or was good enough, in school, among my friends and in my neighborhood.

- No clothes or clothes that did not fit.
- No lunch money
- Electricity & water being turned off
- not being invited to do things bedoring Chris carrier invited everyone but me. She was a friend hog.

Currently (3 years ago) Paula dumped me for a friendship with Laura. Changed my life & effected me more negatively than I could have ever guessed.

God sent me Mary Johannson and Lanny Bell as two great friends!

2

Family Systems

Workbook Keys

1. GOD'S DESIGN FOR FAMILY
2. DYSFUNCTIONAL FAMILY SYSTEM
3. ROLES OF THE FAMILY
4. ROLE BREAKDOWN
5. THE FAMILY IN RECOVERY

Every one of us has been deeply influenced by our family system of origin. Whether they displayed healthy or unhealthy characteristics, the environment and people who raise us, as well as the experiences that occur within that system, have an incredible effect on our character in adulthood. Somewhat like a "marinade" process, the very patterns of behavior, belief systems and relationship skills that were modeled to us are absorbed by us, flavoring every aspect of our lives.

While our childhood experiences are very influential, it's important to understand that as we embark on a journey to recovery, no matter what our earthly experience is, we have a Heavenly Father who seeks to "re-marinade" us in His truth. Since He is the Creator of the family system, He has the ability to supersede anything negative or toxic that we experienced—if we allow Him to.

Why Did God Create the Family?

Just like human beings, God desired a family of His own to care for, love and bestow His provisions and blessings upon. In fact, all of us were created for *God's pleasure* to be loved and to learn to give His love to others. The heart of God is expressed through the family—it shows His character in action as a parent and spouse and is meant to teach us God's very nature and the depth of His love for us. While as human beings we will fail in our family roles at some level, God fulfills His role in our lives perfectly.

On earth, the purpose of the family was designed to provide a safe haven where love, security and well-being allow for the healthy physical, emotional, mental and spiritual growth of each member, but especially for the children. The family trains and prepares its members for the "battlefield" of life. Children use the home above any outside influence to gain skills, to deal with emotions, to learn relationships and to learn how to love. This special institution is meant to be a place of rest amidst a world filled with troubles and pressures. It's a place where we are meant to experience intimacy and find acceptance.

Understanding the First Family

Before we seek to understand the family in our own life, it's important to know that we were at a disadvantage coming into the world. We inherited dysfunctional family skills from our forefathers, and we have been bound by their toxic results ever since. This simply means that, like it or not, our families will have imperfections.

The history of the first family helps to accurately identify our own challenges within our family systems. In the book of Genesis, we find the famous account of God's creation of Adam and Eve where He says, "It is not good for the man to be alone. I will make a companion who will help him" (Genesis 2:18). When God gave Adam a companion, she was meant to be a tremendous blessing. She was designed to be his perfect mate and helper—someone he could relate to and love.

At first, Adam and Eve enjoyed a safe, fulfilling and blessed covenant where they were "one" with God and each other. They experienced love, peace and joy as they shared and enjoyed fellowship in the comfort and perfection of the garden. But it didn't take long before that same blessing was an entry point for Satan to disrupt God's plan for the family.

Eve's choice to disobey God's simple commandment that she not eat from one particular tree in the garden wasn't just a mistake. She chose to believe and trust that what Satan had told her was true and what God had told her was a lie. Not only that, but as she unseated God's position of authority in her life, she proceeded to influence her husband to do the same. Adam's sin wasn't just that he disobeyed God but that he allowed himself to be influenced by his wife through a lie. In essence, Adam gave her permission to be in position of authority over himself and God. His inability to stand up to her in the name of truth cost him dearly. God held him responsible for the sin of them both because Adam was the designated leader.

The Consequences of Sin

The fall in the garden meant that the fellowship with God had been broken, and the original plan for mankind was forever lost. The consequences of separation from God were unbelievably awful. It left a void inside both Adam and Eve and placed a curse on the very relationship God had meant to be literally "wedded bliss." They would now begin to seek to fill that void improperly, continually heeding other enticements. They would also no longer have the resources necessary to make their relationship work because those resources were based directly on their union with God.

And things got worse. Sin would leave a plague and bring pain to the family system from there on out. While not always a popular teaching, God did in fact place a curse on the gender roles as consequences of the disobedience of Adam and Eve. The male was cursed to work the fields, which meant he would bear the burden of responsibility for working and financially supporting his family. This sense of responsibility would extend to more than just material needs, but he would ultimately be held accountable for all their needs. The female was cursed to painful childbearing, and her now fallen nature would "desire" the love of her husband but would simultaneously resent his authority over her. "And though your desire will be for your husband, he will be your master" (Genesis 3:16).

The irony of these two curses is that they portray the very heart of the breakdown we see occurring in many family systems today. The husband rebels against his gender role by being irresponsible and abandoning his family (or by working too much!). The female rebels against her gender role by trying to gain control over her husband (or expecting him to meet all her needs).

To Adam and Eve—now left with the void of separation from God's Spirit, the consequence of the curses, the demands of daily life tasks and the difficulties of the marriage relationship—would be given the responsibility of raising children. And as much of a precious and sweet blessing as they would be, these children would inherit a fallen sin nature and be born in the world separated from God. This means the children they raised and loved would be subject to corruption. In fact, that corruption caused their firstborn, Cain, to murder their second son, Abel. Sin's grip had seeped into Cain's heart. It had first been planted in Adam and Eve and was inherited by the next generation. Sadly, the consequences of sin can extend to future generations.

Whatever our own experience of tragedy, challenge or heartbreak, the reality of living with a fallen human nature in a fallen world is bound to have negative consequences. It may be comforting to understand that the explanation for all our problems can be found through this first family. We inherited the curse of sin. Furthermore, we inherited the curses attached to the consequence of sin. This means we can't possibly get it right or live without negative results, simply because we are human. And our parents couldn't have either.

The good news comes as we realize that just as God cursed Adam and Eve, He also provided a pathway of redemption. The curse wasn't the end of the story. Along with the empty void, the disconnect and the loss of fellowship with God, a plan of redemption was introduced. This plan of salvation would allow all people to individually find a way back to God (see chapter 8). Not only would individual restoration occur but also families would have the chance to be redeemed.

Through Jesus Christ, the very heart of marriage would be exemplified through this plan of redemption—giving it the opportunity to be healed and restored. In fact, the very purpose of marriage would portray the relationship Christ has with His church. In fulfilling this enormous calling, both spouses could come together in pursuit of spiritual maturity, wholeness and intimacy with God—the ultimate and most fulfilling aspect of marriage.

As we look at and seek to understand our own family systems, we must be consciously aware of the two sides: the fallen nature that is plagued with the curse and the redemptive plan of God through the Lord Jesus Christ that is given to us by grace. By being willing to see both sides, we can face some realities, while at the same time find hope. As we look at this chapter, be courageous and ask God to show you what it is you need to see and understand in order to heal.

A Prayer for Revealing Truth

Father God,

My family life has been far from perfect. I don't want to dwell on or blame my past or current family dynamics, but I do want to understand Your will and purpose in my life. Give me the ability to see exactly what I need to see in order to be set free from any damaging belief systems I may have acquired. Help me, Lord. Be my perfect Father right now and lead and guide me into all truth according to Your perfect will in my life. In Jesus's name, amen.

Building the House God's Way

I have not Let God build our home.

Psalm 127:1 says, "Unless the Lord builds a house, the work of the builders is wasted." If we visualize God's perfect home, we will see a delightful place of rest, solace, love, peace and fulfillment. It will be composed of individual family members working in their God-ordained positions to fulfill the purpose and plan for their family. If a home is operating in God's order, some distinct characteristics are bound to appear:

- Jesus Christ will be placed at the foundation as a real person who is given the ability to be sovereign and in control. Therefore, His love and power will affect all aspects of life.
- Grace will permeate the family's environment. Family members will be allowed to expose their faults and weaknesses without the risk of rejection. Value, acceptance, and core worth will be instilled into all members as a result.
- Unconditional love will be present based on God's love working its way through each family member. This means there are no strings attached and no necessary tasks to perform to earn love.
- The heart will be emphasized more than behaviors. Children will be understood to be precious, valuable and loved no matter what they do. (However, negative behaviors are disciplined).

- Roles and responsibilities will be clearly defined and understood, allowing each family member to take responsibility for his or her own actions and allowing others to take responsibility for theirs.
- Boundaries will be clearly stated, defining what is and what is not acceptable. When boundaries are broken, consequences will be enforced to make it clear that the boundary breach wasn't acceptable.
- Communication is real, open and honest; all family members are allowed to express real feelings and share the challenges of life.
- Consistency will exist day to day, promoting a safe and secure environment for everyone.

When these functions are in place in a family system, some positive benefits will result, including these:

- Security, peace and joy are at the foundation. This does not mean painful circumstances are not present, but it means that through all challenges, there is a sense of God's control, faithfulness and love.
- Family members genuinely desire to submit to one another. When the family is loving, the members will want to please and to surrender personal rights just for the sake of expressing that love.
- The home has a spirit of freedom that allows everyone the opportunity to succeed and fail. It allows children the opportunity to safely learn from mistakes. Freedom is in not being allowed to do just anything; it is in being taught the inherent value of living God's way while exercising the gift of a free will.
- The development of healthy boundaries offers the opportunity to learn how to set personal guidelines and to recognize the value of submitting to all rules and regulations.
- Healthy self-esteem is formed where children are able to find their unique personalities, gifts and identities and learn the value of who they are in God's design.
- The maturity process is nurtured and healthy growth takes place spiritually, emotionally and physically.

As we look at this list, we might get overwhelmed. It should be clear that in some way, our own family experience won't always measure up. But the purpose of understanding God's blueprint for the family isn't just to see how we have failed; it's also to understand His design and purpose for it—which are an expression of

His heart. This means that above anything else, we can peer into our Heavenly Father's desire to relate to us.

A Home that Breaks Down

In truth, wherever the family system falls short, that system is no longer operating as God intended, thus it becomes dysfunctional. Because the family is meant to be a representation of how God loves us, when it is damaged it can cut right to the heart of our perceptions and understanding of God Himself.

Visualize a home being built upon a foundation that is cracked or missing altogether. Without that foundation, everything else will be unstable too. Then, imagine if the walls and roofs were left off or barely secured. It certainly doesn't sound like a home that anyone would feel safe occupying. Finally, what might we find if the house had no supporting beam to hold it up and keep it supported? Its external components may look secure, but eventually the house would cave in.

Since the very purpose of the home is to be a safe haven and shelter, a home that has suffered this level of structural damage is functioning outside its purpose. In fact, rather than protect, it would put the occupants in grave danger.

We would think it insane for anyone to occupy a physical house that looks as though it could crumble, yet many of us have occupied that very type of "house" in our own lives. Our family life apart from God can lead to unbelievable levels of dysfunction. Let's look at some of the ways the family system breaks down:

- Family is driven by the selfish need of family member(s); a person dictates the overall operation. Depending on this person's issues, attitudes, beliefs and addictive behavior, the effect of this can turn a home into a fearful and insecure environment.
- Love is conditional—based on performance—so children quickly recognize that what they do matters more than what they truly feel or experience. They do not understand or see their inherent core value and worth. They learn to position themselves to please their parents or rebel when they cannot live up to the standards imposed on them. They learn that love is not free, but instead comes with strings attached.
- The house is covered by guilt, shame and fear. These negative emotions drive the family members to either attempt to overcome the problems through "good behaviors" or rebel against them.
- Roles are undefined and chaotic. (We will discuss this in more detail later.)
- Proper boundaries have not been established, resulting in a lack of respect for the needs of other family members. This produces a sense that individual rights are not protected. Family members will resort to a form of survival rather than developing the ability to engage with one another in a safe and loving way.

(See chapter 11.)
- A lack of consequences and/or discipline can encourage and enable bad behavior. Wrongful and anger-driven discipline can drive a child to rebellion.
- Lack of honest communication leads to the inability to communicate true thoughts and feelings. Everyone is playing a role in a drama, outwardly pretending to live one way while inwardly being and feeling different. Children in these homes will learn these patterns of communication for a lifetime. They will repress emotions, which can drive all sorts of compulsive and addictive behavior.

This dysfunctional family environment produces:
- A sense of shame, insecurity, fear and anger
- The family member's need to rebel or to overly compensate to hold things together
- Poor personal boundaries
- Lack of control/powerlessness and a sense of feeling trapped
- Poor self-esteem and identity
- Emotional and spiritual immaturity
- Inability to have healthy relationships

Wherever we are today in our family systems, we must know that God's intention is always to bring things back to His original design—this is the restoration process that we will emphasize so often throughout this workbook because it's the entire purpose of recovery. While the purpose of this book isn't geared toward marriage and parenting (that process is dealt with through A House that Grace Built by Stephanie Tucker), it is geared toward the codependent's restoration process, which can ultimately affect the entire family system.

Understanding Family Roles

Since a family system is composed of individual members, we can trace a family's dysfunction back to the individual family members and the roles they perform within that system. Most important is the interaction of the husband and wife and their roles in relation to their children.

As we study these roles, keep in mind that we all need to learn our God-given roles regardless of our marital status. If we've been left or abandoned by our spouse or became a single parent because of other choices we made, this lesson still applies to us. It's important to identify our own childhood experiences as well as to be prepared for our future relationships. If we are married, this lesson is especially applicable. But remember, we are all married to God and are members of His family so we all need to learn how to be healthy and whole within a family system.

God's Order in the Building Process in a Marriage

The most important components of building a home God's way is the order and establishment of the roles within the family system. When things go wrong, it's because a family member isn't able to fulfill his or her role appropriately. When we looked at the dysfunctional family, we pictured some of the fundamental ways a house can break down. Let's take that a step further and look at the failure of the family system in terms of role breakdown. According to God's blueprint, there are some necessary ingredients to make a home operate properly. In the same way, when these elements are missing or the order is broken, some serious consequences will result. We are going to look at this order in detail.

1. Jesus Christ is the foundation upon which the home is built.

When Jesus Christ redeemed the human race, He undid the curse on Adam and Eve. This means that those who accept Him need not live in light of the fall, but in light of God's grace. This puts our roles and responsibilities in an entirely different perspective. The book of Ephesians addresses this "mystery."

Out of respect for Christ, be courteously reverent to one another. Wives, understand and support your husbands in ways that show your support for Christ. The husband provides leadership to his wife the way Christ does to his church, not by domineering but by cherishing. So just as the church submits to Christ as he exercises such leadership, wives should likewise submit to their husbands. Husbands, go all out in your love for your wives, exactly as Christ did for the church—a love marked by giving, not getting. Christ's love makes the church whole. His words evoke her beauty. Everything he does and says is designed to bring the best out of her, dressing her in dazzling white silk, radiant with holiness. And that is how husbands ought to love their wives. They're really doing themselves a favor—since they're already "one" in marriage. No one abuses his own body, does he? No, he feeds and pampers it. That's how Christ treats us, the church, since we are part of his body. And this is why a man leaves father and mother and cherishes his wife. No longer two, they become "one flesh." This is a huge mystery, and I don't pretend to understand it all. What is clearest to me is the way Christ treats the church. And this provides a good picture of how each husband is to treat his wife, loving himself in loving her, and how each wife is to honor her husband (Ephesians 5:21–33 MSG).

Throughout this scripture, we see that Christ is the central theme—with Him at the center, the husband and wife love each other through Him and for Him. That means Christian marriages that aren't working properly aren't just a result of living under a curse, but they are an indication that the couple has not given Jesus Christ full dominion over their lives.

Many marriages can be imbalanced spiritually. One spouse may love God while the other doesn't walk or live by Christian principles. What can we do? The Bible tells us if we are married to an unbeliever we should stay in that marriage if our spouse desires to do so. But if the spouse wants to leave, we can let that happen and proceed with our own lives and future marriage relationships (see 1 Corinthians 7:12–15).

If we have a Christian husband or wife, however, we are always called to stay in that marriage (unless infidelity has occurred or, in some cases, extreme forms of abuse that make the relationship dangerous). When our marriage relationship is lopsided, we must be diligent to fulfill our responsibility as if we are serving Christ directly. We must learn to allow Him to meet our needs Himself and go to Him as the source of the components lacking in our marriage. This of course doesn't mean we have to allow sinful or harmful behaviors from our spouse that directly affect our life. In fact, Jesus Christ Himself doesn't condone or allow them without consequences. But we can still find wholeness despite what our partners choose to do. (For more information, please refer to chapter 11 on boundaries. This subject is also discussed in *A House that Grace Built*.)

Overall, the one conclusion we can draw is that the purpose of our own life and the purposes of marriage are to know and love God first.

2. The husband/father represents the basic frame and infrastructure of a home built on the foundation.

Without a supportive and secure foundation, any type of infrastructure built on it will be insecure. God didn't intend for our lives to work without Him, and this certainly includes marriage. The marriage relationship is meant to portray His relationship with us. According to His purposes, the next important component of building the family is the man's role. The male (father/husband figure) represents the structure of the home itself and is the entire covering, including the walls, roof and all other underlying framework. Obviously, if we picture an actual home, this is what makes a house look like a house.

A home without these components is no home at all! So it's obvious that in using this illustration, the male carries some extremely important responsibilities as the "covering." Let's take a closer look.

The Husband's Responsibilities

- **He is the CEO and leader.** A man is the designated leader of his home. God asks him to be like Christ, to portray the same characteristics as He does as the leader of His church. Men are actually called to be "Jesus in skin" to their wives and families. If he leads by example and in love, he greatly blesses his family.

- **He has God-given authority.** The adult male role is one of authority, whether or not he chooses to accept that position. Just as a country needs a leader and a corporation hires a CEO, the husband/father has been ordained by God to be in the position of authority. Therefore, despite how successful he is at it, the role itself never alters. Ultimately, God holds the man accountable for the entire family system. When something is going wrong, God will look to him first for the corrections.

- **He's called to use love, not control.** The husband is called to love his wife as Christ loves the church. This refers to selfless, unconditional love that isn't based on emotion or on how another loves him in return. His love is a biblical command and clearly sets the course of the entire family system. A husband who abuses his position of authority and unfairly uses force and control is greatly harming his position and all other family members. In fact, without his love, the family will fail at some level.

- **He is given the responsibility of provider and protector.** As we previously learned, part of the curse for the man included being required to provide for the needs of his family. But this isn't just a curse; it's also the result of taking ownership and responsibility for the family's needs because he *loves* them. In fact, if love isn't an element, what would even motivate him to take on that responsibility in the first place? God loves us this very same way. When we live under Him, He brings His provision to us. Likewise, when we live under the covering of male leadership, the male is required by God to meet the designated and legitimate needs of the family.

- **He is a lover.** A man is designed to sexually fulfill his wife, caring about her needs more than his own. This is because his sexuality in marriage is to be rooted in love for her, not merely in self-gratification. Anything outside this context will lead to difficulties.

The Husband's Needs

God gave Adam a helper because He had not designed him to live alone. That's not to say that being single isn't a calling. The apostle Paul was single and encouraged others to stay single if that was their gift. But in marriage, a husband is given certain responsibilities and in return needs certain things from his wife and his family:

- Respect for his position of authority and decision making. He thrives when he is honored by his wife and children and they submit to his leadership.
- The affirmation, support and encouragement of his wife. He thrives when he has a helpmate who takes care of details, fulfills the multiple responsibilities of the household and offers words of encouragement and support.
- The structure and "female touch" in his house. A man is designed to need a "beautifier." His wife's wonderful touch of beauty brings satisfaction and fulfillment to him.
- The enjoyment and sexuality of his wife. This isn't based on her external appearance alone but also on the affection he has for her physically, emotionally and spiritually—which is celebrated through the gift of sex.

It's no coincidence that God ordained a position of authority to Adam and at the same time made it his biggest need to be respected by his wife and children. In fact, in marriage, this is a common pattern—God gives us the desire for something our partner is programmed to provide. A man's need for respect is perfectly legitimate. The problems that can arise often aren't based on those legitimate needs: they occur when that need gets twisted and warped and no longer aligns with God's principles.

For example, a man has an inbred desire for and attraction to his wife—at least initially. His need for sexual relations with her was intended exclusively for the marriage relationship. Once he looks elsewhere, he is no longer properly responding to that inbred need but is abusing it impurely.

In marriage, both husband and wife will struggle to align expectations and perceived needs with the biblical facts of marriage. Sometimes, the man's needs are wrongful desires, and imposing them on his partner or looking anywhere outside that marriage relationship would be inappropriate.

When a Man Doesn't Fulfill His Role

Like housing infrastructure, the male role is so important and so influential, that the entire home will be either stable or weak, based on his availability and fulfillment of that role. All men are prone to fail in this. Men who don't know God and don't have a personal relationship with Jesus Christ have no foundation to build upon and therefore could never fulfill the role as God intends. Even a Christian man will find this task overwhelming and difficult, a challenge he is simply incapable of meeting without depending on the guidance of the Holy Spirit.

These are some of the most significant ways a man warps his role:

- Instead of focusing on loving his wife, he is on the receiving end of her love toward him. In truth, he is meant to be the instigator of love—to chase after her and cover her with it. Her love should be a response to that.
- Instead of protecting, he controls the members of his family in a dictatorial fashion whereby he threatens or abuses them. This will create a hostile environment where family members rebel or seek protection.
- Instead of leading, he avoids his responsibility or allows his wife to be in control.
- Instead of being a provider, he looks to his wife or someone else to provide for him. (There are always exceptions to this in employment hardships, physical disabilities, career pathways, and other issues) He may also focus so much on "providing" that he is unavailable for anything else except his work, thus neglecting other facets of his responsibility (such as love).
- Instead of being sexually faithful to his wife, he engages in relationships outside the marriage.
- Instead of being a steadfast and stable infrastructure, he neglects and abandons the needs of his family. Other than unfaithfulness, a man leaving his family is the biggest tragedy of any in his role.

The loss of this male figure in a family system is as destructive as the loss of the walls and roof of a house. It leaves the family members vulnerable, unprotected, and in a state of chaos and neglect. Usually, in an extreme form, the wife or children will compensate to keep things running or operating smoothly. This compensation role is often at the heart of codependence as we discussed in chapter 1. If the family members don't make up for what's missing, it seems they are bound to suffer devastation and loss.

Being Restored God's Way

If a man has suffered defeat in his position as a husband/father, it's never too late for him to get it right. If you have a husband (or father) who is letting you down, begin to pray for a breakthrough in his life, and learn your part in the relationship.

When he wants to make things right, he must come to understand that he is incapable of fulfilling this role apart from God's power, love and grace operating in his own life. When the man begins to exhibit godly leadership, the entire family system will most certainly be radically influenced as a result. Since the very nature of the man's role is give-based, he must be receiving strength and support from his Father in heaven on a regular basis; otherwise he'll have nothing to offer and will eventually wear out or "check out."

If a man hasn't been operating by godly principles but begins to submit to change, he can't expect the entire family to come into line immediately. For example, a man may have been using drugs and alcohol, causing chaos and pain to the family. If he gets clean and sober through Jesus Christ, he will automatically begin to desire to fulfill his role responsibly. At first, this may not be well received. The family will have spent so much time adjusting to his absence, they may not necessarily want to restore his position of authority. He will need to be steadfast, to rely on the Lord and to understand the power of love. If he does, he will most likely see results. But if he does not, he must learn to cover his family in prayer, to continue to be responsible in his position regardless of their response, and to surrender them daily to God.

Application Point:
Answer the following about the father in your life.

How did my dad love my mother and me?

_____
_____
_____

How did he not love my mother and me?

_____
_____
_____

How did I try to get my dad's love?

_____
_____
_____

How did I respond/rebel to my dad's love efforts?

_____
_____
_____

How did my dad provide for my mother and me?

_____

_____

_____

How did my dad neglect to provide for my needs and for those of my mother?

_____

_____

_____

How did my dad lead my mother and me?

_____

_____

_____

How did he fail to lead my mother and me?

_____

_____

_____

How did I compensate as a result?

_____

_____

_____

How did my dad protect me?

_____

_____

_____

How did my dad fail to protect my mother or me?

_____

_____

_____

What, if anything, did this make me feel?

_____

_____

1. *If you are a female and a wife, go back and answer the questions replacing "dad" with "husband"; then replace "mother" with yourself.*
2. *If you are a male and a husband, go back and answer the questions replacing "dad" with "I"; and "mother" with your wife.*

3. The wife represents the supporting beam or pillar.

The position of a wife is critical in holding the home together. She maintains the overall structure of the home by standing firm in her supportive roles. She can be seen as a decorative pillar that both supports the home's infrastructure and offers a beautifying element. If she leaves her position, the home will be unstable, unsupported and prone to falling apart.

God designed Eve to be Adam's helper. The role of a helper, by definition, describes a supportive role. Most people in our culture view the traditional role of a female to be demeaning and offensive, as if submitting to the male explains that we are "less than." The only thing that makes a female weaker than the male is perhaps her physical strength, and she may be more prone to emotional deceit. But we could interpret *supportive* to mean the strength behind the overall system. It's helpful to see it in this context because a woman's role has extraordinary value in maintaining the function of the family system as a whole. Proverbs 14:1 says, "A wise woman builds her home, but a foolish woman tears it down with her own hands." Her position is not weak. In fact, it is so influential that this scripture says she single-handedly has the potential to either build or destroy her home.

In most corporations, the CEO doesn't perform the day-to-day operations; he oversees and provides the direction, financial goals and future vision of the organization. While he makes all the important decisions, the key operational staff do the majority of the work. Often, those staff members implement the plans and vision of the CEO but have some level of independence and ability to make decisions based on pre-determined boundaries.

In reality, the corporation couldn't operate effectively if those staff members opted instead to fulfill their own goals and agenda. If the CEO is irresponsible or unavailable, those staff members may not have any other choice than to make things work. But without leadership, chaos would result, and the organization could fail.

It's no different with a family system. The supportive role of a wife is critical in implementing the day-to-day routine, in keeping the emotional health of the family in tact and in addressing the basic needs of each member. She may not be the overall boss, but her job is loaded with responsibility. If she were unavailable, the family would suffer loss just as a company with a CEO but no staff to implement his agenda would suffer.

It's important to understand that the female role in its core function is one of *receiving*, just as the male's primary function is one of *giving*. While the husband carries the weight of responsibility, the wife is in a much more vulnerable position. She must receive what the man in her life gives in order to function properly in her role. That doesn't mean she isn't a healthy and whole individual; it simply means that her own responsibilities depend on whether or not he fulfills his. Many times women want financial independence and other freedoms in a marriage for this very reason—they'd rather not have to depend on the husband. However logical it may sound (and women who have been hurt by a man may have a very justifiable reason), this attitude will never lead to the type of marriage God intended. That's because her role is different from the man's. If they are both in the same roles, the female role may be neglected and the male role might be diminished.

The Responsibilities of the Female

- **She is required to be submitted and respectful.** Just as the man is commanded to love his wife, God calls the wife above all else to respect her husband's authority. If we have a difficult time with this, it might be comforting to remember that Jesus Christ submitted to His Father (His authority figure) in all aspects of His life on earth. Submission is key—and God requires that in some areas we submit to each other constantly. The notion of submission is a big challenge for a woman, and she may rebel against her husband, especially when he lacks love. It's helpful to know that she doesn't need to submit to wrongful behaviors of a spouse, just to the position itself.

- **She is a supporter and encourager.** The female role is invaluable in its general nature of support. She is a cheerleader, an encourager, and has the ability to hold many things together simultaneously to keep the home operating properly. Her supporting role helps build the entire family, but her disconnection and lack of support will have the opposite effect. A woman's power lies in her tongue—her words. She can use those words to build up or tear down those around her.

- **She is a beautifier.** A woman possesses a certain quality that allows her to decorate and dress things up to be beautiful, warm and inviting. While not every female may exhibit these characteristics, as a whole this attribute is more common than not. Like a strong pillar, she is a strength in the home yet brings beauty.

- **She is called to nurture.** A female is called to nurture the emotional and spiritual development of her children—making a heart connection and teaching and guiding them in the principles of God's Word. She is often a gifted teacher and, by design, will enjoy interacting and sharing the things she learns with those around her.

- **She is a lover.** A female is designed to be her husband's lover. She is to be desired by him and is to please him, which in turn brings pleasure and love back to her. The picture of a woman's sexuality is one of giving herself to her husband. It's important to know that often a female seeks sexuality for love more so than mere physical pleasure.

The Needs of the Female

When God created a female, He made her with certain needs. She was a different kind of species than Adam. Since God made her to be Adam's helper, she was actually created to "fit" with him. This means what he needed, she could provide. But what she needed, he could provide. This is, of course, not to be confused with the divine and spiritual needs that come from God alone.

- She needs to be given loving leadership—she thrives under a strong infrastructure. However, when the husband doesn't fulfill his responsibilities, she is prone to become angry and bitter, or may exhibit strong codependent tendencies.
- She needs to find acceptance and be shown affection, approval and love by her husband—she thrives under the assurance of his care and appreciation. Since she was created to be his helper, by her very nature she desires his love. This is normal and legitimate in the context of marriage when it isn't interfering with or replacing God's love.
- She needs to be provided for and protected—she thrives when she feels secure and taken care of. A woman is the picture of someone who gets "rescued" or "swept away" by her prince charming. If he doesn't do this, she often attempts to take over his role, but, sadly, she loses that feminine role in the process. In her codependence, she will often attempt to protect, save or rescue him instead.

Just as a man has an inbred need for respect, a woman has an inbred need to be loved. She will always thrive the most under love's influence and rebel the most when it is missing.

When the Female Role Breaks Down

Women who have been abandoned by men may find the previous list to be offensive. Yet all women, if they are honest, want a man to chase after them, love them passionately and provide for them responsibly. It's simply a part of a woman's genetic make-up to desire this. If the man abandons his role at any level, she may be inclined to focus more on completing his masculine role. This is because, without infrastructure, the home can't be maintained or survive.

Even if he's not neglectful of his role, the woman may still want to step into his shoes and take on roles he is meant to fill.

The most significant ways a female may mismanage her role include these:

- She attempts to be the provider and protector of the house in place of her husband. This causes her to see herself in the masculine rather than the feminine position.
- She assumes a position of authority and leadership over her husband. This is at the heart of the fall in the garden. Whether or not her husband is fulfilling his role or not isn't the issue; he is ordained to be in that position, and when the female tries to take over, negative results will follow.
- She is prone to manipulate a man to get him to love her and provide the things she desires. She can be deceitful and charming to get the things she wants, which is a subtle attempt to gain the controlling role in the relationship.
- She fails to nurture the emotional needs of the family. Her lack of ability to teach and nurture her babies and children will greatly affect their emotional maturity and sense of security.
- She neglects or rebels against managing the home and doesn't care about its overall sense of order and beauty. A chaotic home will hurt the entire family.
- She uses her own beauty and/or sexuality to attract or invite the attention of other men. Her beauty is a gift for her husband, not other males. It's okay for men to find her attractive, but she is responsible for how she projects herself to a degree.

Seeing our own breakdown might be painful for some and leave others screaming, "What am I supposed to do if my husband is gone, or if he is unavailable?" The truthful answer is that sometimes a female has to fulfill the masculine role to compensate for what a man isn't doing. If she is single, this is simply a necessary way of life. But if done without an understanding of the importance of her God-given gender role, it can have a profound effect on her identity, how she sees herself and how she engages in all future relationships. It can take her further and further away from a desire to be in a feminine role. In truth, when a woman takes on the masculine role she often wants the control and authority that come with it. Giving up this role once it has been taken can be quite difficult. If you struggle, you are not alone; don't allow that to hinder you from your recovery.

Being Restored God's Way

The wife/mom will blossom when she learns to see herself in a marriage with Jesus Christ—and count on Him as the Lover, Provider, Protector and Giver of what she needs.

True, she may be affected by her husband's absence or failures (if applicable), but she can continue to be the pillar of strength. A woman is admired in our culture when she takes on the man's responsibilities. But if we see it from God's perspective, He approves of a woman with a gracious spirit—a woman with a spirit of submission (see 1 Peter 3:4). That doesn't mean she can't be strong, but neither does she need always to take charge. In fact, her controlling spirit is her biggest character defect. To counter that, her biggest weapon is her relationship with Jesus Christ and her ability to pray for the needs of her husband and children.

A female is an amazing creation. To the degree she can align herself to her identity and purpose in Christ Jesus, she will be able to appreciate her beautiful design as a female. God can and does make up for absent husbands, but He is also capable of restoring them. Change has to start with one person, and she can be that incredible godly influence on her husband simply by demonstrating an intimate relationship with her perfect, loving husband, Jesus Christ. This takes time and requires a deeper understanding of recovery, so give yourself patience and time (this process is discussed in *A House that Grace Built*).

For men and women alike, these roles break down as we learn how to survive without the necessary resources or guidance. That's why we don't have to run away from the things we see in our gender role that may be faulty; we simply need to become aware of what has occurred. Remember, we can't change our *behavior*—God must change our *heart*. The purpose of this workbook is to uproot, expose and deal with the things we need to change and surrender to the things we need to accept. In the process, we get to see and understand who God is, why He made us and the radical love He has for us. Isn't that worth it?

Application Point:
Answer the following about the mother in your life:
How did my mom show respect to my dad?

_____

_____

_____

How did she rebel against his authority?

_____

_____

_____

How did my mom encourage, nurture and support my dad and me?

_____

_____

_____

How did she fail to encourage, nurture and support my dad and me?

_____

_____

_____

As female or a male, what did she teach me about beauty and femininity ?

_____

_____

_____

How do I view the female gender as a whole?

_____

_____

_____

Did my mom possess masculine characteristics? Which ones?

_____

_____

_____

What do I see as unfair or wrong with being a female? (if applicable)

_____

_____

_____

1. *If you are a husband, go back and answer the questions replacing "mom" with "wife" and "dad" with you.*
2. *If you are a wife, go back and replace "mom" with "I" and "dad" with your husband (or significant other).*

The Roles of Children

Children represent future generations. They are brought into the world with basic needs: to be loved, valued and accepted by their parents. While they are born separated from God, they are still by nature precious and innocent. In fact, Jesus said we need to come to Him like a little child.

Children come into the world as helpless, dependent babies who need to rely on their parents to care for them. If they are not cared for and do not bond properly with their parents, they may have bonding and relationship issues their entire lives. In fact, they are most vulnerable and dependent the first three years of life. That's why these are the most formative years of any in developing their sense of security, trust and overall sense of value. Children will be deeply and astonishingly influenced by the marriage relationship and the role and gender models their mom and dad offer. But more than anything else, the ways of loving and relating they learned as children will be brought directly into their adult relationships in areas such as these:

- Mothers teach little girls how to love and care for men.
- Mothers teach little boys how to be loved and be cared for by women.
- Fathers teach little girls how to be loved and cared for by men.
- Fathers teach little boys how to love and care for women.

The roles of the male and female become distorted in various ways, but the effect of these warped roles on children can be permanent. Furthermore, in the extremely dysfunctional family system, children may experience neglect and perhaps even abuse. They may experience the divorce of their parents, be raised by a single parent or be exposed to all sorts of immoral behaviors.

Whenever a parent leaves the position of being responsible, the child will learn how to compensate in some way. If a parent can't or doesn't provide the emotional, physical or spiritual needs of the child, the child will need to learn how to get those needs met on his or her own. This survival mode is often at the very heart of both codependent and the BCAP patterns of behavior.

The Responsibility of Children

Children are to be in a kind of "school" that prepares them for life. They are being trained to be husbands, wives, parents, responsible workers, etc. Children may be given a range of responsibilities as they get older but are overall in the position of learning and being equipped. That's why expecting a child to perform adult roles is so unfair—they are simply incapable of it.

Above all, God asks that children honor, obey and respect their parents' position of authority. In fact, one of the Ten Commandments is based on this very principle.

In unhealthy families, however, children face difficult challenges. They may have parents who seemingly don't deserve any form of respect. If their parents don't offer much of anything, the children become more "adult" than their parents. Should children respect their parents in those situations? Like a spouse, children don't have to accept a parent's bad behavior, but they do need to honor the parental position. The problem is that children don't know the difference. Therefore, in attempting to love and accept a parent, a child often unknowingly accepts the parent's bad behaviors as being okay and therefore is prone to repeat that behavior. This could be biblically considered a "generational curse" where the same negative strongholds are passed on from one generation to the next.

The Needs of Children

- Above all, children need love. They will blossom and mature in the security of knowing that, despite what they do, the people in their lives truly love them. If love is lacking, their entire sense of security and purpose may be damaged at some level.
- As children grow, they need to be disciplined and understand the difference between right and wrong. A parent who "loves" a child by trying to please him or her and never assigns consequences for bad behavior isn't loving that child at all. Discipline is love.
- Children need to be taught. In healthy family systems, children are given plenty of room to make mistakes and fail in the learning process. However, if the environment is strict or shame-based, they may never understand the general nature of learning and be prone to perfectionism, performance-based approval and/or rebellion. In other environments, children aren't taught at all and thus go through life attempting to figure things out.

How Children's Roles Become Distorted

Children in dysfunctional situations will act out in a variety of ways. Children whose needs are not met or aren't loved properly will need to learn to survive somehow. They may do some of the following:

- **Try to take on adult roles and responsibilities, becoming "mini-adults."** These children will suffer from enormous disconnection and denial of their true needs and desires. They will not learn to see or value themselves but will focus on their "job" to help and resolve the problems of those around them. (This is the development of the codependent personality.)
- **Rebel against the entire family system and behave in noticeably disrespectful ways.** These children may begin to use drugs and alcohol at a young age or become pregnant as teenagers. The parents may become ashamed of this child and blame the child for all the problems, but in a dysfunctional environment, rebellious children are often acting out the true nature of what is taking place

in the home. Even though they are pegged the "bad" one, they are often more emotionally honest than the other members. (This is the development of the BCAP.)

- **Withdraw and hide, isolating themselves from the family and from other relationships.** These children are very fearful and will have a difficult time socializing or interacting in relationships at any level. They may be prone to take on an addicted personality.

Let's look at Jesse's family. As a young girl, her father was an alcoholic who eventually abandoned his role and left the family altogether. But while he still lived in the home, Jesse's mom took over most of the daily tasks. She was the financial earner and did all the hands-on tasks of operating the home. Jesse's dad, on the other hand, was often out drinking with his friends. He hopped from job to job and was never able to hold a responsible position. He became violent and angry when drunk, and as a result, Jesse developed a deep and overwhelming fear of his presence in the home.

Watching her mom suffer, Jesse felt an obligation to help her. Jesse took on adult responsibilities from a young age. Her mom depended on Jesse not just for the functional aspects of running the house but also often used her for her own emotional support system. Because of this, Jesse always felt she had slid into an adult role and therefore abandoned her own childlike needs. Rather than receive from a parent, she was prone to think about family responsibilities. This taught Jesse some twisted and warped belief systems about the roles of the husband/father and wife/mother, including these:

- A male figure was unavailable to her—causing her to believe that she wasn't worthy of being provided for, protected or loved by a man.
- A female figure modeled the masculine role—causing her to believe that a female's role was authoritative, provisionary, protective, etc. She ended up "mothering" men rather than expecting them to lead.
- Her childhood role was one of acting and behaving like an adult, causing her to believe she wasn't entitled to the needs other children had, and therefore she bypassed childhood altogether.

Jesse grew up to marry a chemically dependent man who showed her a great deal of love initially but eventually took on many of the same characteristics as her father. She naturally mothered him, took care of him and felt the obligation to support the family financially and practically.

Jesse was living under the curse of her own familial experience. While her intentions were entirely good, she wound up repeating the same family roles in her adult life as she espoused in her childhood. Furthermore, because she was asked to carry the weight of a parent's needs physically, financially and emotionally, she not only denied her own needs but was also asked to perform mature roles while still immature. She didn't "grow up too fast" but in some sense never grew up at all.

The Family in Recovery

In recovery, Jesse would learn to recognize how her own family experience had shaped her belief systems. She saw how the comfort and familiarity of skewed roles transferred into her future marriage relationship, even though at first it seemed "packaged" so differently. She would also learn God's intent and purpose for her family and marriage role and, slowly, she would allow God to transform her personality.

Just as every family member has learned to adjust and cope in a negative way, each family member must address his or her own issues and learn to align life according to God's principles. There is no quick fix to this process, but for the codependent, change is entirely possible. Even with just the codependent offering changes, the family has more potential to become healthy.

Whatever you have experienced in your own family life, or are currently experiencing, remember that God is a restorer. This means we don't need to get it right the first time for God to intervene and make something (or someone) that was broken, whole again.

If you are dealing with past issues in your family, it is important that you properly deal with the circumstances that occurred and actually grieve for what was lost (we will address this in chapters 6–9). You may need to grieve over abuse or neglect. You may need to grieve over abandonment and loss. But your ultimate healing will come in understanding the heart of your Heavenly Father. As we will learn, this Heavenly Father is capable of replacing each and every need we lost in our childhood. He can mend every wound. Nothing our earthly parents did or didn't do can permanently hurt us.

If you are dealing with current family issues, remember that a family will never change by the members attempting to change or fix each other. This is often what happens, and it only escalates and aggravates the core problems. God alone has the power to change our family members (see chapter 5). Sometimes the only way we can remain healthy and find personal restoration in an unhealthy family system is by setting boundaries and adhering to them (see chapter 11). This can even include separation for a period.

What is the real weapon? Prayer! When we embrace the understanding that we are powerless over our family members, we can at the same time recognize that God is more powerful. Therefore, prayer alone is our greatest weapon in dealing with the difficult behaviors of a family member. Even when we don't see the evidence of it, we know that God is faithful in answering the cries of His children. He is after all, the perfect Father. We can depend on His love even when our own family has seemingly deserted us.

Remember these important steps in trying to understand how families are restored:

1. The family is composed of individuals who each contribute to the healthiness or unhealthiness of the system.
2. Change happens only by recognizing a problem.
3. Family members can be responsible only for changing themselves, not the other members.
4. God is the only one with the ability to change our hearts.

The Family of God

As Christians, we are brought into the body of Christ and are in fact married to Jesus Christ. Within this family, God is our Father. This turns fellow Christians into our brothers and sisters in Christ. If we have difficult or imbalanced family systems, the church is a new family where we can find godly examples, be encouraged in our own biblical roles and learn how to work out these principles with others who are like-minded. Now, that doesn't mean there won't be dysfunctional church families—some churches can also be unhealthy. So if you are looking for a church family, be sure to find a good match. Also, seek out the support of Christian recovery groups such as Celebrate Recovery. These wonderful places of support can also be a spiritual family to you as you go through your journey.

God intended His church, including Christian recovery, to be the place where we put all these principles into action. But it's also a place where God can make up for the losses and absences in our own life by giving us spiritual parents, spiritual children, spiritual gender models and close friends. Make finding a healthy church part of your recovery goal.

A Prayer for My Family

Father God,

I am so grateful to know that You are the source of truth. As painful as it can be to see how my own family life has fallen short of this plan You provide, I have so much hope that You are already in the process of restoring that which has been broken. Teach me, Father, how to end generational sin and cycles of behavior that are harmful. Help me to fulfill the role You designed for me.

I am grateful that You already see me as Your perfect child. Change my heart, not merely my outward actions. Lead me into the life You intended and show me anything and everything that is not of You so I can make it right.

I also pray for my family members. Lord, I hold them up to You. You alone have the ability to restore my family. I thank You in advance and praise Your name. You are good. You are in control.

In Jesus's name, amen.

Application Points:

Describe your family system as you were growing up.

_____

_____

_____

How was God seen in your family? Was He someone to be feared or loved, or was He non-existent?

_____

_____

_____

Describe your current family system.

_____

_____

_____

What do you see working in your life that is functional?

_____

_____

_____

What do you see working in your life that is dysfunctional?

_____

_____

_____

3

Emotional Strongholds

Workbook Keys

- EXPLAIN THE PURPOSE OF EMOTIONS
- EXPLAIN THE DIFFERENT TYPE OF EMOTIONS
- HOW CAN WE OVERCOME DIFFICULT EMOTIONS?

Most of us reached a point where the emotional pain in our lives drove us to seek help. We picked up this book, began a program or just prayed that God would remove our pain. At the beginning of this journey, we are often filled with so many negative emotions that we don't even know where to begin. Like popping an aspirin for a headache, we are looking for the shortest and quickest fix that can take the pain away. For the codependent, our attempts to medicate and deal with pain are usually quite subtle. Unlike the chemically dependent, we may not have recognizable addictions in our life, but we have developed other unhealthy mechanisms in an attempt to overcome pain.

As difficult as they can seem, emotions really do have a purpose. Furthermore, as we learn to properly identify them, we can gain some perspective, thus making them lose their intensity. While this entire workbook will deal with this area, we are going to take a glimpse of some of the most common emotional strongholds. But just as important, we are going to learn about the purpose of emotions and the overall strategies we can begin to develop to cope with them.

Are Emotions Bad?

We may have been taught that emotions are wrong or something we aren't allowed to express. We may have learned to cover them over. We may have even been taught by Christianity that all emotions are "bad," but clearly this isn't the case. Since we are created in the image of God, we should first understand that emotions are simply part of what makes us human beings. God gave us emotions so we could feel, be passionate and experience the fullness of life. God also exhibited emotions (see Psalms 33:5; 95:10; Isaiah 49:1516; 61:8; Zephaniah 3:17). If God Himself has emotions, clearly they cannot always be wrong in and of themselves. However, just like anything else, our emotions can get twisted and skewed. When we are living apart from God's plan, there are many negative consequences. Emotional pain is one of those consequences.

The Purpose of Emotions

Emotions are like the engine light in a vehicle. When emotions go off, we must understand that something is happening "in our engine" and the emotion is a warning sign. If we learn of sad news, the normal reaction should be sadness and grief. If we feel conviction that we've done something wrong, we need to get right with God. Our emotions aren't the issue. They are merely an expression of the issue.

Imagine life if we didn't feel. Imagine if we didn't have the capacity to respond and experience life with emotion. Life would be dull and shallow at best, to the point of being meaningless. If we didn't feel, we'd be no different from a computer or a robot.

On the other hand, we can be completely imprisoned by our emotions. When we've lost control of our emotions, we no longer understand or identify the issues that drive them, and we allow them to reign and rule in our life.

The Origin of Negative Emotions

Most negative emotions come from faulty beliefs and faulty thinking. Believing something that is rooted in our flesh—Satan's lies or the philosophy and systems of the world—leads to faulty thinking. What we think affects how we feel. What we feel influences our behaviors. It looks something like this:

Beliefs →Thoughts→Feelings→Behaviors

It's important to understand that while our thoughts and beliefs are a choice based on our free will, emotions are irrational. If someone tells us to "stop feeling that way," we wouldn't be able to. Instead, we would need to stop believing or thinking that way.

To put it into perspective, imagine you just found out someone you loved had been in a terrible car accident. If you chose to believe that, your emotional response would be great sorrow and anxiety. You might run to the hospital or begin to make phone calls to alert others to the news. Now imagine you discovered you were misinformed. In fact, the loved one in your life is perfectly fine! Once you learned the family member was safe, your emotions would stabilize and your behavior would instantly change.

If your emotions are causing you continual pain and suffering, it's imperative that you learn more about them and what might be driving them. The purpose of later chapters is to diagnose those driving roots. For now, let's seek to understand some of the most common emotional challenges we face.

Anger: The Emotion of Defense

Anger is a defensive emotion that arises when we feel our boundaries and sense of rights have been somehow violated. Anger is an attempt to hold on to what we have, to validate how we feel or to protect what we feel entitled to possess. Thus, it's a form of self-preservation. We can also experience anger when our own sense of worth is threatened, our basic needs are not properly met or we feel our beliefs are under attack. Anger is normally a secondary emotion—it is driven by a deeper emotion that masks the initial emotion.

Most people who suffer from codependence experience a lot of anger. Because we are attempting to balance imbalanced relationships, a sense of violation and being used is likely to result, even if we don't express those feelings outwardly. When anger results in violence, rage and other erratic behaviors, it's easy to recognize, but not all anger escalates to those levels. Sometimes anger can be very subtle and hidden. Many people say, "I'm so frustrated" or "This is really taking a toll on me," but don't recognize that anger.

Identifying Anger

Anger can arise in these circumstances (and more):

- We feel ignored.
- We feel worthless.
- We feel powerless.
- We feel our safety threatened.
- We feel that our basic needs won't be met.
- We feel unloved.
- We feel rejected.
- We feel unappreciated.
- We feel violated.
- We feel disrespected for our moral beliefs.
- We feel we aren't being taken seriously.
- We feel we are being ridiculed.
- We feel abandoned.
- We feel used.

Examples of Anger

- A wife and mom takes care of her family's needs. She says little and expects little in return. She would be described by everyone who knows her as being friendly. But she is frustrated and lonely on the inside, and no one really knows it—including herself.
- A successful worker tries hard to attain his goals and perform well in his job. However, despite his efforts, his boss never says anything positive and is chronically negative and sarcastic. Since he strives so hard, he feels unappreciated and harbors deep resentments.
- A husband comes home from a difficult day to find his dinner not yet ready to be served. He immediately lashes out at his wife for being incompetent and yells at the children. He uses his anger in an attempt to bring the environment under control.

Is Anger Wrong?

When anger is managed properly, it doesn't cause a problem. God's Word says, "'And don't sin by letting anger control you.' Don't let the sun go down while you are still angry, for anger gives a foothold to the devil" (Ephesians 4:26–27).

When we feel angry, it's comforting to know that God also displayed this emotion. God clearly was angry at evil. He hated it, and we are allowed to hate it too. But we are not allowed to be angry with people to the point where our hearts are filled with bitterness and resentment. The clear distinction between righteous anger and the type of anger that leads to many levels of sinful behavior is the ability to separate the person from the act. Since most people don't do this, at least initially, an unrighteous anger takes over.

Anger can cripple us. It can lead us down pathways of rage-filled, abusive and violent behaviors. It can cause us to drown in misery and result in deep depression. There is nothing to take lightly about anger. It must be removed if there is any hope of recovery.

While anger can sound ugly, just like anything else we learn in recovery, it has a purpose, an explanation and a solution. Anger is usually connected with many other emotions. Often we have to find the raw emotion that triggered the anger. Remember, anger is actually the need to preserve something we feel afraid of losing, including our self-worth.

Ways We Use Anger Defensively

Using anger to defend and protect ourselves is unhealthy. It can become a wrong method of coping with our pain and is connected to the need to dominate or control others. It's also the "I'll deal with this pain my own way" emotion.

Anger literally causes our heart to harden and assume a combative or defensive position. It can even act like a drug. When we become angry, we don't have to feel the pain that prompted the anger, but we won't feel any good feelings either. Taken to extremes, anger seems to empower us to change the circumstances that threatened us to begin with.

God wants us to be angry at ungodly and immoral things in life, and He especially wants us to be motivated to keep those things out of our life. A righteous form of anger can motivate us to change or can initiate movements such as the American Revolution. When we use righteous anger, we take that energy and apply it to a solution.

Application Point:
List the manifestations of anger you see in your life right now or have experienced in the past.

_____

_____

_____

_____

Rejection

Being rejected by someone is perhaps the most painful thing we can experience. Yet rejection is a reality of life. If we've experienced a painful childhood with a lot of rejection, facing rejection in adulthood can be that much more difficult. A root of rejection can cause much pain and lead to all sorts of dysfunctional thinking, feeling and behaving. At the core, the person with a root of rejection has actually believed, "I'm not good enough. I'm not worth much. Who could love me?" Whenever a situation reinforces those negative beliefs, the feeling of rejection kicks in.

Rejection and Anger

Since rejection is often too painful to cope with, many people go directly from feeling rejected to feeling anger.

Here are some examples:
- A woman is rejected by a boyfriend and begins to verbally attack all the ways he let her down in their relationship.
- A church member feels betrayed by another member who seems to have lost interest in their friendship. She begins gossiping about that person's personal life as a subtle form of punishment.
- A wife feels rejected by her husband because of his chemical addiction. While subtly attempting to change him, she complains incessantly to him and uses

threats that don't work. She calls her friends to complain about what a terrible husband he is.

At the core of these situations, everyone portrayed felt the initial blow of rejection but quickly turned it into anger in order to cope. When we experience rejection, we often counter it with a need to find fault in the person or circumstance that caused it. We may never even realize that when we do this, we are actually in the defensive mode of anger.

Rejection and People Pleasing

Other times, rejection can drive us to compulsively find a way to be more acceptable. This leads to the behaviors of codependence and people pleasing. We begin to believe that the person who rejected us is right and therefore we need to adjust, compensate or change to get that person to accept us. The above examples, let's now show how a people-pleasing person responds:

- A woman is rejected by a boyfriend and tries to figure out how to change herself and win him back. Or else she looks to the next relationship and does everything possible to ensure that the new boyfriend won't reject her in the same way.
- A church member feels betrayed by another member who seems to have lost interest in their friendship. She begins flattering that church member every time she sees her, brings gifts to her, and goes out of her way to praise her in the group. She hopes that in this way the church member will be won over.
- A wife feels rejected by her husband because of his chemical addiction. In an effort to gain his acceptance and love, she works hard every day to compensate, to please him and meet his every need. She tries very hard not to do anything that might upset or anger him.

It's important to know that when people embrace this type of system in coping with rejection, they have adopted an external reference point to determine who they are or what they should do. Essentially, that means they use another person as their guiding influence. Therefore, they have placed that person in God's position.

Properly Dealing with Rejection

As we deal with rejection, we must first ask ourselves a difficult question: *Am I doing anything or behaving in any way that might be unattractive or unacceptable?* For example, we may feel rejected by a poor performance review at a job. But perhaps it was legitimate. This type of rejection is disciplinary in nature—there is something about our behavior (not necessarily our character) that deserves to be rejected. Other forms of rejection, however, have nothing to do with our own behavior or actions and everything to do with the way another person, because of their own issues, mistreats or abandons us. This might be based on a distorted point of view, emotional baggage or skewed perspectives. In the dysfunctional family system, for example, a child can be continually rejected because of unreasonable and unfair meet the expectations of unhealthy parents.

How do we learn to face and accept rejection when it can be so painful? When we feel rejected by others, we need to attempt to accurately identify the situation, identify the other person and identify ourselves. And then we need to embrace God's perspective. We are not responsible for how people choose to see us; rather, we must stand firm in who we know we are (see chapter 10). This is where the battle is always won or lost.

Here are some questions we can ask ourselves when feeling rejected :
1. What is the nature of the rejection?
2. Is the rejection based on reality or my own feelings?
3. Have I done something that could have possibly contributed to the rejection?
4. Is this person unhealthy and perhaps projecting their own issues onto me ?
5. How can I deal with this ?

We aren't perfect, and perhaps we have qualities in us that people will reject, but we still have inherent worth and value. As we will continue to learn in other sections, we must learn to see ourselves in the light of how God sees us. God says, "I will never fail you. I will never abandon you" (Hebrews 13:5).

Application Points:
Do you recognize a pattern of rejection in your life?

_____

_____

_____

Can you recognize how you might cope with rejection?

_____

_____

_____

Find a scriptural promise that answers your rejection.

_____

_____

_____

Fear

Fear comes from a threat of danger and a sense of insecurity. Sometimes fear is real: a storm is about to hit our home; we nearly get into a car accident; we find we have an illness. But often fear is irrational, meaning it has no basis in fact. We can be afraid of people and events that will never affect us. We can fear failure and never try anything new or challenging. We can fear rejection and never pursue satisfying relationships. People who are fear-based most likely didn't experience security and safety in childhood or adulthood. They perhaps didn't feel a sense of protection and the hope and assurance of support when a dangerous, or less than comfortable, situation arose. People who are fear-based don't have the proper understanding of God or don't know how He relates to us as the perfect Father, Provider, Protector, Lover, Giver.

Fear can completely paralyze a person. A person bound by fear is a person who doesn't want to do much of anything. They literally hide under a shell, detach and withdraw. It might not be a physical detachment, but often that detachment happens at an emotional level.

Fear also has the ability to drive codependence. We just spent time understanding rejection, but the *fear* of rejection can provoke the same negative feelings. What is the difference? If we are rejected, we need to face that reality. But if we *fear* being rejected, it has not yet happened. Our fear could prevent us from pursuing a relationship or cause us to do irrational things. Fear can sometimes be obvious, but often it is disguised:

- A woman works overtime and takes on multiple job roles because deep down she constantly fears that if she doesn't do much more than required, someone better could replace her. She feels unappreciated and used.
- A young lady never socializes or makes efforts to make new friends, always finding excuses for her time. Secretly she craves friendships but feels insecure about her social skills. She is angry that her social life doesn't exist.
- A man doesn't know how to talk to women so he goes to a bar and drinks some beer to find more "courage." He meets women who use him and then dump him, leaving him feeling rejected and angry.

Each of these situations has fear at its root, which also overlaps feelings of rejection. In these examples, fear also led to anger, which became the secondary emotion.

How do we define fear? As with anger, we need to inventory our actual fears. The Bible tells us there is no acceptable fear except the "fear of the Lord." Fear is of the Enemy, not of God. In fact, we also learn that "perfect love expels all fear" (1 John 4:18). Therefore, it's safe to conclude that when we have fear, we lack love.

Just as identifying fear is so important, it is important to realize we need more time nurturing our relationship with the Lord. We must seek Him, look to Him and believe He is our Protector and Defender in all ways and in all situations. Unlike other emotions, fear is always illegitimate. We are reminded hundreds of times in God's Word not to fear. We must choose to believe God's truth.

Application Point:

Here are the fears I recognize in my life:

_____

_____

_____

I can claim the following promise when I'm faced with fear:

_____

_____

_____

Loneliness

Loneliness isn't necessarily being alone. It means we feel isolated and disconnected from others. Loneliness says, "I'm the only person going through this." Many people go through life lonely and are never able to identify loneliness as a problem. They fill life with things, busy activities and social calendars, yet feel that void and disconnect.

God created us to be in relationships, but they were always designed in such a way that He would come first (chapter 4). Anytime we are disconnected with our need to be in a relationship with God first, we'll experience loneliness.

Loneliness can lead to anger, or it can lead to other conditions such as depression. Since relationship problems are at the heart of codependence, this can be a deeply challenging obstacle to overcome.

Examples of Ways Loneliness Can Be Manifested

- A nurse spends her busy day with patients working twelve-hour shifts every day and arrives home feeling empty and unfulfilled.
- A woman runs frantically about her day stuffing her calendar full of things to do, people to visit, ways to be of service and church responsibilities. Despite all her activity, she feels disengaged and is unknowingly experiencing loneliness.

- A young woman comes home from college and finds herself disappointed and disconnected. She realizes her family isn't emotionally bonded, and that causes her to feel immense loneliness while in her own home.

Entering recovery can be lonely if we need to give up relationships that are no longer healthy, or our own family members don't understand what we are going through. It is essential to connect with people who can encourage us and understand where we are.

In reality, the process of recovery and healing is one of connecting. First, God repairs our connection to Him. Ultimately, that connection will give us the ability to connect to others in healthy ways.

Even so, we must be willing to experience loneliness as part of being human. Sometimes, we'll just feel lonely and need to use those times for solitude with God rather than isolate ourselves from others. By identifying our loneliness, we can begin to hand over that feeling to God. We can use those times for prayer, reading God's Word and simply just being with Him. As we focus on Him, we find that the sweetness of His presence engulfs us. Rather than feeling alone, we feel connected to Him. Jesus said, "I will never abandon you" (Hebrews 13:5). How comforting it is to know this when we feel abandoned or left to ourselves.

Application Points:
Explain how you experience loneliness.

_____
_____
_____

Explain what you do to cope with loneliness.

_____
_____

Powerlessness

When we are powerless, we are unable to help ourselves. We are unable to change our circumstances because something more powerful than we are overtakes us. It can be positively frightening to be powerless in negative situations—particularly when there is a direct need or dependency concerning the person involved (spouse, family member, employer). Powerlessness can also happen when someone violates us or maliciously attacks our character. It can be felt in childhood when we have unhealthy and controlling families. If we have experienced a lot of powerlessness in our life, a defensive reaction may occur almost immediately when we are put into any circumstances remotely similar.

Examples of Powerlessness

- A woman feels dependent on her employment yet must tolerate an abusive and demeaning boss.
- A man comes home to find his wife drunk after she promises she would quit drinking.
- A young lady ends a relationship only to find that the man destroyed her character on the college campus by spreading false and malicious rumors about her.

Powerlessness is at the core of many anger issues. When we feel unable to help ourselves or change our circumstances, we may protect ourselves through anger. We may also attempt to control things through our own efforts, directly or indirectly. Many times, in powerless situations we try even harder. The effort to keep trying can be seen especially in a codependent.

In reality, powerlessness is not the problem. The way we *deal with* powerlessness is the larger problem. Our own efforts, our angry and vengeful reactions or our depression can't change a thing. When we learn to identify the emotion of powerlessness, we can come to a point of true surrender. Along with real powerlessness (minus any efforts to change anything!) there needs to be the attitude that God is more powerful than whatever obstacle we face. Instead of trying so hard, the ability to surrender it to Him is where we find victory. In the midst of the strain and pain of feeling so out of control, we can rely on this stabilizing truth: "For I can do everything with the help of Christ who gives me the strength I need" (Philippians 4:13).

Feeling powerless is sometimes the result of a lack of healthy boundaries. While boundaries aren't intended to control our environment, they help us gain a sense of sanity and peace. We'll spend more time on boundaries in chapter 11.

Application Points:

Do you recognize a sense of powerlessness in your life?

_____

_____

_____

What can you biblically claim in order to overcome that sense of powerlessness?

_____

_____

_____

Shame and Guilt

Shame is the inherent sense that "something is wrong with me." Guilt is the sense that we committed a wrongful act. Shame and guilt are by-products of the Enemy. They can be the result of sinful choices or of someone else's sins or unrealistic expectations. It's important to establish that as a child of God, there's no room for either of these emotions. Even though we continue to sin, we are no longer guilty: "So now there is no condemnation for those who belong to Christ Jesus" (Romans 8:1). The cross bore the shame of our sins, and that shame was taken away once and for all.

At the same time, we should be able to feel the pain of doing something wrong without the root of shame and guilt. God uses something called "conviction" to show us the error of our ways. God's conviction is a good thing. He uses conviction in the life of believers so we will repent and come back to Him. When He places us under conviction, we can feel pretty horrible, but it is a loving rebuke that calls us back to Him.

Satan uses the weapons of shame and guilt in a different way, however. He wants to make us believe we aren't good enough and don't have what it takes to live the Christian life. He wants us to give up and walk away from God. Just as the purpose of conviction is to draw us to God, shame and guilt cause us to run and hide. When we are experiencing shame and guilt of this sort, be certain it is always of the Enemy and never from the Lord.

If we were raised in a family that used shame and guilt as a method of control, we may think that God operates the same way. He does not. God allows only the type of pain that will motivate us to run back to Him. He is and always will be the perfect, loving, gracious Father.

How to Deal with Shame

We will discuss shame in detail in chapter 7. For now, understand that shame becomes an identity issue. Continually feeling that we aren't good enough, that we don't measure up and that the very essence of our being is not acceptable places chains around our soul. Shame is so toxic, and many of us don't even realize it is dominating our lives. The true healing in our lives occurs when that shame is removed. In fact, the entire healing process revolves around the removal of shame. This workbook is designed to walk us through that process.

Overcoming Painful Emotions

Is there any way to step out of the emotion in the heat of the moment? Dealing with emotions can be the most difficult challenge we face. Simply "getting over them" is difficult and won't just happen right away, but we can begin to learn how to stabilize our emotions in the following ways:

1. Remember that emotions are indicators, not facts.

Emotions reflect what is happening in our heart. They should not be ignored, nor should they be taken as factual truth. Understanding they are essentially a response and not the actual problem can help us put things in the proper perspective. If we are grieving the loss of a failed relationship, those feelings of pain and sadness are a by-product. It is normal and healthy to experience grief. People who try to repress and deny emotions wind up with bigger problems. However, as we go through grief and learn to accept and move on beyond that loss, we have the chance to continue living a healthy life. We can reflect on our mistakes and find hope in what we have learned.

On the other hand, if we continually focus on the loss of that relationship and never try to move past it, we become imprisoned by sadness and despair, which can become paralyzing. This disrupts our ability to ever live a life of joy and peace or to be able to experience all God's blessings in our lives. This emotion is no longer a healthy state of grieving—it is a form of bondage.

2. Identify the belief system that drove the emotion.

When emotions become intense, we need to step back and identify the origin of the circumstance, thought, idea or belief that triggered the emotion. We usually cannot stop feeling. In the example above, the loss of relationship can truly seem devastating. But over time, the feelings of despair may be directed by false messages such as, "I can't live without that person. Life isn't worth it." Those are the beliefs that need to be understood and recognized because underlying those beliefs is a lie. In reality, we did experience loss. It does hurt. But we can and will survive and heal. Often, we have entire belief systems about life, love and relationship that need to be transformed. So finding these beliefs may lead us to the revelation that we need an enormous amount of healing, far beyond that one relationship. If you find yourself at this point, rejoice and don't despair. God's greatest work is done when we reach this place of recognition. This workbook will continually address this area.

3. Identify when we transfer responsibility.

We must realize that another person isn't responsible for how we feel. Emotions are influenced by our *own* thoughts and beliefs. That doesn't negate the fact that people can genuinely hurt us. However, by owning our emotions we can begin to deflect negative messages. For example, if someone tells us we are stupid, we can internally say, "No, I'm not stupid. I'm actually quite intelligent." As long as we are humble about it, we've just refused to allow those words to penetrate. We may still feel a bit hurt, but we know the comment was false. On the other hand, we could have chosen to believe we actually are stupid. If we received that as truth, we made it a part of our internal self-talk that can lead to feelings of worthlessness, rejection and anger.

4. Recognize Satan's part.

We can't discount the element of spiritual attack in our emotional challenges. Satan can't make us "feel" anything, but he knows how vulnerable we are. He works overtime, trying to tempt us into thinking false things about ourselves and others, knowing if we "take the bait" we will eventually wind up in bondage to our emotions and sinful reactions. The Bible talks about the weapons of spiritual warfare in the removal of strongholds:

> We are human, but we don't wage war as humans do. We use God's mighty weapons, not worldly weapons, to knock down the strongholds of human reasoning and to destroy false arguments. We destroy every proud obstacle that keeps people from knowing God. We capture their rebellious thoughts and teach them to obey Christ. - (2 Corinthians 10:3–5)

5. Claim God's promises to defeat negative emotions.

Whenever we feel a negative emotion, we can find a solution to that emotion in the Word of God. Claiming a promise against the emotion doesn't change the circumstance. We need to address that situation for what it is. But claiming a promise against the emotion means that instead of dwelling on the pain that provoked the emotion, we are going to dwell on God's glorious supplies to meet our need, whatever it might be.

Learning to respond to painful emotions biblically is a growth process, so, depending on our maturity level, it may take time before we see significant change. Eventually, as we learn to respond to our emotions in a healthy way, they are put in their proper place. For example, when we feel fear, we can cling to one of God's comforting promises. As we dwell on God's truth, we invite the power of God through the Holy Spirit into our situation. Rather than allowing fear to consume us, we begin to experience God's peace and joy. As we practice this discipline in all areas of our life, eventually our thinking, feeling and behaving are radically altered.

Table 2: Beliefs, Emotions, and Behavior Chart

We may make hundreds of decisions every day that affect how we think, feel and act. These are normally reactions to given situations. The goal in recovery is for us to eventually identify the belief and thought patterns in our life so we can respond based on reality, God's truth. Below is a chart to help us identify some of the feelings driven by faulty beliefs.

Faulty Beliefs	Driving Emotions	Behavioral Reaction	Truth-Based Response
I have to feel this way.	Powerlessness, anger.	I can't choose my emotional responses. Life just happens to me, and I'm a victim of my circumstances.	My emotions don't reflect reality. I need to be grounded on what God says is true. If I learn to dwell on God's promises, my emotions can change.
I can't accept myself without the love and/or approval of those around me. I'm lovable if others think I'm lovable. I must work hard to make them love me.	Fear of rejection, shame.	The central goal of my life is to focus on the needs of others and to try to please them. I also work hard to make people see me a certain way.	I can accept myself without the love or approval of anyone. I am loved and approved in Christ Jesus. My only goal in life is to please God.
If I don't do everything exactly right, I'm a complete failure and feel worthless.	Shame, guilt, fear (of rejection and failure).	I have a standard of perfection in all things I do. I impose high standards on others. If I can't do something perfectly, I won't do it at all.	I can calmly accept myself regardless of what I do or how I perform. I will do my best and leave the results to God. I learn to walk in grace.
Other people or things outside of me make me experience the emotions I feel.	Powerlessness, anger.	I demand people make me feel good or blame them when I feel bad. I try to change the way others feel. I get angry when people don't meet my needs.	I, and I alone, choose to believe and think the way I do. How I think affects how I feel. When I base my thoughts on God's truth, my feelings stabilize.

Faulty Beliefs	Driving Emotions	Behavioral Reaction	Truth-Based Response
I get angry when people don't behave in ways I think they should. It's my job to get them to understand the error of their ways.	Anger, powerlessness.	I attempt to control other people's behavior so they will measure up to my own standards.	It's the Holy Spirit's job to bring conviction to change someone else's behavior. I can set healthy boundaries in my life but have no right to attempt to change or control another person's behaviors.
I need to be ultra-responsible for others. I don't think they can handle things and things will fall apart if I don't assume the responsibility.	Fear, powerlessness.	I do things for other people and prevent the people in my life from having to face negative consequences (enablement).	I am responsible for myself and need to allow others the opportunity to be responsible for their own choices. I often stand in God's way by intervening and attempting to "help" and "fix" others.

Faulty Beliefs	Driving Emotions	Behavioral Reaction	Truth-Based Response
I can overcome someone's bad behavior by being the good one.	Shame, fear, anger, powerlessness.	I work hard to be good and follow all rules. My efforts will attempt to correct everything "wrong" around me.	I have no ability to undo someone else's behavior, including my own. Only God can do that through His grace and the power of His redemptive blood. My good acts must be from Jesus for them to hold power.

A Prayer to Deal with My Emotions

Dear Father,

I come to You with a broken heart. I have been hurting but unable to identify the source of that hurt. Anger is often my method of coping with the deeper pain on the inside. I realize You have solutions for dealing with that pain. I just don't yet know how to claim them in the heat of the battle. Please help me. Bring the ability to discern the source of my emotional pain. Help me see how negative beliefs are causing me to think, feel and react to situations inappropriately. And most important, please fix those things in me that are broken, and give me the ability to understand that other people, no matter how much they have hurt me, aren't responsible for my feelings. I thank You, Father, that you are going to do for me what I cannot do for myself.

In Jesus's name, amen.

Application Points:

Describe the nature of your emotional turmoil right now.

_____

_____

What circumstances or people have you blamed for your emotions?

_____

_____

_____

Develop a plan to "capture your thoughts." Start a journal with categories listed below. If you don't know where to begin, try to identify the emotions or feelings first. If you feel angry, sad or lonely, try to trace it back to what you are thinking. If you notice your feelings or thoughts drive certain behaviors, write that down too. If you can't put it all together, just wait and leave it blank.

If you are able to capture a thought that is a lie, replace it with truth in Scripture. Now keep a journal over the next 24 hours to practice this lesson in identifying thoughts, feelings and behaviors in order to align them with God's truth.

I think:

_____

_____

_____

I feel:

_____

_____

_____

I act:

_____

_____

The lie I believed:

_____

_____

_____

The truth I replace it with: (find a biblical promise)

_____

_____

_____

4

Love Systems

Before you begin to read this lesson, write out your definition of love. What drives you to love people? Do you feel loved? How do you receive love?

_____

_____

_____

_____

_____

_____

God created us with an inherent need for love. It is even more important than the air we breathe and the food we eat. Just as our physical body would eventually die without nutrition, a lack of love will disrupt our ability to grow emotionally or spiritually. The very reason for our existence is carved out of love—we were designed to receive and give love as the basis for all relationships. Without love, we can never fulfill our God-given purpose. Furthermore, we will never be satisfied, healthy or whole.

As we learned in chapter 2, God used our parents to provide this much needed love before we were able to know Him personally. They were our first examples of how we would learn to interpret, give and receive love in relationships. The type and amount of love we received as children will deeply affect our ability to love in adult relationships. If we were not loved properly, we will go through life with a need for love and an empty heart. We may also acquire countless false beliefs regarding love that will directly spill over into all our relationships.

A lack of love in our upbringing leaves us terribly vulnerable to attempting to improperly gain and buy love. Our methods of compensation or survival and our controlling tendencies are merely efforts to get the love we desire.

What Is Love, Anyway?

It's important to understand that the Bible describes three different types of love. Just as we have a three-part being (body, soul and spirit), these forms can be broken down as physical, emotional and spiritual love.

Eros (physical love). This love is usually based on physical attraction to another person. Typically, in the dating process, eros is what draws us to someone at an external level. This form of love can be romantic or sexual. It also tends to drive the more carnal forms of attraction that can lead to deep levels of bondage. However, within the context of marriage, this type of love plays an important role. Attraction and sexual bonding are important and necessary. But if they are separated from a deeper form of love, they are shallow and misused for selfish gratification. If eros is the only love present, it isn't real love at all.

Philia (emotional love). This love is based in the soul in the area of emotions. It can be found in friendships and romantic relationships. It is a sense of caring and sharing with another person as feelings are exchanged and a level of intimacy is developed. Functioning properly, philia should include the mutual ability to give and receive. For a marriage to become healthy, philia is necessary. It has nothing to do with the physical attraction and everything to do with the ability to connect and bond at a deeper level through talking, sharing, listening and empathizing.

Emotions do change, and therefore philia can change with the emotions. Emotions aren't always stabilized in healthy thought patterns or in truth. Thus, just as eros can manifest in wrongful lust, philia can be similar in the area of emotions. In unhealthy relationships, two people can be in bondage to emotional strongholds. They can be feeding off each other to meet their own emotional needs. Or the relationship can be imbalanced, with only one person doing all the giving. Codependence is rooted in a skewed form of emotional love that actually becomes emotional bondage.

Agape (spiritual love). Agape is God's love. Agape is derived from the Holy Spirit living within; therefore, it isn't human at all. It is a completely unselfish, giving-based form of love. This type of love can love a person despite any physical or emotional challenges. It is explained in 1 Corinthians 13:4–7: "Love is patient and kind. Love is not jealous or boastful or proud or rude. It does not demand its own way. It is not irritable, and it keeps no record of being wronged. It does not rejoice about injustice but rejoices whenever the truth wins out. Love never gives up, never loses faith, is always hopeful, and endures through every circumstance."

We are going to focus primarily on agape, as it has the power to completely undo and change those negative love systems in our life. God intended our life to be impregnated with agape. The moment we are born again, the Holy Spirit indwells us and we are connected with agape. But for many of us, an experience of love hasn't occurred. For the codependent, those past beliefs regarding love block the ability to truly understand and experience God's love. We may be afraid of intimacy with God because we do not understand how He operates. Sometimes we are filled deep within with bitterness and unforgiveness that prevent the Holy Spirit's ability to gain access. Like a blockage in a drain, the Holy Spirit is blocked and prevented from reigning and ruling. His love is there, but we can't experience it because we aren't able to let it flow freely in our lives. In essence, we grieve the Spirit.

The remarkable thing about codependence recovery is that love is both the problem and the cure. The journey of this workbook teaches some concepts, but the true power behind recovery is your being able to connect with the God who created you and loves you. In that love, you will find peace, wholeness and the ability to function in healthy relationships. But this change doesn't happen immediately; it is a process, so don't lose faith. If you seek Him with all your heart, you will find Him.

Understanding Love Systems

In this next section, we are going to be looking at love systems. The purpose is to understand what motivates and drives our need to love and be loved by God, others and ourselves.

God's Love System

Jesus replied, "'You must love the Lord your God with all your heart, all your soul, and all your mind.' This is the first and greatest commandment. A second is equally important: 'Love your neighbor as yourself.'" (Matthew 22:37–39)

"So now I am giving you a new commandment: Love each other. Just as I have loved you, you should love each other. Your love for one another will prove to the world that you are my disciples." (John 13:34–35)

In these pieces of scripture, God lays out His system of love. He gives us a particular "formula" to follow to fulfill the greatest of all His commandments: love God, others and yourself.

1. **Love (agape) God above everything and everyone.** This means we must put Him first and seek Him most. God's love will provide the love we need to care for our own love needs and be able to pour out love to others. We love God because He first loved us. We love others just as God loves us.
2. **Love yourself.** Most of us think humble Christians wouldn't love themselves; it sounds so selfish! Yet God intended that we receive His love and love the person He made us to be.
3. **Love others.** It's clear that there is a relationship between self-love and the way we love others. This scripture says that we love others as ourselves. Therefore, it's possible that if we don't love ourselves, we won't love others.

Loving God First

The codependent usually has extremely skewed views regarding love, which are unknowingly transferred to God. For codependents, so many price tags have come attached to love that receiving love without paying a cost is something they have a difficult time comprehending. They believe love is something to work for and earn, much like a job with a paycheck. Codependents' behavior is mostly founded on a works-based mentality: "If I do this, then I'll get that in return."

If we believe God requires us to do special things to earn love from Him, we become performance-oriented. We will be prone to thinking, "God is mad at me." If we measure ourselves by His laws rather than by His grace, we will always see ourselves as failures. But the problem goes even deeper. When we are in a performance mode with God, our actions and behaviors try to win His approval to make ourselves feel acceptable. We don't give Him what He truly desires, which is our burdens, pain, and sin. Instead, we are too busy trying to make ourselves worthy of Him.

The reason this cycle of behavior is so dangerous is that God's love doesn't rest on our efforts or attempts to be acceptable. It isn't what we do that can make us worthy or unworthy in His sight. It's what He did for us.

Application Point:

Have you ever stopped and honestly assessed how you think God loves you? Take a moment to reflect on that right now. As He looks into your innermost being, as He watches you, how does it move His heart? Is He pleased with you? Is He distant? Do you know without doubt that He loves you? And if so, exactly what does that mean? Write out your thoughts.

_____

_____

_____

_____

_____

_____

If we look at the mountains of issues in our lives, it would be convenient to try to find a remedy that could tell us "step by step" what to do. However, the how-to guides on relationships don't seem to work very well. Even if we attempted to change our external behaviors, or get someone else to change, those same issues would continue to rear their ugly heads.

In reality, the solution to every relationship issue we face is to learn how God relates to us through His love. In fact, true recovery only happens when we embrace, understand and allow God's love to flow through us. If we developed and nurtured a personal relationship with God for the rest of our lives, He could perfectly teach us how to love in each of our relationships. Not only that, but if the people in our lives had that same knowledge and experience of God's love, they would pour love back into us as well. Just imagine this working itself out—God's love at the center and everyone pouring His love into each other. Sounds too perfect and almost ridiculous, right? Ironically, that is God's plan and purpose. Anything different from that is outside the will of God!

Before we can even address love, we need to take a look at the "Author's" definition of it. Here are some general characteristics:

God's love is based on grace—it is a free gift that we cannot purchase (see Ephesians 2:8–9). If we try to purchase it, we won't be able to receive or experience it. God's love is based on what He did for us, not what we can do for Him. This grace isn't accessed just at our point of salvation; rather, it's something we must live and walk in on a daily basis.

Meditation point: Do you try to bring gifts to God to please Him, such as a checklist of all the good things you've done?

_____

_____

God's love is based on choice. He doesn't demand or force us to do anything (see James 1:15; Deuteronomy 30:19; Matthew 6:24). God is the giver and respecter of free will. We can receive His love and enter into a relationship. We can reject His love and live our life separated from Him. If God merely controlled us, we would be robots. Instead, God intended that we engage in relationships where love is the driving force. Because codependents are operating under the influence of a person's control and even exercising that control over others, this principle of an all-powerful God who loves us by choice is difficult for them to comprehend.

Meditation points: Do you feel you have the fundamental right to choice in your relationship? Can you see patterns of control in order to "survive" in the relationship? How does that translate to your relationship with God?

_____

_____

_____

God's love is given out of true sacrifice. It cost Him dearly to show His love to us (see John 10:11, 15–18; John 15:13; 3:16; 1 John 3:16). He laid down the life of His Son and painfully imposed the shame and grief of our sin on Him. Jesus Christ agreed to hurt, to bleed, to suffer and to die on our behalf only for the sake of His love for us. There was no direct benefit attached to that other than to rescue and redeem us. This type of love is incredible, and when we encounter it, it can only bring forth joy, thankfulness and worship.

Meditation points: How do you see God's sacrifice in your life? Do you recognize your efforts to sacrifice for others? What do you think your driving motive is? Contrast that motive with God's motive.

_____

_____

_____

God's love is unconditional. There is nothing we can do to take it away or change it (see 1 John 4:7–10; Romans 8:38–39). This is the essential hallmark of agape love. Its source comes from the giver, not the receiver. In other words, unconditional love has nothing to do with what's on the inside or the outside of the other person. It is a love that comes from an affectionate desire to love, which is an outpouring of the heart of God. That love can love us when we are doing things right. . . or doing things wrong. It can love us when we are at our best . . . or at our worst. However, God does establish consequences for sinful choices. He'll continue loving us in our bad places, but He does not approve and reward negative behaviors. We cannot mistake unconditional love for an acceptance of sin—God's love despises anything evil. Similarly, God's blessings are conditional. "If we, then He'll" is a theme in the Bible. We access God's blessings based on our willingness to obey Him.

Meditation points: Do you think God loves you more when you are "doing the right things?" How does your own condition affect how people love you? How does their condition affect how you love them?

_____

_____

God's love seeks an admission of sin so He can forgive and restore those areas of our lives (see Luke 16:15; Matthew 23:25–28; Isaiah 64:6; Romans 10:3). God doesn't want us to offer our good behaviors to impress or please Him. In fact, He will reject them. Why? That is called self-righteousness and He says in Isaiah 64:6 that our self-righteousness is "filthy rags" in His eyes. If our ability to follow God's rules and be good all the time worked, we wouldn't need a Savior. We wouldn't need to be forgiven because then we'd be perfect!

So often, we have learned that mistakes are bad. That failure is embarrassing and unacceptable but an inevitable part of the human experience. In fact, the only hope we have of becoming more and more righteous is through a close and intimate walk with our Lord. Unlike the mindset of perfectionism, God isn't interested in our efforts to get everything just right. He's more interested in our ability to be honest and authentic in His presence by laying our sin, grief and despair at His feet. That is the place where He can heal our hearts through the power of His forgiveness and ultimately teach us how to forgive others.

Meditation points: Do you try to do everything just right? Do you fear failure? Are you more prone to presenting your goodness, or your sin, to God?

God's love seeks intimacy with the "real you" (see Psalm 139; Isaiah 43:4; 1 John 4:18). God loves the real us, with all our flaws and weaknesses. He seeks intimacy and close connection—where we see Him and He sees us. We may attempt to run and hide, not because of who we are in God's eyes but because of what sin has produced in us—either our own sin or the sin someone else imposed on us (through abuse, rejection, neglect, or other issues). When we hide our true selves because we feel unworthy, it simply means we don't understand grace. We haven't yet grasped that God is our Creator and our true Father and that He designed us with His own hand and heart. Therefore, He is interested in relating only to our real self. He wants to take away the sin, pain and defects that have prevented us from being the people He made us to be. We must learn to grasp that we truly are precious in His sight.

Meditation points: Have you gotten real before God, or do you still fear Him seeing inside you? Do you try to hide from Him? Do you try to hide from others? What scares you most about intimacy?

God's love gives from the abundance of His heart—never out of constraint, fear, guilt or necessity (see 1 Corinthians 13). God loves us merely for the sake of loving us. He doesn't need to love us. If we were accustomed to feeling that our needs imposed unpleasant burdens on others, or as though loving us was a hassle or chore, we may think God loves us in a similar manner. But God's heart is pure, and He loves us from a pure heart. There is no "shadow or shifting in Him." We are never a burden to Him. We are His beloved children whom He may need to discipline but will never reject.

Meditation points: Do you feel that God is bothered by you and hassled by your requests? Do you constantly apologize to people, always concerned you are being a burden or trouble? Do you "love" people because you feel obligated or pressured to do so?

_____

_____

_____

Our best efforts to produce anything close to agape will always fall short. Remember, true love—agape—is a resource of the Holy Spirit, and we can access it only through a relationship with Him. We will learn more about this further on in the lesson.

Unhealthy Love Systems

As we look at the heart of God and discover He is filled with grace, love, and kindness toward us, it should move us to desire to love and serve Him more. Often this doesn't happen because deep down we are still blocked by faulty belief systems regarding love. When our earthly experience has been unloving, we may find it difficult to understand God's love. God is our real Father. He is the One who made us, and therefore, His acceptance and love will conquer any and all negative earthly experiences.

To better understand how a negative love system can develop, we will look at two examples. As you read, attempt to identify any of these areas that are skewed in your own life.

Eleanor

By all outward appearances, Eleanor's family was healthy and normal. Her parents had important responsibilities in church, and life centered around church activity. Since her mom and dad were so "important," Eleanor felt pressured to be a little better than the other kids at church. While Eleanor's parents were so occupied with church functions, at home they were uninvolved and uninterested in Eleanor. Eleanor, therefore, learned to seek her parents' approval in the limelight of the church. She tried to understand the people at church, including their expectations, so she could appropriately respond and react. The goal? For people to notice and send good reports to her parents.

While Eleanor heard messages about the Bible, God and Jesus, her only concern was making sure that she was a "good girl" for the sake of her parents' reputation. Despite her efforts, Eleanor's mom was easily embarrassed if Eleanor's dress was wrinkled, if her hair came untied or if she acted nervously or foolishly in front of people.

Subconsciously, Eleanor began to learn that as hard as she tried, she was never good enough in the church environment. As a young girl she felt sad, lonely and flawed, unable to understand how she could reach that place where she would make her parents truly proud of her.

In her teen years, Eleanor gave up on church altogether. Eventually, she withdrew from any understanding of a personal God who loved her. She decided, instead, that He probably didn't approve of her either. She felt better and stronger living life trying to be "good" and "successful" based on her own achievements.

As an adult, Eleanor was a successful businesswoman. She seemed to constantly take on more and more projects at her firm and had impeccable standards in work. Her driven, aggressive tendencies were countered by deep fears of losing her position, of being seen as incompetent or of failing altogether. While her outward act was so impressive that no one saw any cracks or flaws whatsoever, inside, Eleanor was unknowingly still living as that scared, small child who was unaccepted and unloved. Eleanor created her own poisonous and toxic bubble of maintaining outward control, while inwardly feeling like a complete failure.

Eleanor's Love System

- Eleanor never engaged in any form of self-love.
- Eleanor learned she was lovable if she acted appropriately.
- Rather than love others, Eleanor feared them and looked at how they might judge her.
- Eleanor replaced the ability to relate to others with unrealistic standards and work ethics that others found impossible to meet.
- Eleanor transferred her work-based system of beliefs onto God. She felt that no matter how hard she tried, she failed to meet His standard.

The Results

- Eleanor was trapped by perfectionism and performance.
- Eleanor believed that what she did made people love her. Since she failed at love, she focused more on trying harder to do.
- Eleanor used work to avoid relationships.
- Eleanor's relationship style was merely defensive; she didn't know how to let

someone close to her, much less love her.

- Eleanor was alone.
- Eleanor did not know how to receive or give love properly.

John

John was raised in an abusive, alcoholic home. When John was twelve, his father abandoned him, his mom and his brother. After his dad left, his mom was always very sad and became occupied with drinking and men. And with his dad gone, John felt the need to be the "man of the house." He worried about his mom all the time and went to great lengths to help her. When her boyfriend physically abused her, John tried to defend her. He always failed, and instead of being concerned for him, his mom always defended the abusive boyfriend.

John worked hard to love his mother, reasoning that if he could love her enough, she wouldn't need those other men. Since she always chose another man, he felt inadequate.

John took care of the house and helped raise his younger brother. He was always very responsible, and didn't laugh or play like the other kids. Life was serious business. Unlike his brother who began drinking and using drugs at an early age, John chose to take the straight and narrow path. He followed rules, never drank and always made responsible choices. He was hailed a class leader in academics and took on other leadership roles that led him to a fully paid scholarship through college.

While John seemed like a bright and shining success story, inside he felt completely inadequate and was always waiting for the bottom to fall out. His mom often bragged about him to friends but never spent time with him and always chose her boyfriend over him. Because John couldn't win his mom over and change her ways no matter what he did, he believed he was a failure.

With what appeared to be the start of an exciting and prosperous new life, John became paralyzed under his own skin in his adulthood. He was drawn to a woman with drinking problems, and in his marriage he functioned in much the same way as in his childhood. He attempted to rescue his wife from addictive issues and once again fell into the despair of seeing his best-laid plans fail. Eventually, he began to drink. Unable to understand what was missing in his life or how to undo the things he had done wrong, he felt hopeless. His standards were always so high, his choices so measured, and his intentions so good—to end up like this meant there was no point in trying.

John's Love System

- John didn't learn his value or that he deserved to be loved. He saw himself as a person who had to work hard in his relationship with his mom to earn love.

- John used methods of compensation and survival to deal with parents who abandoned him in different ways.
- John believed he had the capability to change others through his "love" efforts.
- John believed he could undo the bad through his love efforts.
- John equated being good with deserving love based on something he did.
- John did not know or experience God's love.

The Results

- John was unable to connect emotionally in relationships because deep down he felt so inadequate and unworthy of receiving love.
- John went through life feeling guilty and responsible for the choices and emotions of others.
- John measured himself by his success. Failure of any sort led to complete despair.
- John tried to save and rescue others but didn't know he needed a Savior.

These examples may seem dramatic, but they are ever so common among the codependent. They denote some of the fundamental flawed belief systems regarding love. And sadly, they illustrate how deeply tainted love becomes when it has been inadequately developed during childhood.

Could John and Eleanor get beyond their childhood experiences and adult strongholds to unleash a life of hope, purpose and the ability to give and receive love? Truthfully, without intervention or change, they are doomed to a pathway of much pain and loneliness. Love systems become deeply embedded in our character and have a way of continually being passed on from one generation to the next. The only way to break this cycle is to learn to love God's way.

To do this, we must

1. Be willing to understand our love system up until this point. How do I give love? How do I love myself? How do I love God? How does God love me?
2. Be willing to learn *truth* based on God's Word about what God intended for love and relationships. We need to sift through the actual truth of the Bible and compare it with our current belief systems.
3. Be intimately connected with God as He takes those truths about love and makes them real in our heart—bit by bit, piece by piece transforming us to live by His love. Intimacy with God begins with brokenness, vulnerability and trust.
4. Learn to love others through our relationship with God. We learn we can't "do" love; we must "become" love. We can only become love through that relationship with Jesus Christ—there is no other way.

How We Love Improperly

How do you interpret your world? Through our own senses and experience, we unknowingly have inside of us thousands, probably millions, of "tapes." Even as little babes, these tapes were recording messages that told us who we are, how to love, how to be loved and more. Children raised in emotionally healthy homes may be able to replay tapes to recall lessons their parents taught them. But children raised in emotionally unhealthy homes may have messages that tell them, "You aren't lovable. . . something is wrong with you . . . you're not good enough for my love." These messages are terribly damaging and destructive. For the child who hears and believes these messages, they have the power to damage his or her entire perspective on love and relationships for a lifetime.

As we begin to face our codependence, it can become difficult to realize that some of our behaviors and actions, even if filled with good intentions, result from responding to these dysfunctional messages, not the healthy demeanor we had attempted to create. As we've wrapped ourselves externally in a package that seems impressive, likeable and filled with good measures, it can be unbelievably painful to realize that our efforts to fix, help and compensate come from our own pain, unmet love needs and fears. When love hasn't nurtured us properly and we've developed faulty belief systems regarding love, it can be expressed in many unhealthy ways.

Below are some of the common ways a codependent develops maladaptive behaviors to enable him or her to function in a relationship that lacks true love. Most of these outward behaviors are driven by inward brokenness but occur at an unconscious level. That means we don't intentionally live out this system of love; somehow, it has been recorded on our tapes as the way of functioning in relationships.

Proving Our Worth

For the codependent, part of the obsession is in working hard to convince other people we have value, goodness and worth. Needing to do this means we are in a defensive position—feeling obliged to prove ourselves. This system of thinking is highly destructive. It says, "Something is wrong with me, but I'm going to try to prove [to myself and others] that I'm okay."

Sometimes our need to prove ourselves shows in an aggressive, over-achieving manner and we try to out-do everyone else. Workaholics often fall into this category, and it can lead to an extremely prideful lifestyle, even though the roots are derived from insecurity, not confidence.

When we use self-effort, personal achievement, good deeds or anything external to measure our worth as a human being, we are in the bondage of codependence and self-centered living. God's system of love says, "You have a spiritual need for Me and through My relationship with you, you have value and worth. You're okay just as you are. You are secure in Me."

Meditation points: How do you prove your worth to others? How do you see your worth in God's eyes?

_____

_____

_____

People Pleasing

Typically, one of the driving forces behind a codependent person is the compulsive need to please people, especially people who seemingly hold a place of importance in our life. In people pleasing, codependents give a great deal of power to another person. We believe that we are acceptable and worthy if we can find approval from someone else we care about or respect.

Like the notion of trying to prove our worth, in people pleasing we are obsessed with the need for approval. We believe our good efforts will earn favor with others. In a certain sense, we are trying to buy people through good deeds, gifts, flattery and similar acts. Most people pleasers don't even recognize that they have an agenda of their own. However, if they don't receive the desired response for their good efforts, they usually respond with bitterness or with a compulsive, obsessive need to try harder. This is where the true root of people pleasing can be found. There is an agenda attached to the act of "kindness."

People pleasing is one of the pathways toward burnout. We find that no matter how diligent our efforts, pleasing everyone is impossible. Furthermore, we end up living our life based on other people's desires and preferences to the point where we don't even know what or how to choose for ourselves anymore.

God does call us to serve others, but through a Spirit-filled walk with our Lord where He is directing us. In reality, when we obey God, not everyone will be pleased. We might even have to let people go without and say no. But if we are doing it through the Lord, we are pleasing Him, which is our final goal.

Meditation point: Are you consumed with trying to please people? How so?

_____

_____

_____

Perfectionism

As codependents, we are often perfectionists who hold ourselves to an extraordinarily high standard and must convince others we have it all down perfectly. We may equate one mistake with total failure and become overwhelmingly embarrassed, ashamed or humiliated when people witness our failure at any level. In our world, we need to be strong, to never let anyone down and to never show any signs of weakness. We seem to think that somehow people want us to be perfect and that if we attain perfection, we will be loved and accepted. In our quest to get everything right, we often isolate ourselves from others. We can also be discouraged perfectionists in some areas of life and reason that if we don't do it perfectly, why even bother?

God never asks us to be perfect. He asks that we get honest. He knows the basis of a relationship with Him and others must be based on grace and forgiveness. We all make mistakes. We all have faults. And when we learn to love ourselves, we will realize that being human is okay. God loves us and paid a price for us. Thank God, we don't have to measure up to a standard of perfection to be accepted by Him.

Meditation points: Are you a perfectionist? What happens when you fail? What standards does God judge you by? How is this in complete contrast with God's love?

_____

_____

_____

Disassociation

As codependent, we eventually learn how to present an outward facade while our inward life leaves us with a sense of being unknown, unseen and unheard. Trapped within our own skin, a separation occurs that leaves us acting one way on the outside while feeling something altogether within. This emotional dishonesty, which we most likely learned in our upbringing or in unhealthy relationships, is deadly. It has left us vulnerable to making poor choices, to allowing people to mistreat us and to participating in unhealthy situations, all while claiming our actions were done "in the name of love." This breakdown looks something like this:

Table 3: Outward versus Inward Persona

Outward Persona	Inward Persona
Try to be who people want me to be.	Reject myself. "No one would want me this way."
Together, strong, focused on others' needs.	In need of support and guidance. Screaming on the inside for someone to love me.
Giving, kind, and nice.	Terrified that you'll reject me if I don't "bring enough to the table."

In recovery, we find that, above all else, God wants us to dispose of the phony masks and facades we hide behind. He is interested in the real person. As we learn to be accepted and complete in God, we are able to offer our authentic selves in relationships. Authenticity is a key ingredient of any healthy relationship. Whenever we are phony, we will be unable to connect, thus leaving us vulnerable to unhealthy relationship systems.

Meditation points: Have you developed an outward persona, even though you think and feel differently inwardly? Explain.

Is Self-Love Selfish?

Most of us who struggle with codependence see ourselves negatively at a core level, whether or not we are aware of it. Because we are unable to understand our self-rejection and self-loathing, we are unconsciously driven by strategies to get love. "If only I can do that, then I'll be loved" may be an unrecognized motivation. When we choose to find our own methods of dealing with our sense of unworthiness, we take matters into our own hands. It may seem innocent, but our decisions are done independently of God. As difficult as it may be to face this reality, we are essentially fooling ourselves by believing "I" can overcome my problems and the problems of others. While we may not love ourselves, we become exceedingly self-reliant. This is called pride. It is always self-centered, never God-centered.

Seeing that we are selfish and prideful can be enormously difficult. After all, we seem to be living sacrificial lives. Everyone else seems to be selfish! Yet, if we get honest with ourselves, we are often (not always) motivated by the need to self-protect, to get emotional needs met and to control outcomes of other people's behavior. Those are all self-serving motives and survival strategies that are independent of God. Thus, pride is at the root.

Pride is simply "I can do it on my own." It's not necessarily feeling puffed up about ourselves. Pride also tends to make us compare ourselves with others, leaving us "better than," or "less than" others. We are selfish by default. Pride makes us see everything in life from our own point of view, needs and desires. Selfish people are very capable of doing nice things for others—they are simply motivated by selfish purposes.

Admitting our selfishness is a vital key toward genuine change. It can lead to a true sense of brokenness and the realization of our need for God to operate in our lives at a foundational level. If you recognize this as a problem, you are one step closer to a solution.

When we are finally able to get ourselves out of the way and let God in, we will experience the type of self-love that leads to healthy relationship skills. God teaches us how to see the world and ourselves through His perspective. We discover that, in Him, we have immeasurable value, worth and a unique set of skills (see chapter 10). We also find that He created us for a specific purpose, to accomplish something that only we can do. The revelation of this has the potential to completely transfer our love system from a self-centered foundation to a Christ-centered foundation.

If we don't see our value in who we are in Christ, we aren't "humble"—we're actually allowing ourselves to stay in that self-centered mindset. Without a Christ-centered attitude, we can continue to replay the tapes in our minds of what our parents or friends told us. We become bound by trying to overcome those negative perceptions of ourselves and become consumed with self; thus, the negative cycle perpetuates itself. Let's differentiate between healthy self-love and selfish pride.

Table 4: Healthy Self-Love versus Selfishness and Pride

Healthy Self-Love	Selfishness and Pride
I have the ability to accept the person God made me to be, with all my strengths and weaknesses.	I focus on myself and all my insecurities and flaws and believe everyone else is focusing on them too.
Since I am forgiven by God, I have the ability to forgive myself. I understand that "who I am" and "what I do" are separate.	Since I haven't fully grasped God's forgiveness for me, I am unable to forgive myself or others. I feel I must pay the price for my actions or attempt to undo them independently. I feel my actions or the actions of others against me justify my sense of worthlessness.
I am able to recognize and embrace my skills, abilities and authentic identity, knowing that everything I am is to be used for God's glory.	I am attempting to measure myself by the people around me, constantly searching to see whether I have enough to offer. I often feel either "too good" in some situations or "not good enough" in others (pride).
I understand I have inherent worth, value and ability to love and be loved based on my righteous standing in Christ Jesus through His shed blood on Calvary.	I try to measure my worth by the things I do, the sense of accomplishment I attain, my efforts to fix people and my own attempt to be "a good person."
I am dependent on Jesus Christ and I can do all things through Him.	I am dependent on myself, and others are dependent on me too.

Meditation points: Do you see pride and selfish motives in your life? Explain them.

_____

_____

_____

Giving and Receiving Love

How many times have we tried to make an imbalanced relationship work? How many efforts to change people have failed? Many of us bypassed the first two ingredients of God's system of love: putting God's love first and loving ourselves. Since that left us empty and with so many needs, when we enter into a relationship, we put an enormous amount of pressure on that relationship. Not only does it need to satisfy our self-need for love and acceptance, but it also essentially needs to replace God!

To illustrate this, think of a watering can. Its purpose is to sprinkle water onto plants, grass and flowers. It is a mere vessel to hold water from another source. It can't fill itself up; it can only give out what it has been given. If it isn't filled up, it is useless.

We are intended only to be vessels of God's love. In fact, we don't have the capability to produce love on our own since it is a by-product of God's Spirit. His love in us nourishes us and allows us the ability to properly give love away. This "water" is life giving—not because of the vessel that carries it but because of the Source that provides it.

Often we misplace and misappropriate the getting and giving of love. We go through life feeling empty. Our "waterer" is dry. We start to look to people to fill us up. Instead of functioning as "sprinklers," we actually become more like a vacuum—looking for something on the outside to fill our needs on the inside. But people are not the source of love—they are mere sprinklers. However, we often illegitimately ask them to satisfy the needs that only God can meet. This leads to much devastation and pain. If a family, community, church or organization is filled with people who are empty and looking for their own needs to be fulfilled, it will quickly become sick and possibly even eventually die.

God designed relationships to be fulfilling, satisfying and mutually beneficial. He designed us to need and love each other to a degree, meaning we are to be interdependent within our community, churches and homes. In interdependence, we are connected and even intimate with those around us, but at no point do we lose our own identity. In interdependence, we are not in a state of needing, but one of giving. When we link with others who are willing and ready to meet our needs, harmony, wholeness and true love bind our hearts together.

Functioning properly, our needs actually give others around us the opportunity to pour into us. Their needs allow us this same opportunity. This is how God designed His church to function—the parts of His body functioning to form one unified body (see 1 Corinthians 12:12).

Codependence and Giving in Relationships

Codependence brings an array of relationship challenges in the area of giving love and receiving love. Since codependents primarily focus on ways to earn love through giving, the very function of "giving" is equated with "getting." This isn't intentional; it is a learned pattern of behavior, usually formed earlier in childhood. Despite its origin, it means that the emotion driving codependence is based on self-needs. As we learned already, that opposes the very definition of God's love.

If we evaluate the operating system of love in our life, we may become painfully aware that giving was our way of avoiding some painful realities. Rather than face a legitimate missing need (see chapter 6), we tried to compensate for what was missing. Or we used giving as a way to purchase something else in return.

Not only is this system self-centered and self-seeking, but when this occurs, we can be giving things wrongfully, things that could even harm the receiver!

Some Examples
- An addict or alcoholic may receive much "help" to offset his or her addictive behavior. The giver of this "help" isn't benefitting the receiver at all. In fact, this kind of giving is encouraging and enabling negative behaviors that allow the addict or alcoholic to remain in an addiction. What would be "giving?" In this situation, the addict or alcoholic requires tough love and defined boundaries. Love needs to say, "I will not accept this behavior."
- A child may get many material gifts from an emotionally unavailable parent. The child needs love and attention but instead is coaxed by "things." The child can learn that things matter most in life. That form of giving doesn't help the receiver at all. What that parent needs to give is time, attention, discipline and love. No thing can replace that.

We can only become true givers when we have God's love in us. Then we become carriers of that love and can offer it to the people who need God's resources. Most of us come empty-hearted from a lack of love poured into us. That need is genuine, and we must believe that God has the capability to fill our hearts and make up for whatever is missing from the past. God knows exactly what we need, and He knows what others need too. He allows us to participate in giving so He can help and bless others through us. He uses people to do the same for us. This cycle of giving and receiving truly reflects and expresses the heart of God.

Meditation point: How do I use giving in my relationships with God and others?

Codependence and Receiving

Being on the receiving end in any relationship is very difficult for the codependent. At times, being in the position of needing to receive can become almost humiliating. It can be so awkward to face a need and allow someone to help us, we might even rather go without receiving help altogether. Why such a fear of receiving? We may not realize that as givers, we place ourselves in the position of control. Our self-reliant nature (pride) finds it humiliating to receive. Working for something means "I earned it." Receiving something out of need has nothing to do with "what I have to offer."

However, codependents are also prone to being overly needy with some relationships, while exhausting themselves in other relationships. We may gladly give away that control to someone we believe can fix or change us. Receiving becomes skewed anytime God's order in our life gets misplaced. We might look for people to meet the needs only God can fill. Or we may simply think we are not lovable enough to receive. Whatever the reason may be, one of the sweet and satisfying experiences in life is being the receiver of gifts and true acts of kindness. If we never needed anything from anyone, we would be self-reliant. But God did not create us that way.

Independence does not lead to recovery. Interdependence must be the goal.

Meditation point: How do I exercise "receiving" in relationships with God and others?

Table 5: Giving and Receiving: Codependence versus God's Love System

"Codependence" Driving "Giving" in Relationships:	"God's Love" Driving "Giving" in Relationships:
I need to bring something to you. I feel obligated to seek out how to fill your need. I want your validation and acceptance. It helps me feel in control. (selfish motives)	I give this to you because God gave it to me first, and He desires that I share it with you. I want to bless you. (loving motives)

"Codependence" Driving "Receiving" in Relationships:	"God's Love" Driving "Receiving" in Relationships:
I don't know how to receive. It is embarrassing and shameful for me. Instead, if you do offer something, I will look for ways I can pay you back. After all, isn't that what you are looking for me to do? (selfish response)	I am in need, and the way you blessed me to meet my need showed me how much God loves and provides for me in my life. I am so thankful and grateful to you and to Him. (God-centered response)

Application Point:

Take some time to evaluate your own love system. Write out specifically how you give and receive in relationships. What motivates and drives you? Why?

_____

_____

_____

_____

_____

_____

_____

_____

_____

_____

_____

_____

_____

_____

_____

_____

_____

Encountering Real Love

What has held you back from receiving God's love? Do you have it in your head, but not your heart? The way you love others right now is a direct reflection of your current belief systems regarding love. It also reflects your love for God. However, if you were told to start loving today, you wouldn't be able to. We are not capable of learning how to truly love except by experience. God doesn't require us to give out anything He hasn't already provided to us. Therefore, you can only give out God's love, in its true form, by receiving it first.

If we have a bunch of head knowledge but no experience, it's time to empty it out and truly look at our belief systems regarding God's love. Therefore, the first thing to do is to admit the current condition of our heart. Am I selfish? Am I people pleasing rather than God pleasing? What motivates my behaviors, good or bad?

Admitting is the first step, and repenting comes next. Once we see our patterns of behaviors, we must admit them and ask God to change us so we don't continue to repeat them. This change will not necessarily happen immediately; we must also learn what it means to walk by grace. Moment by moment, day by day, we need to focus on how God loves us, meditate on His promises to us and establish a new foundation based on Him.

The apostle Paul (when he was "Saul") wasn't necessarily codependent, but he struggled in similar ways. He believed life was about doing things externally and religiously. He used a sense of morality as his compass to determine if he was "okay" on the inside. He thought he was following God, only to discover that his system of living and loving stood in complete opposition to the ways of God.

Our own story might not be so dramatic, but when we are living by a sense of needing to prove and perform, earn and buy love, we have a false understanding of God. We need divine intervention to place us on the pathway toward understanding God's love. Paul had such an intervention in his life, and out of his experience came foundational truths that apply to our own lives.

I once thought all these things were so very important [following the "outward" rules to gain the approval of God], but now I consider them worthless because of what Christ has done [being approved by His grace]. Yes, everything else is worthless when compared with the priceless gain of knowing Christ Jesus my Lord. I have discarded everything else, counting it all as garbage [my efforts to please people, my emotional needs], so that I may have Christ and become one [intimate] with him. I no longer count on my own goodness [my codependent efforts] or my ability to obey God's law [externally follow rules], but I trust Christ to save me. For God's way of making us right with himself depends on faith [based on my position in Christ, not my efforts]. As a result, I can really know Christ and experience the mighty power that raised him from the dead [an experience of love, not just head knowledge]. I can learn what it means to suffer with him, sharing in his death. [I learn how to sacrifice and suffer with Him —thereby identifying with His love.] (Philippians 3:7–10. Words in brackets added by author for emphasis.)

According to this scripture, how do we convert from an unhealthy love system to the love system God intends?

- We must have our hearts broken of self, including self-efforts, self-benefit, and more.
- We must realize our deep need for God to live in us and receive His grace and forgiveness.
- We must discard our outward acts by which we try to prove our worthiness to self, others or God.
- We must adopt a new system where we find our worthiness in Christ.
- We must personally identify with Jesus Christ in order to "know Him" and "be one with Him," including His sufferings, His death and His resurrection power. This means:
  - We experience the type of love that will suffer and sacrifice for the benefit of someone else to accomplish the will of God.
  - We are able to die to self, including the selfish intents of our heart (we don't die to the authentic person God created us to be).
  - We are anointed with the power of the Holy Spirit to live our life through Him—this is the same power that resurrected Jesus Christ from the dead.

The truth of God's love means little or nothing in itself if we never activate it in our lives. We must receive it and open it like a gift before we can use it. How can we receive God's love? Like Paul, we need a personal encounter with the Lord where He reveals truth to us. In this transaction, we must be able to stand before God and realize we are empty handed, bringing our empty "love cup" and acknowledging in His presence, "I need your love—even though I have nothing to give you for it. Please do for me what I cannot do for myself." (The next chapter will deal with the concept of surrender in detail.) Then, unlike the mindset of "I must do," "I must work," receiving God's love is a restful process (John 15:5). We simply stand in His presence, allowing Him to mentor, guide, teach, counsel, instruct, nurture, comfort and heal us. We don't do anything other than simply make ourselves available to Him and learn to trust and obey Him. We find that in Him, we become His love. This is the mystery of God, and it is the longing we all have in our heart. This love then translates and spills over into our relationship with others and ourselves.

The Test of Love

How can we identify the presence of authentic love in our life? The Bible tells us that when it is operating in our lives properly, it will be evident:

> We know what real love is because Jesus gave up his life for us. So we also ought to give up our lives for our brothers and sisters. If someone has enough money to live well and sees a brother or sister in need but shows no compassion—how

can God's love be in that person? Dear children, let's not merely say that we love each other; let us show the truth by our actions. Our actions will show that we belong to the truth, so we will be confident when we stand before God. (1 John 3:16–19)

Dear friends, let us continue to love one another, for love comes from God. Anyone who loves is a child of God and knows God. But anyone who does not love does not know God, for God is love. God showed how much he loved us by sending his one and only Son into the world so that we might have eternal life through him. This is real love—not that we loved God, but that he loved us and sent his Son as a sacrifice to take away our sins. Dear friends, since God loved us that much, we surely ought to love each other. No one has ever seen God. But if we love each other, God lives in us, and his love is brought to full expression in us. And God has given us his Spirit as proof that we live in him and he in us. Furthermore, we have seen with our own eyes and now testify that the Father sent his Son to be the Savior of the world. All who confess that Jesus is the Son of God have God living in them, and they live in God. We know how much God loves us, and we have put our trust in his love. God is love, and all who live in love live in God, and God lives in them. And as we live in God, our love grows more perfect. So we will not be afraid on the day of judgment, but we can face him with confidence because we live like Jesus here in this world. Such love has no fear, because perfect love expels all fear. If we are afraid, it is for fear of punishment, and this shows that we have not fully experienced his perfect love. We love each other because he loved us first. If someone says, "I love God," but hates a Christian brother or sister, that person is a liar; for if we don't love people we can see, how can we love God, whom we cannot see? And he has given us this command: Those who love God must also love their Christian brothers and sisters. (1 John 4:9–21)

These remarkable scriptures tell us that love is action oriented, not feeling oriented. They explain that we are to love just as Christ loves us—sacrificially—even if it hurts or costs us. The difference is that when we truly love, we are doing it through Him. And ultimately, we are doing it to glorify and honor the name of Jesus Christ. It is Christ-centered, not self-centered.

As we get ready to conclude this chapter, notice an amazing revelation in these scriptures. In codependence, our love is twisted and our motives are wrong. When we find God's love, it transforms our heart. It helps us properly see ourselves through God's perspective and eventually pours itself out to others. In this scripture, John isn't talking about codependent love that is based on mere outward acts for selfish benefits. He is talking about the true love of God (agape) that comes from an intimate relationship with Him. Not only are we called to love others, but we also find that the benchmark of our love for God is measured by how we love others!

Are you ready to measure your love source? If you were to take a litmus test on the amount of God's love in you, what would you find? The reality is that God already knows. However, He isn't standing in heaven pointing a finger at you in anger. He has seen every hurt and painful thing that has ever happened to you. He has seen everything wrong you have ever done too. He has a remedy for all of it. He just wants you to come to Him and rest (see Matthew 11:28).

The surgical hand of God Almighty may feel painful at times, but it is coated with a healing ointment of the Holy Spirit, which above all is filled with love. Our obsessive need to playact can be stripped off in His presence, transferred into His loving care where we can breathe in His grace, His acceptance and His love. We don't have to act for Him. And it is through Him we are going to be made right. We love God not by doing things for Him. We love Him by allowing His love to dwell in us, thus having the desire and ability to be what He calls us to be and love how He calls us to love.

If you've been striving to love and be loved by your own efforts, say a prayer like this:

A Prayer to Find Authentic Love
Dear Father,

I realize I've focused on myself and what I can do for You and others in order to make my life work. I realize now that I have little to offer apart from You. I also know that my life is about what You did for me when You saved me. And that You want to use me or work through me to touch others. I realize I have not always loved from a pure heart. I realize I don't always love myself. And I realize I often do not love You first. Apart from You, I am completely powerless to change. I acknowledge, confess and repent of any negative love systems I created to survive. I am ready to allow You to love me deeply and heal where I wasn't loved properly or was hurt by others. I embrace and receive the truth of Your love for me from today and forever more.
In Jesus's name, amen.

Application Points:
What do you see as blockages in your life right now? Have you been able to identify any belief systems you carry regarding love? Write them down.

_____

_____

_____

Do you see God's love for the people in your life? Do you love them through Him, or do you use your own efforts?

_____

_____

_____

5

The Surrendered Life: A Battle for Control

Workbook Keys

1. WHY IS SURRENDER IMPORTANT?
2. HOW DO WE TRUST GOD?
3. DESCRIBE CONTROLLING PATTERNS
4. DESCRIBE DEPENDENCIES
5. DESCRIBE SURRENDER

No concept is harder for people to grasp than what it means to surrender. We often hear we should "just let it go" or "give it to God." It sounds so simple, yet it is so profoundly difficult. As sad as it sounds, many (maybe even most) Christians never truly experience the brokenness that leads to true surrender. We learned in the last lesson that we access God's love through this same broken condition. In reality, the pathway to surrender *is* the pathway to experiencing and receiving God's love. The two are interchangeable and can't be separated.

Our willingness to be broken of self, to realize our need for God, to receive God's forgiveness and to enter into a new relationship with Him based on grace (not our effort) is what surrender is all about. Surrender is the doorway toward a life of freedom. We often think of it in terms of "what I have to give up." We associate surrender with defeat or loss. Yet true surrender is an act of receiving and being able to give love. We realize, as we walk through the death of self, that self was an imposter preventing us from being the person God intended us to be. Self was in a survival mode—trying to hang on and get needs met in various ways.

While salvation determines our eternal destiny, surrender doesn't affect our standing in God. We could choose to live our lives for ourselves and never truly surrender, and God would accept us as His children nonetheless (if we really knew Him). What we would lose, however, would be our true purpose and identity while here on earth. Instead of fulfilling our divine destinies, our lack of surrender would keep us fighting battles and attempting to make life work on our terms—with little success.

Everything we learn in our dysfunctional pattern of living and relationship styles is that God has a better way. We don't go through this process for any other reason than to become aware, to be able to repent and to ask God to give us the power to change what needs to be changed. Sometimes, as we face our codependence, we can feel overwhelmed. We must remember that God has a better plan. We aren't just survivors; we are children of God. He wants the best for His kids. To hunger for what God has in store for us, we must be willing to walk out in faith and conform our will to God's will. To say, "Go ahead, Lord, have your way in me."

What do we see in a surrendered, not just a saved, soul? The characteristics are distinctive:

- They filter their perspective through what Christ has done for them—they never want to take credit for anything in their life.
- They have indescribable peace.
- They seem to have joy in the midst of challenging circumstances and praise and thank God despite those circumstances.
- They speak to God, and about God, in an intimate and personal way.
- They speak to others with love, showing grace and mercy to people struggling or hurting.

Most everyone who fits this description can tell you a story. Usually personal effort, self-reliance and life choices failed. They needed Someone higher than themselves who could restore their lives. They came into contact with this through the Person of Jesus Christ.

Arriving at this point truly requires divine intervention. We need to both become broken of self and made aware of a God who loves us and has a plan for our life. Some of us have reached this place, only to find ourselves taking back control. Others of us never really learned how to let go in the first place.

In this next lesson, we are going to look at a variety of factors related to the notion of surrendering ourselves, our lives and the people in our life over to God. As you go through the material in this chapter, remember what you learned in the previous lesson. God LOVES you. Even if you have to face things in yourself you don't like or have to see other people's behaviors that hurt you, God's entire purpose today and always is to restore you to the person He intended you be and teach you how to love God's way.

Trusting God

God is a giver and respecter of free will. He will not force Himself on anyone. He will not make us give our will to Him. All of us by our sinful flesh are programmed to want to live independently of God. It is only through that personal relationship and the indwelling of the Holy Spirit that we are made aware of our need to depend on God.

There can be a huge wall of separation between knowing we need to depend on God and actually transferring our trust to Him. We don't trust God for various reasons. A tainted parental experience may have clouded our perception of God. The term *father* could have negative or painful implications. We may not have taken the time to nurture a personal relationship with God and simply do not know Him. We may have learned about God in a religious sense and still see Him as someone who cares more about how we are breaking rules than what concerns our heart. And, most commonly, we may blame God for allowing certain circumstances to happen in our life. After all, if He controls everything, then how could He let us be hurt?

Because God operates by a system of free will, He doesn't always interfere with the consequences of a human being's sinful choices. A God who is in control in one sense but operating by a free will on the other hand can be difficult to comprehend. We can't even begin to try to understand the world from God's perspective, so all we can depend on is the purity, the love and goodness of His character. We can rely on His Word and trust that it is true. So true, in fact, that we can take it to the "spiritual bank" of heaven and cash in every promise. For example, we can read Romans 8:28, which says, "And we know that God causes everything to work together for the good of those who love God and are called according to his purpose for them" and realize that right now, as we place our trust in Him, He is orchestrating redemption. He may not have "willed" for some of the things to happen in our lives, but He can still allow us to benefit somehow.

The Word of God is filled, absolutely packed, with passages on trusting God. In fact, next to actual salvation, our ability to trust in God determines the entire outcome of our lives. Here are some important things God says to us about the benefits of trusting Him:

Trust in the Lord with all your heart; do not depend on your own understanding. Seek his will in all you do, and he will show you which path to take. (Proverbs 3:5–6)

It is better to take refuge in the Lord than to trust in people. (Psalm 118:8)

I love you, Lord; you are my strength. The Lord is my rock, my fortress, and my savior; my God is my rock, in whom I find protection. He is my shield, the power that saves me, and my place of safety. I called on the Lord, who is worthy of praise, and He saved me from my enemies. (Psalm 18:1–3)

But when I am afraid, I will put my trust in you. I will praise God for what he has promised. I trust in God, so why should I be afraid? What can mere mortals do to me? (Psalm 56:3–4)

We are confident of all this because of our great trust in God through Christ. It is not that we think we are qualified to do anything on our own. Our qualification comes from God. (2 Corinthians 3:4–5)

The Lord is a shelter for the oppressed, a refuge in times of trouble. Those who know your name trust in you, for you, O Lord, do not abandon those who search for you. (Psalm 9:9–10)

Taste and see that the Lord is good. Oh, the joys of those who take refuge in him! Fear the Lord, you his godly people, for those who fear him will have all they need. (Psalm 34:8–9)

Trust in the Lord and do good. Then you will live safely in the land and prosper. Take delight in the Lord, and he will give you your heart's desires. (Psalm 37:3–5)

Clearly these pieces of scripture provide but a glimpse of the amazing victory we find when we trust in God. It's obvious that trusting Him gives us access into the heart of His loving plans and purposes for us. With so many promises God has given, what stops us? Why don't we believe that God is able?

Trusting in a God we can't see requires faith (see Hebrews 11:1). For most of us, people have let us down or hurt us. Our ability to trust people in our earthly experience has been shattered. How could we possibly trust in a God we can't even see? Yet, we can trust in God because He is mightier, more powerful and above everything that has gone wrong in our life. He despises the wrongs committed against us, but He has promised us redemption. He grieves over the sin and bondage in our heart—but He has a method of deliverance for us. If you are struggling with trust, before you continue, say a prayer like this:

A Prayer to Trust God

Father,

I realize that I struggle with trusting You. Please forgive me and change me. Your Word contains endless descriptions of who You are and the way You love me. I am declaring these truths in Your Word as the activating power in my life. I desire to be set free from anything and everything that I am clinging to other than You. Teach me, Lord, to believe what Your Word says and to transfer my trust to You. Teach me, Father, to surrender to You.

I want to live the life that You designed for me to live. I don't want to waste another minute. Please, Lord, have Your way in my life.

In Jesus's name, amen.

Application Points:

Do I see God as a real person in my life: involved, active, loving and concerned? Or do I see God as someone distant and angry, detached and uninterested in my problems?

_____

_____

_____

How have I trusted Him in the past? What has He done for me as a result?

_____

_____

_____

Do I feel disappointed or angry with God for prayers He seemingly never answered or situations He brought into my life that seem unfair? Explain.

_____

_____

_____

Am I willing to let go and let Him have His way, or am I still trying to convince Him to allow me to tell Him how I think things should be in my life? Explain.

_____

_____

_____

What do I fear if I release my life to Him? Do I think He will take things away? Explain.

_____

_____

_____

How does God view me? What is His opinion of me and my situation?

_____

_____

Identifying Our Dependencies and Controlling Tendencies

All forms of unhealthy dependency and control are the direct result of not trusting God. Anything other than God that captures our dependency can only lead us into bondage. This means that as we look at these behaviors in this chapter, we can find comfort in the reality that they can be swallowed up through learning how to grow by trusting the Lord.

To begin this section, it's important that we understand where, and in whom, we currently place our trust. Take some time to meditate on the following:

What, or who, drives and influences my thoughts, feelings, and behaviors—or in others words, whom do I live for?

_____

_____

_____

Where do I get my needs met for love, acceptance, value and worth?

_____

_____

_____

Whom do I turn to and trust in times of trouble?

_____

_____

_____

Where do I find my security and strength when I need it?

_____

_____

_____

Where do I find validation?

_____

_____

Whom do I depend on to meet my financial and material needs?

_____

_____

_____

Self-Dependency

Most of us who have identified with codependent behaviors have needed to survive in a variety of ways to simply have needs met. We may have learned that we ultimately needed to care for our own situations in life because other people were unavailable. Unknowingly, our operating system, or the person we placed our trust in, was *self.* Trusting in self is such a normal way of living—most of us are unaware that something is even wrong with it. Self-effort, self-strength, self-attempts and self-security seem natural ways to function in everyday life. Listed below are some of the ways we are self-sufficient in codependence:

- A need to defend myself and my children from irresponsible or abusive people in my life, feeling it's up to me to maintain peace, control and sanity in my house (usually in the chemically dependent family system)
- A need to hold everything together in my life because I can't depend on others to help me
- A belief that "my way is right" and people should see and conform to that standard
- A need to handle problems on my own because I don't have a support system I can trust
- A need to work hard to become a good person, being proud of my effort to live a moral life and feeling disgusted by people who don't live by the same standards
- A need to find a sense of justice, often feeling that life and the injustices of others aren't fair and need to be "settled" correctly
- A belief that with enough willpower and strength, I can get through difficult times

If we have extremely self-sufficient tendencies, we may have a difficult time trusting in anyone. If people were perceived to be untrustworthy in our lives, self-sufficiency became a means of survival. Self-sufficiency leads us to try to control every aspect of our life and often the lives of those around us. Unknowingly, we are unable to even trust in God when we have this mindset. We trust more in self-righteousness than in the grace of God. We somehow believe that everything is up to us and if we don't keep things under our thumb, they will fall apart.

Because we feel the need to manage life, we bear a tremendous amount of stress and pressure. We may suffer physical problems because we neglect self-care. We may have other addiction issues: alcohol, eating disorders, or others—all compulsive behaviors that we exhibit amidst an obsessive need to maintain control. Not understanding that the controlling position we have placed ourselves in is not what God intended, a vicious cycle of self-expectation and survival techniques drives us to carry the weight of the world on our shoulders.

If this applies to you, it's important that you simply understand that, for whatever reason, you learned that life was up to you. Many of us were even taught that to act this way was responsible and proper. Sometimes a skewed perception of God can leave us vulnerable to self-survival, as we discussed in the previous section. However we got to this point, it's time to think and ask God to reveal why and where we learned self-survival skills.

At some point, if we let self die so Christ can reign, we will find the most tremendous relief from burdens we could imagine—namely, the sufficiency of Christ.

Meditation points: Am I a self-sufficient person? How did I learn this? Have I always believed it was a noble and strong characteristic? How do I see it now?

_____

_____

_____

People Dependency

While codependents are self-sufficient in many ways, we primarily are identified as having dependent personalities. Dependent people overly latch onto the significant people in their life, believing their own security rests on those people (or situations, jobs or a variety of other things). They go to great measures to find stability in those relationships, believing they will satisfy their craving for love security, and other emotional needs. While dependent people are driven by those needs, they want dependency to be mutual in the relationship. In other words, they don't just seek dependency in a person. They feel secure in relationships where that same person is also dependent on them in return.

What are the implications of dependency? Where dependency on anything or anyone exists, the person or thing that meets the need of the dependent gains power over that person. Chemical addictions have power over people, for example. In our relationship with the Lord, dependency on Him places Him in the position of power. This is good—He should be granted that position of power and authority. But when we overly depend on other people, we place them in a position of power over us. In some ways, we can unknowingly make them our "gods." To counter that, we find areas where we can gain control in that same relationship. If we can be depended on in certain areas, we gain our own power (control) in that relationship.

This power struggle happens behind the scenes, and we usually have no idea what is taking place. We see only the outward results. These relationships are need-driven and control-based. As codependents, we wind up in relationships where we are looking to have our needs met (leading us to dependency), while also feeling the need to "rescue" that same person we are seeking to be dependent upon (gaining their dependency).

What's sad about this vicious cycle is that it stands in complete opposition to a relationship that is love based and free (chapter 4). Let's look at some examples:

- A husband needs the validation and approval of his wife and goes to great lengths to manage her and make her feel dependent on him. Deep down, he is dependent on the emotional security of having her tell him how much she needs him. Often, she rejects the dependency he tries to create, which frustrates him. He is unknowingly dependent-based, not love based.
- A thirty-year-old man still lives with his parents and functions under parent/child dynamics because he feels unable and unequipped to live any other way. He is financially and materially dependent on them and has no interest in taking responsibility for doing anything else. His parents unknowingly encourage this because his dependency on them makes them feel secure and needed. The relationship is dependent-based, not love based (where personal responsibility and accountability would be encouraged).
- A wife has feelings of insecurity in her life that are fed when she plays the role of being helpless and needy. She orchestrates ways for her husband to be forced to assist her. At the same time, she "mothers" him, manages and attempts to compensate for areas of his personal weakness due to his alcoholism. She knows that he needs her in order to function. The relationship is based on needs and personal weaknesses to create a perceived mutual dependency. This is in opposition to a healthy marriage where two secure people give to each other out of love.

Dependency versus Authority

It's important to note that some forms of dependency are appropriate. For example, children are supposed to be dependent on parents until adulthood. It's not "a power kick"—it's a position of authority and responsibility. In the same way, a wife places herself under the authority of her husband when she marries him. He is meant to take responsibility for her needs, thus making her dependent. So where then do we draw the line? How can we distinguish, especially in a marriage, when healthy and authoritative dependency is in place or when dependency is in fact a power kick?

Whenever we face questions about relationships, we must go to the Word of God. We begin by looking at how God relates to us, His children. We know He is in a position of authority yet continues to respect our free will. We learned in chapter 4 that He wants a relationship with us based on mutual love and submission, not force, coercion and control.

As we look into our own situation, we have to evaluate the fruits. We are going to look at the manifestation of this in more detail in these next sections.

Control in Relationships

It should be clear by now that unhealthy dependency and control go hand-in-hand. Most codependents, by definition, have an ultra-need to control people and circumstances. More often than not, our controlling tendencies are expressed unconsciously. Even if we are obviously and purposefully attempting to control people and circumstances, we may actually believe it's our job to do so! We may even be the recipients of someone else's harsh control over us and use our own control in much more subtle ways to cope and survive.

In reality, all forms of control apart from the Holy Spirit are tools of the Enemy. Control stands in complete opposition to the godly characteristic of free will (a right to choose). Whenever we use control to get people to respond or behave in a certain way, it is evidence that the relationship lacks the understanding of true love. In reality, our need to control seeks to satisfy self, and people become a means to that end, whatever it may be. Whether our efforts to control are subtle attempts to defend, self-protect, get our needs met indirectly, gain love, find happiness, maintain peace and so forth, these efforts result from not trusting in God above all else.

It's so important that we don't water down the tragedy of control. It leads to horrific cycles of relationship pain. Wherever control exists, the relationship cannot grow or thrive. In fact, it is destined to some form of death: emotional or spiritual.

Understanding Controlling Patterns

Most people fall into three basic types of controlling patterns: aggressive (domination), passive (submission), or passive-aggressive (combination of both). We are going to look at dominant and passive controlling patterns. As we look at both sides of control, keep in mind that many of us are both passive and aggressive. That simply means we stay more passive and use more subtle and indirect forms of control but can hit a point where we've had enough and blow up and show more aggressive tendencies.

Dominant/Aggressive Controller

Aggressive people control by force. They actually see a person as someone to own or possess. This form of control revolves around a perverted sense of the right to dominate another person's will, personal rights and behaviors.

Aggressive people want power and want to make people fear that power. They are continually implementing strategies to increase a personal sense of superiority and domination over others. These types of aggressors are usually very recognizable. They might even use physical aggression as a means of seeking the subordination of others. They can be strategic and manipulative when in need of something specific. They want what they want, and they will run over other people to get it.

The methods of aggressive people are not always that straightforward. Some aggressors use emotional and intellectual head games to trap people into submission. For example, an aggressor can twist the reality of a situation and blame and shame people to belittle them. They can also use correcting, criticizing, fault-finding, condemnation, confrontation, silent treatments and demeaning as tools of control.

Often aggressors seek to develop dependencies upon them to gain control. Dictatorship nations that come to power often initially seize on the vulnerabilities of people to gain control over them. While at first their efforts seem good, dictators lure people into dependency, which ultimately translates into power. It is no different in relationships. Aggressors may know a person's weaknesses and play upon them. They may even offer ways to initially meet those needs. Eventually, they will be in the position to say, "You could never live without me." Once the dependent state is established, they have power (control) over that person.

While aggressors appear strong, they are actually weak and fear abandonment and rejection. Unhealthy as it is, this personality will benefit only from God's intervention, not human intervention. Sympathizing or seeking to "fix" this type of personality could take us down.

There are no limits to how dark and manipulative an aggressor can become. These behaviors all open doors to satanic influences. Anyone who has been under the influence of an aggressor may have battle scars. They may have suffered physical, mental, emotional and spiritual abuse.

Submissive/Passive

Codependents can take on aggressive controlling tendencies over time. If they were subjected to control, they may eventually opt for the more intensive form. However, more often, codependents tend to be at the receiving end of the dominant/aggressive control. They also tend to counter-control as a means of survival. This plays out in a form of control that is much different. It is subtle and often filled with nice actions, but it nonetheless seeks to manipulate and change outcomes in people and circumstances.

To better understand the difference between the dominant and the submissive controller, let's look at the story of Jane, a woman attempting to overcome her codependent behaviors. Jane grew up in an alcoholic environment. Everything revolved around her father's drinking and abusive tendencies. His angry, aggressive approach in the home led to frantic attempts to appease him. The goal of the family was to make sure dad didn't get upset. Even more so, it was Jane's desire to earn her father's favor and affection, although that never happened.

The Cycle of Control

Controlling influence: Jane's dad aggressively controlled the entire atmosphere. The focus of the home was his "needs," and abusive behaviors dominated the home.

Counter-controlling: Jane unknowingly sought to control how her dad felt and acted. For example, an episode of rage was to be avoided at all costs, so Jane would do anything in her power to please, bring peace or accommodate her father.

Jane grew up unknowingly controlled by her father's unhealthy emotions and drinking, and she unknowingly developed a counter-controlling mentality. She carried this same system into her adult relationships as she "read" the needs and emotional problems of those around her so she could respond appropriately. Her response was an attempt either to protect herself or to indirectly get her needs met. Since this was a "normal" childhood experience, she didn't know any other way and therefore repeated the behavior in her marriage. Her life was governed by either feeling controlled by someone or counter-controlling to get what she needed to survive.

In this example, Jane's counter-control is typical of someone trying to function in the survival mode of an oppressive situation. If we look at these behaviors side by side, it would appear fair to say that Jane is the victim. Rightly so, except that Jane's counter-controlling tendencies would become a very unhealthy operating system in her life. With this system in place, Jane cannot participate in healthy love of any form. Certainly, her behaviors aren't as noticeably bad, but the root driving force behind them is actually the same problem as her dad's: self is trying to get self-needs met.

Counter-controllers normally have a more passive personality. Control may be a form of protection or survival and the way to meet physical, emotional or spiritual needs.

For example, they may take any of these actions:
- Attempt to control someone else's feelings or protect someone from bad feelings (the faulty belief: I have the power to change or affect someone else's feelings)
- Attempt to control the way a person perceives, likes or responds to them (the faulty belief: I have the ability to control how a person sees me)
- Follow rules and moral behavior strictly to gain a sense of goodness, thus feeling superior to people who are perceived as "bad" (the faulty belief: I can earn my own righteousness)
- Use subtle comments that include guilt-giving statements: "You should have done this but didn't"; or shaming statements: "What is wrong with you?" (the faulty belief: pointing out their wrongs indirectly will make that person change)
- Tell lies to maintain a reputation or be perceived more positively (the faulty belief: it's okay to tell lies if people will think better of me)

- Use flattery or gifts to buy the affection or approval of someone (the faulty belief: I can influence the way people think about me)
- Try to earn love by doing anything they think would cause someone to love them (the faulty belief: your love can be earned through my efforts)

Passive control is extremely difficult to recognize when it has been etched into a person's character from a young age. These controlling patterns often seem normal, therefore almost impossible to detect. All passive control is expressed through manipulation, which can be very artful and disguised. The use of guilt and shame specifically tends to be taught through the family of origin. Influencing people and getting them to act the way we want them to act becomes a learned relationship skill.

A codependent who adopts passive but controlling mentalities is prone to pass these off in unhealthy ways that will cause damage in relationships. Let's look at another example, a man who is seeking help for his addiction to drugs, alcohol, sex and gambling.

Henry

Henry grew up in a Christian home. Rules, lists and expectations were drawn by his mother to ensure that his behavior was appropriate. Henry learned to measure himself by his mother's approval. If he didn't measure up to her expectations, she made comments such as "You know better" or "What's wrong with you, Henry?" Since he lived life trying to measure himself by his mother's standards, he didn't know how to make his own choices based on his personal ideas, conscience, perceptions or needs.

Although he didn't realize it, Henry's world was totally controlled by his mom. He became a by-product of whatever she wanted him to be. He felt obliged to appease her and sought to avoid the shame he felt when he let her down. He also used her favor to get special gifts that his other siblings didn't enjoy.

As he grew older, he found less and less satisfaction from earning his mother's approval. He began to secretly find ways to break from her and participate in behaviors and activities she would oppose. He began to drink and party, while at the same time played the role of mama's boy.

The Cycle of Control

Controlling influence: Henry's mom imprisoned him with expectations built around her own needs and desired outcomes of his behavior. She used guilt and shame in an attempt to control his behavior. Deep down, she suffered from an internal sense of feeling inadequate and out of control. She feared losing him.

Counter-controlling: Henry felt powerless and confined by his mother's control.

He eventually tried to break from her control by leading a double lifestyle. This ability to fool his mom gave him a sense of control over his own ability to make decisions or to feel good. He learned how to use his relationship with his mother to get whatever material needs he wanted.

Henry grew to become a full-fledged alcoholic and attracted a codependent wife who tried to manage him in much the same way his mom had. While this pattern of relationship was entirely unhealthy, it was a reality from the past that he carried into future relationships. He learned to feed his wife's emotional need to be validated by him in order to gain her favor, while selfishly seeking whatever he desired outside the relationship: sex, gambling, partying. Eventually, Henry was completely unavailable and the family system became desperately broken down.

Here we see how Henry's unhealthy dependency on his mother, driven by her strong controlling behaviors, prompted him to develop other counter-controlling behaviors. The "fruit" of Henry's mom's attempts to control the outcome of his behavior produced the fertile soil for addiction and rebellion. Of course, she wasn't directly responsible, but that environment seems the most likely to breed those characteristics. It's ironic to note that our controlling attempts often actually produce the opposite of what we want.

Application Points:
Try to identify controlling patterns in your own life.

Have you been oppressed or felt controlled by someone? Was it through dominant or more subtle approaches? Explain.

_____
_____

_____

Do you recognize any ways in which you may have attempted to use control in your relationships? Was it dominant or subtle? Explain.

_____
_____

_____

The Pathway of Surrender

All human relationship problems can be traced to some form of control. Based on what we have learned so far, it should be obvious that human beings attempting to control other human beings doesn't work. As we learned in the last lesson, the foundation of a healthy relationship is intended to be love. And the very fabric of love is that it produces a spirit of freedom, not control. When we try to control people, we are in fact in direct competition with the Holy Spirit. In 1 Corinthians 2:11, the Bible tells us that no one knows a man but the Spirit that lives in him. As human beings, whenever we take the position of trying to control someone else's thoughts, emotions or behaviors, we are essentially trying to stand in God's shoes.

Many times we are unaware how we try to control others and how we have allowed others to control us in relationships. If we are oppressed and dependent on those who control us, it can be extremely challenging and paralyzing. What we must decide is to believe that the power of God truly can overcome those circumstances. We cannot change people, but God can. He can also deliver us from oppression or simply change our own heart so we have the tools and resources to deal with the circumstances appropriately. Normally, as we learn how to cease control in our own relationships, we begin to see that the problems are not just other people but that we in fact have our own dysfunction. God will reveal to us our faulty beliefs and the negative systems we use to make relationships work.

Letting go comes with a realization that we will be empty handed, at least for a period. In the long term, the idea of a healthy form of letting go is that there is something better to cling to. It's a realization that whatever we are holding on to doesn't really belong to us, and we need to be willing to set it free from our grip. Parents sometimes need to learn this with maturing children who enter adulthood. At some point, that child can still be loved, but not held on to. For the codependent, hanging on means "I can fix it, change it, manage it or make it right." Letting go is an act of admitting our own power didn't work, leaving us with a sense of powerlessness.

Realizing that it is impossible to control other people and our own circumstances can be very painful and frightening. In fact, if we lived under that reality in and of itself, we would feel helpless and hopeless. However, a codependent who experiences powerlessness has made the most difficult step toward healing. It is at this arrival place, otherwise known as brokenness, where God can divinely intervene in our life.

A true brokenness is a divine appointment only God can orchestrate. Through the various situations, God is pleading with us to realize our helplessness and thus realize our need for Him. When this occurs, it gives us the ability to transfer control. When and if we are ready to surrender, we must make two basic transactions:

1. Die to self. What does that mean? We choose to cease control. We choose to strip off our own defense mechanisms and strategies of battle, recognizing we were losing the war. The death of self is not the death of our God-given destination, identity, personality and giftedness. It's the death of our self-will (flesh) that is programmed to meet needs independent of God.

2. Allow God to take control of our life. That means we no longer call the shots based on our own needs, perceptions, survival strategies, and so forth. Instead,

we let God call the shots for us. We allow Him to lead and guide us into His ultimate plan and purpose for our life.

While this sounds simple enough, it can be a fierce internal struggle. By nature, we are prone to be in the mode of self-survival and self-defense. The codependent, especially, has had to learn self-survival strategies to simply function in life. Being asked to abandon those strategies, admit defeat and truly surrender can leave us with a complete sense of vulnerability. So what would motivate us to do such a thing?

John 12:24–26 provides a summary of the purpose and goal of true surrender (brackets enclose author's words used for emphasis).

> I tell you the truth, unless a kernel of wheat is planted in the soil and dies [our self-will], it remains alone. But its death will produce many new kernels—a plentiful harvest of new lives [a life surrendered]. Those who love their life in this world will lose it [those who choose to live independently of God]. Those who care nothing for their life in this world will keep it for eternity [those who give God control]. Anyone who wants to be my disciple must follow me, because my servants must be where I am. And the Father will honor anyone who serves me.

Through this scripture, we learn that ultimately the entire destination of our lives rests upon our willingness to die to self so Christ can live through us. But we must understand what this entails. Living for God brings amazing blessings—the access to all God's resources and an endless supply of His love, mercy, grace and power. As the diagram on page 117 shows, giving God control simply puts us and the people in our lives under God's sovereign provision and protection. (Refer to diagram "Ceasing Control: Giving God Control" on Page 117.)

Not every person gets "broken." In fact, it's sad to say that more people probably never get broken by God in this fashion. By nature, codependents tend to be extremely strong-willed and able to withstand difficult circumstances through a learned system of survival. Our toughness and ability to persevere certainly appear to be noble qualities. Yet that mentality will keep us fighting battles in our own strength, battles God never intended us to fight. Like soldiers in a war, we are in a battlefield unaided and without weapons, fighting to overcome things we have neither the power nor the ability to overcome.

The codependent actually needs to go through a process to understand that God wants our weaknesses, not our strengths. Since we are by nature fighters, this can take some time. In 2 Corinthians 12:9–10, we read about the relationship between our weakness and God's strength.

Each time he said, "My grace is all you need. My power works best in weakness." So now I am glad to boast about my weaknesses, so that the power of Christ can work through me. That's why I take pleasure in my weaknesses, and in the insult, hardships, persecutions, and troubles that I suffer for Christ. For when I am weak, then I am strong.

One of the secrets we learn in walking with Jesus is that when we give Him control, in our weakness we are strong. Why? Because He has control and He is strong! However, if we are trying to be strong and in control, we are very weak. Every resource we need to live life is found in our relationship with God. When we surrender control to Him, we come under His provision and His protection.

If you still think life depends on your own strength, you are not quite ready to relinquish control and give it over to God. However, when you feel defeated and tired, giving your life and will over to God can be the most incredible experience of your life. If you are facing trials and tribulations right now, God might be crying out to you, "Come to Me." When you scream out, "I CAN'T, HELP ME GOD," it is at that point, the very point of your need, that God begins to work. Asking Him to help is just the beginning. He wants not only to bring blessing into our lives and relationships but also to remove strongholds and our controlling mentalities and replace them with love. We still may be in difficult and oppressive situations, but we have a new perspective. (In chapter 11 we will learn the importance of boundaries in dealing with control.)

Are you believing God? Do you trust Him? Is His control better than your own? Claim this promise: "Now all glory to God, who is able, through his mighty power at work within us, to accomplish infinitely more than we might ask or think" (Ephesians 3:20).

A Prayer to Let Go

Dear Heavenly Father,

I need You in my life right now. I realize I cannot manage my life without You. I see my self-dependency and my dependency on other people. I have tried to change people and fix their problems. I have carried the weight of the world on my shoulders. I have tried to rule my world. I realize now that it isn't my job, and the journey from here on out is determined by my willingness to let You break me. I ask You, Lord, to reveal or remove anything that might be hindering me from coming to You. I want to become like a child, willing to be led by You. Parent me, nurture me, guide and keep me in Your care. Enter into my heart at my point of need right now. Be not only my Savior, but also my Lord. Heal me where I'm wounded and love me where I'm broken. If I don't see or understand my needs right now, please reveal them to me. Thank You in advance for your goodness and Your grace. I release my tight grasp on my life and instead put my hand in Yours. In Jesus's name, amen.

Application Points:

What can you do today to focus more on the exercise of letting go and allowing God to control your life?

_____

_____

_____

Does this act of transferring your will to God's will confuse, frustrate or anger you? Are you excited, ready and willing?

_____

_____

_____

People Control Me - I Control People

Self

I am in denial of my needs

I allow people to control and influence my feelings and behavior

I don't think I deserve better

Others

I try to fix and change others

I focus on other people's problems

I try to please people

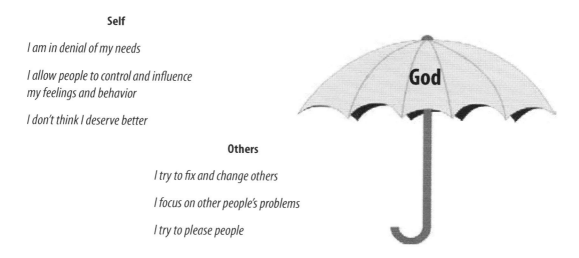

When people hold power and God is displaced, my own power lies in my efforts, leaving me exhausted, frustrated and angry. I am not under God's protection because I'm not trusting Him. I get in the way of God because I think I have the tools to change others.

God is Control

Self

I cease control

I focus on my own need for change

I receive God's love and rest in Him

Others

I stop my efforts to please and fix others

I surrender the people in my life to God

I pray for others

When God is in control, His power is released. My ability to admit my weakness places me under the supernatural protection and providence of God. I surrender the people in my life to Him and give God the ability to work on their behalf. I experience His presence, peace, joy and hope.

6

Breaking Free From Denial

Workbook Keys

1. WHAT IS THE DANGER OF DENIAL?
2. WHAT ARE WAYS WE CAN BE IN DENIAL?
3. WHY MUST WE FACE UNMET NEEDS?
4. WHAT IS THE PURPOSE OF TRUTH-FINDING?

Our codependence is a filter by which we have viewed the world, ourselves, others and God in a toxic and harmful manner. This filter has told us things that aren't true. This filter has made us see things that aren't there, while at the same time blinding us to things that really do exist. It's no wonder, then, that the most difficult thing about recovery from codependence is *seeing things as they are*. That means pulling off the filter, peeling back the masks and getting to the raw layers of what our experience up to this point has *actually* been. While it sounds scary, it can be summed up in one word—truth. Jesus said, "And you will know the truth and the truth will set you free" (John 8:32). We avoid truth, yet truth brings the freedom we so desperately need. We often create a reality of how we wish things would be, or we cover over things through our skills of compensation. This distortion of reality is a safety net that allows us to hide behind a facade that states, "Everything is fine." It creates an illusion, a false impression, that may seem to satisfy others but leaves us barely hanging on.

Denial is the blinder. Denial is the killer that prevents us from living the life God intends for us. As human beings, our natural reaction to the damaging consequences of sin, hurt and pain is denial. Satan knows that as long as we don't believe a problem exists, we will never be able to find a solution. He will use whatever forces possible to keep us in denial.

If we were able to get honest, we'd admit that we've been hurt, we've felt used, and we've carried a lot of burdens. Deep down, we crave for someone to understand and know where we've been. Yet because our defense mechanisms have continued to be built throughout our lifetime, we rarely, if ever, have been able to do so. This next lesson is where we are asked to take an honest look at ourselves, including our experiences, relationships and sin issues. The purpose is to fight against the real enemy of our souls—the lies we believe that bring us some form of death while on earth.

To begin, we are going to seek to understand more about the ways we participate in denial of both actions (behaviors) and needs. Denial can mean many different things to different people, but for the codependent, it often includes these:

- Denial of the way others have hurt us. We may simply not want to face that pain and have therefore hidden it in our unconscious mind.
- Denial of who we really are. We feel unworthy and scared to face ourselves. Usually this is a result of deeper shame messages that were planted into our lives.
- Denial of the behaviors of others. We are not in touch with the reality of other people's behaviors. For example, we may see an addict's behavior as bad but have grown to accept it and adjust around it. After some time, we don't even realize how dysfunctional it may be. Some people in denial blatantly deny the wrongful acts of another and even protect that person.
- Denial of our own behaviors. We may not be able to accurately assess how our own behaviors may cause damage to others if we are more focused on how others have hurt us. Or we might overly condemn ourselves when we haven't actually done anything wrong in a relationship.
- Denial of our feelings. A person who becomes detached grows emotionally cold. We may have feelings toward a variety of things, but we cannot connect those emotions to what is taking place on the inside.
- Denial of the imbalance of our relationships. We work so hard to compensate that we don't realize we overly give and rarely receive. We may have other relationships where this pattern is reversed.

There are different levels of denial, depending on the nature of traumatic and difficult experiences we have encountered throughout our lifetime. The more extreme forms of denial include these:

Denial by Substitution. This type of denial allows us to suppress the true reality of a situation and instead try to substitute another reality for it. We might create a fantasy version of our past life. Or we might focus on changing our current circumstances so we never have to see them as they really are. For example, Al is still concerned with pleasing his parents, although he is well into adulthood. Al has always put his dad on a pedestal and believes his dad is a loving and wonderful man. In reality, Al's dad was extremely abusive to him in childhood and through his adolescent years. Al's dad also abused his sister, who has since sunk deeply into addictive behavior. Al is offended whenever someone mentions anything negative about his dad, especially when it is coming from his sister. Al adamantly defends his dad and loyally works to make sure everyone thinks his dad is the hero he has believed him to be.

Repression. This is the ability to "stuff" things, burying the event, trauma or emotions in the unconscious mind. When we repress something, we seem to not be affected by that issue, but in reality, the repression drives a variety of negative thoughts, emotions and compulsive behaviors. Since that driving root is not dealt with, a person with a lot of repression is trapped and unable to identify the true issues. For example, Jenny cannot recall accurately a period of her life when she was experiencing significant loss and abandonment. If asked, she is vaguely aware of what she experienced and tries to discount or block those memories as simply "being in the past." However, she suffers from an eating disorder and an extreme form of codependence.

Disassociation. This is the ability to completely disconnect from an event where there is no memory whatsoever of trauma that occurred. When a child is disassociated, retrieving the memory of that event will not happen easily. Only the Holy Spirit can retrieve these memories as they have been completely removed from any conscious state. For example, a child may have been sexually abused and completely "checked out" to cope and survive. In a way, the child disappeared in that event and has no ability to retrieve it at a conscious level. A person who has suffered this type of trauma may require the assistance of a qualified Christian counselor or pastor in the initial phases.

Being able to expose and dispose of denial is a foundational and necessary ingredient for any change to take place or for freedom to be found. For children, denial, repression and disassociation give them the ability to cope in overwhelming situations. Just as the physical body goes into shock to allow it to function under trauma, children who have been exposed to extreme emotional pain are often able to disconnect from the situation enough to be able to function. Had they not been able to repress some of the trauma, the pain would have been too much for them to bear. Therefore, it could be thought of as a defense mechanism that acts to protect a child (and sometimes adults). While this is a much needed survival mechanism, there comes a point when the issue must be addressed properly for healing to take place. The only safe and effective way for this to occur is alongside Jesus. Certainly, a human counselor can provide guidance, but only the True Counselor can extract those deeper and more traumatizing situations and uncover the true impact.

How can we face things that we never could before? What could give us the courage to look beyond the outward reality we've created and trade it for inward truth? Over and over again we must come back to the purpose of our lives. We are made in the image of a Creator. We aren't made as some generic "cookie cutter" of the human race, but we have been formed and hand-designed by that Creator, with uniqueness, giftedness, significance and worth. God desires to remove the things keeping us from becoming that person. Going through this process restores us to our original design.

Here are a few of the things God says about us:

"For I know the plans I have for you," says the Lord. "They are plans for good and not for disaster, to give you a future and a hope." (Jeremiah 29:11)

"I knew you before I formed you in your mother's womb. Before you were born I set you apart." (Jeremiah 1:5)

"O Lord, you have examined my heart and know everything about me. You know when I sit down or stand up. You know my thoughts even when I'm far away. You see me when I travel and when I rest at home. You know everything I do. You know what I am going to say even before I say it, Lord. You go before me and follow me. You place your hand of blessing on my head. "(Psalm 139:1–5)

Application Points:
Do you see right now how denial may have skewed your view of life? Where are you prone to denial?

_____

_____

_____

Are you afraid of truth? Why?

_____

_____

_____

Assessing Unmet Needs

Just as we need to uncover forms of denial that conceal the events and things that happened to us, we must recognize the absence of God-given needs. People can hurt us by what they do to us; they also hurt us by what they don't do. For many of us, a root of abandonment and neglect is responsible for our wounds.

As human beings, we have basic needs including these:

- The need to be loved
- The need to be accepted
- The need to have significance

Children who grew up in a dysfunctional home may never have had these needs met, or they were met through false messages of what it meant to be loved, accepted and significant (instead earning acceptance or working for it). Often, in unhealthy family systems, there is an unspoken message that having needs at any level is embarrassing or shameful. Why? In reality, when parents aren't able to provide basic needs, they may in turn blame the child for expecting or demanding too much. Children from these homes are often told they should know how to survive and function without any direction or guidance. You could say these children are asked to grow up on their own and are then criticized for not understanding how life works. When this happens, children are taught that their basic needs are wrong. They learn they must cope by themselves.

How does a child survive? As we discussed in chapter 2, they will learn from an early age how to function and survive to get needs met indirectly, which may result in various unhealthy behaviors including manipulation. If they adopt codependence as adults, they will spend most of their time focusing on the needs of others, while consistently having their own needs neglected. In some ways, codependents end up doing for others what they wished someone would do for them. But the bottom line of that behavior is that it makes them falsely feel in control, as we discussed in detail in chapter 5. Actually, these needs are perfectly legitimate and placed in us by the heart of God. Not having essentials such as the need for love met is devastating (chapter 4).

How Do I Identity Unmet Needs?

The unmet needs of codependents need to be properly understood and identified. One of the only ways we can understand our unmet needs is to work through and identify true needs openly with God. Many times felt needs are far from actual needs. We need the guidance of the Holy Spirit to show us the difference. Let's review some of the areas where we are prone to experiencing the neglect of legitimate needs:

- **Genuine experience of love.** As we saw in chapter 4, the absence of love is devastating and the root cause behind our codependent behaviors. When relationships lack love, they are replaced by dependency and control (chapter 5). When we are in a survival mode, these issues develop automatically, and we build walls of denial so we can function. You may have already discovered your own skewed loved systems. If you have not yet done so, it's time to acknowledge that the unmet need for love is legitimate.

- **Life nurturing and guidance.** Children must be taught life in a variety of ways. From the smallest and most basic things to the larger and more complicated things, a parent's job is to be continually teaching a child and equipping him or her to become a mature adult. The problem is that not every parent is able to do this. Not every parent is emotionally available to give the child the time and attention required to take on that mentoring role. By not nurturing a child, yet expecting him or her to "know life," parents send their children false messages about God-given and legitimate needs.

- **A sense of protection.** Children require the safety of healthy boundaries and protection from outside threats. If a parent is unavailable or in their own forms of denial or addiction, they may knowingly or unknowingly allow a child to be violated by an outside or inside perpetrator. If one parent is abusive, the child may be confused about why the other parent allows this to happen. In more subtle ways, a child can feel unprotected when a parent does not provide a watchful eye over him or her. The child may do things that are dangerous and harmful. This sends a message to the child that the parent simply doesn't care, isn't interested or doesn't have time to "bother."

- **Healthy forms of discipline.** Discipline teaches a child proper boundaries and a sense that actions have consequences. Abusive discipline is very damaging, but just the same, no discipline at all leaves a child unable to learn cause and effect.

- **Nurturing of identity and gender role.** Many of us didn't have strong gender role models. Even if we did, we may have been taught misconceptions about our identity and roles as males or females. We may feel disconnected with our gender role, feeling more masculine or feminine. This distortion can lead us into many levels of relationship and sexual identity problems.

- **Acceptance as a valuable and precious child.** Children are valuable and precious by their very existence. If a child is seen as a burden, a problem or continually not measuring up to a standard, that child will have no sense of acceptance and no sense of being truly precious. The root of shame will be planted, and that child will continually try to prove worthiness or will simply give up.

- **The loss of a carefree and fun childhood.** Children aren't meant to carry adult problems, yet in dysfunctional families, some children carry all the adult problems because the adults have checked out. Children from these families have no understanding of the fun and carefree lifestyle a child was intended to live. Life is serious. The pressure and overwhelming sense of responsibility will disrupt a child's maturity and lead to lifelong emotional and relationship problems. We often hear people say, "I was never able to grow up."

- **The instilling of self-esteem.** A healthy self-esteem ensures a child has an accurate and balanced perspective of self. That means they don't feel an exaggerated sense of self but they don't encounter self-hatred, self-rejection or self-loathing either.
- **Encouragement.** Like those with a coach, we need to be encouraged to be our best. We sometimes need someone who simply says, "I believe in you." If we never had anyone speak positively into our hearts in our childhood, we may have believed that nothing about us made us special. Some of us were even told, "You won't amount to anything." How tragic. We all have a God-given destiny, and if you have never received encouragement, we pray you will receive it right now. You are precious. You are God's child. You have a significant purpose because God says so.

When we've had unmet needs in childhood (or adulthood), we must recognize and grieve what we lost. Children, especially, must understand that something they desired or needed was not available. That precious child we all were at one time did what he or she had to do to survive.

However, today we have new choices. We don't have to continue down destructive paths trying to replace the things we lost. By grieving over our losses, we can move on in a healthy way and ask God to make up for our unmet needs. If we ignore and stay in denial of those needs, we unknowingly continue trying to replace what was lost. Here are two examples:

- A woman might be attracted to an abusive, alcoholic man just like her father, believing this time around she can fix or change him.
- A man might look to his wife to replace a mother who abandoned him, unknowingly boxing his wife in by behaving overly possessive out of fear of her leaving.

The difficult thing is that when we realize we are recycling past needs through current relationships, we'll at some point need to grieve our losses in those current relationships. In the above example, the woman needs to grieve her issues with her father (the root), but she'll also need to grieve the losses within her current unhealthy relationships and all the devastation they caused (the effect).

You'll be asked to write out your specific unmet needs. In chapter 9, you'll learn exactly what it means to grieve your pain and losses. When we truly do grieve, we can break the cycle of wrongly trying to replace those needs indirectly or through another person.

As we go through this process, the amazing thing about our God is that He meets us at the point of our need, even when we don't understand it. God provides the core needs of our life for love, acceptance and significance. There is not a person in the world who is able to give us exactly what we need except God Himself. And we can claim the promise of Philippians 4:19: "And this same God who takes care of me will supply all your needs from his glorious riches, which have been given to us in Christ Jesus" and cash it into heaven. But remember, God will meet your *true* needs, not necessarily your *perceived* needs. Do you trust Him?

Application Point:
Do you feel uncomfortable admitting your needs to people? Why?

_____

_____

_____

Self-Confrontation: Developing an Inventory

How do we know if we are in denial? How can we assess our unmet needs? Usually, all of us entering into recovery have many layers of denial. However, the intensity of that denial can range immensely. That's why an honest assessment process is necessary. Developing inventories of life experiences and relationship issues is an effective tool in overcoming denial. We will spend the rest of this chapter preparing to begin this inventory process.

While this process can lead to significant levels of growth, we must understand that it may take time. We must set realistic expectations as we approach an inventory. At times, God may touch us and give us the ability to feel a supernatural healing instantly. But often in the healing process, God simply exposes lies that we have accepted as truth. He takes that truth and makes it a reality within us so we are walking in the light rather than the darkness of the deceit and lies we carried. No matter our background, this process requires maturity and growth. After we begin to expose issues in our life, a lengthy amount of time may be required to completely process them.

Whatever your experience has been, be assured that the God who made and loves you will walk you through this process. Because of your unique experiences, He will probably work with you differently from how He works with someone else. That's why we can never compare this process with that of another—our healing may be on a different time line.

Breaking Free: No More Denial

In this next section, we are going to be developing the actual inventory of the issues in our life (refer to page 129). They will include issues such as these:

- **Ways you have been violated (sinned against).** This list should include all acts of violations and sins committed against you. Try to begin at the earliest memory and work your way forward to recent experiences. Use specific things rather than generalizations. Focus on the actual sin/violation, not the person. (For example, whether or not the person intended to harm you doesn't matter at this point. It's important to simply see and face the violation and the effect it had on your life). If you are having a difficult time organizing, go relationship to relationship, focusing on the key areas of violations. Be as all-inclusive as possible.

- **Immoral and sinful behaviors you committed.** This is a list of things you have done that violated God's Word, yourself or another person (it could be all three). Try to begin at the earliest memory and work your way forward to recent experiences. These should be specific acts, not general. If you have a difficult time organizing this list, go from relationship to relationship (mom, dad, siblings, friend, and so forth), focusing on the key ways you wronged someone else. Be as all-inclusive as possible.

- **Painful and traumatic experiences.** Traumatic and life-altering events can shape our lives tremendously. These are typically major issues such as a parent's death, divorce or sexual assault. These should be specific rather than generalizations. Be as all-inclusive as possible.

- **Relationship patterns.** This is a list of love skills (give and take) in relationships. It is intended to highlight those relational patterns so we can understand where unhealthy dynamics exist. Include all-important relationships in the family of origin and all-important adult relationships.

- **Unmet Needs.** This is a list of things you needed and didn't receive or had and then lost. It's important to connect with these items and at some point go through an actual grieving process (see chapter 9). Use specific things rather than generalizations. Be as all-inclusive as possible.

Before you attempt this project, spend time in prayer and meditation. If you need to take a break and come back, remember to open up in prayer again. Only God can reveal these things to us and He must be present for this to be effective.

Dr. Tucker, Director of New Life Spirit Recovery, uses this process firsthand in the counseling environment. As the client sifts through memories, he asks them to visualize themselves going hand-in-hand with Jesus as their Guide. He encourages them to ask God to allow them to experience whatever senses are necessary to connect to the event or situation. That means that they might need to remember the sight, sound, touch, taste and smell.

As an example, "Linda" was asked to recall a memory of an alcoholic dad. Dr. Tucker's goal in her counseling session was to actually connect with the emotions of that event. To do this, he asked her to remember the smell of his breath, the sound of his voice and the sting of him knocking her against a wall. Ultimately, as she sifted through these memories in that manner, she found herself deeply impacted by the nature of her trauma. She was overwhelmed by grief but at the same time realized how she was experiencing a sense of God's peace and comfort. This was the objective.

We look back only to emotionally connect with life experiences that had been repressed, disassociated or not otherwise properly dealt with. In essence, we must "feel to heal." Our inability to feel led us to compulsive behaviors in the first place. Now, instead, we face those things we have hidden from by learning to embrace the True Comforter. "Linda" and many like her experienced a newfound freedom. She faced the pain of her past yet discovered a new understanding of a God who loved her infinitively more than she could even comprehend. She realized, as we all must, that God carried her grief, and as she courageously allowed God to reveal truth, He was in the process of healing her.

This is a very powerful process, but it can be painful. The process of sifting through the past is to remove "death," including lies, denial and false messages acquired. When we read that Jesus Christ came to bring us an abundant life, it literally meant HIS life! (see John 10:10). Through the power of the Holy Spirit, "His life" is the fulfillment of all the promises we find in Scripture.

Jesus Christ is the Prince of Peace and the True Counselor. However, if you've had some significant pain and suffering, we encourage you to find a qualified counselor, mentor or sponsor who has a Spirit-led walk and an understanding of the love, power and grace of our Lord.

A Prayer to Break Denial
Father God,

Denial is a scary word. It means I have been deceived somehow. I ask You right now to remove the blinders from my heart. Please show me anything that has kept me from being the real person You made me to be. If there are wounds I need to address, show me. If I have been locked up on the inside while living differently on the outside, rescue me. I believe according to Your Word that you love me perfectly. And in that perfect love, I know I can face the things in my life I need to face. Be with me, Lord. Guide me. Expose the things that have held me in bondage, but do so lovingly and graciously. I pray against the tactics of the Enemy. I know he would tempt me to feel shame. Instead, let me see how much You love me and desire to set me free.

In Jesus's name, amen.

Violations & Sins Committed Against You

The categories are as follows:

Incident: Describe the actual sin or violation committed

Person: Write the person or people that committed the act

Internal Message Received: How did the sin/violation "register" within me - what did it say?

Emotional reactions: Check the boxes that apply

This Led Me To: describe your response following the violation

Incident	Person	Internal Message Received	Shame	Loss/Abandonment	Rejection	Resentment	Unworthiness	This Led Me To
Physically abused when my father was drinking	Dad	I was not lovable, dad did not care about me, something was wrong with me.	x	x	x	x		Go through life trying to prove myself to men. Repeated the cycle with future husband.

Behavioral Inventory of Immoral or Sinful Acts

Behaviors: Describe the thing you did

Person I Violated: Write the person who it violated

How It Affected that Person: Explain how your behavior may have hurt or affected that person

How You Should Deal with It: Check the boxes that apply

How It's Affected You: describe your response following the violation

Behaviors	Person I Violated (God, self, or others)	How It Affected that Person	Need to Confess	Need to Receive Forgiveness	Prepare to Make Amends	How This Affected Me
Verbally abusive to spouse	Myself, spouse	Hurt deeply	x	x	x	I've carried guilt and shame

Trauma & Life Altering Events

Event: Describe

How it Affected Me: As a result of this incident, what changed in me?

Person I Blame: Name the person you feel made this event occur (God, self or others)

Emotional reactions: Check the boxes that apply

Event	How it Affected Me	Person I Blamed	Denial	Disassociation	Repression	Anger	Rejection	Abandonment

Unmet Need or Losses

Unmet Needs or Loss: Describe

How I Attempted to Get that Need Met on My Own: As a result of not having a need met, or having lost something, how did you attempt to compensate? How did you make up for it or try to get it met in another way?

Person I Blamed: Who did I actually feel was responsible for this loss or unmet need? (Self, God, others)

Emotional reactions: Check the boxes that apply

Unmet Need or Loss	How I Attempted to Get that Need Met on My Own	Person I Blamed	Denial	Anger	Abandoned	Unsupported	Unforgiveness	Rejected

Love Skills & Codependence

Name of Person: Person in the relationship
How I gave: Explain how you loved in the relationshp
How I received: Explain how you received love in the relationship
Emotions Checklist: Check all that applied in the relationships

Name of Person:	How I loved/gave in relationship	How I was loved/received in relationship	Overcompensated	Felt Needy	Felt Rejected	Felt Unloved	Felt Abandoned

7

Exposing Shame

Workbook Keys

- DEFINE SHAME
- WHERE DOES SHAME COME FROM?
- HOW IS SHAME REMOVED?

God is in the business of restoration. It is through the life of His Spirit that we are brought back to wholeness. Nothing that has occurred in our past is allowed to have sovereign reign in our life when we summon the God of the Universe for assistance. Those parts of our lives that have been broken, emptied or invalidated are precious to God. The Word of God tells us how God is intimately involved with our pain: "You keep track of all my sorrows. You have collected all my tears in your bottle. You have recorded each one in your book" (Psalm 56:8). How amazing to realize that God has His own inventory of each one of our burdens. Imagine—He already authored a list that records our tears, not our wrongdoing! It is with that understanding of God's mercy and compassion that we are able to deal with the issues in our life. God's love toward us enables us to step out in faith and seek redemption. In fact, we are promised that nothing can separate us from God's love or take it away—nothing in the past, present or future, including all the experiences we have had (see Roman 8:38–39).

As we continue down the pathway toward healing, we must be willing to face the very things that caused us so much pain. We must also face our own wrongful behaviors. It is at this point that people either grow weary and give up or move on toward freedom. If we are courageous enough to move through this process, we won't be disappointed. It leads us into God's peace—a place where we can abide and rest in Him despite anything that occurs externally around us. But to get there, we must be willing to remove the turbulence that created so much conflict. We must be willing to face shame.

Shame: The Poison of Our Soul

Shame is the most lethal and toxic weapon of the soul because it prevents us from knowing or experiencing the love and grace of God. It operates by the realization that we missed the mark, we failed or we didn't measure up to a standard. It accompanies a feeling of being dirty and unacceptable. Shame disrupts a sense of normalcy and wreaks havoc on our ability to be healthy and whole. Satan will work hard to accuse, torment and make us believe we don't measure up to God's standard, creating within us feelings of worthlessness, hopelessness, grief, depression and chronic anxiety. When Satan captures our minds through these shame messages, he in essence has control over our lives.

As we will learn, the Word of God deals very specifically with shame. In fact, Jesus didn't just come to remove our sin; He also came to remove the harmful effects of shame. In recovery, we are taught that in order to heal, we must bring to light the very things we tried to hide. Bringing God's revealing light into our life can initially be quite uncomfortable. However, by exposing these issues, the Holy Spirit seeks to cover us with God's grace. It is in this condition that shame loses all power over us as we are covered in the reality of God's forgiveness, freedom and acceptance.

Identifying Shame Messages

Identifying the shame in our lives may not come easily. Even if we begin to see events, sins, trauma, abuse, and other issues, we may be unable to see how shame took root. We often think shame is directly correlated with the things we have done. However, shame is also usually a by-product of the way others have imposed standards on us and the very acts of abuse or neglect committed against us. For example, someone violating us may have instilled a belief in us that said, "This is what you deserve. Who would love you?" When someone violated us, neglected us, said painful words to us or shamed us, they sent a message direct into our head and heart. The act itself was bad, but the message it sent had the potential to affect us for the rest of our life.

Shameful messages can also say, "You're bad, you're stupid, you're fat, you're ugly." For example, Kelly was told she was overweight by her perfectionist mother with high standards. In reality, Kelly was a normal, healthy teenage girl. However, because she believed she was fat, she became ashamed of her weight and body image. Over time, Kelly developed compulsive behaviors in her attempt to control and lose weight. She eventually became anorexic and no matter what her weight was believed she was fat.

Kelly's problems stemmed from more than just her mother's words, but the mother's shame message planted a seed. That seed took root in Kelly's life; thus she allowed it to control her thoughts, feelings and behaviors.

Does that make it her mother's fault? Not exactly. Kelly chose to receive the message as truth. The problem is that as children we often automatically believe what our parents say. Eventually, we might reject those messages, but in our early years, we might believe whatever we are told.

While Kelly's mom may seem to be cruel, she was a carrier of shame. If we could look into her life, we'd see that she had a very rigid standard of weight because of the abuse and teasing she, herself, suffered in childhood.

Sadly, when we carry shame, we unknowingly superimpose it on others. Shame is often passed from one generation to the next. In this next section we will be learning how to identify and get rid of shame.

Application Points:
When you wrote or reviewed your inventory list, did you feel any shame? Explain.

_____
_____
_____

As you think upon your life up until this point, can you identify any specific relationship where shame was superimposed upon you? (The sense that you didn't measure up.)

_____
_____
_____

As you think upon your life up until this point, can you identify any relationships where you imposed shame on someone? If so, why did you?

_____
_____
_____

Name an area in your life you are extremely embarrassed and ashamed of. Can you trace the "message" behind it?

_____
_____
_____

How Does Shame Enter Our Life?

As we will learn, we must remember that shame is a by-product of hell. God does not use shame. He uses conviction in the life of the believer. Therefore, all shame is dangerous and needs to be removed. We will be dealing in depth with the riddance of shame in the next two chapters. In this chapter, we will learn how it is imposed, and in the chapters to follow we will learn how shame can be permanently removed. First, let's look at the three ways shame enters:

1. We are born into a family and a world that is filled with expectations and pressures. We learn to measure ourselves by a certain level or standard. Shame is produced when we feel unable to live up to our own standard or the standards of those around us.
2. We experience shame if we commit sin and do not deal with it biblically.
3. Shame is also produced when people sin against us. Through violations, shame is placed on us and cuts to the very core of our self-worth.

Shame Enters When We Don't Measure Up to Standards

Every person, family, corporation, church and society has a built-in system of standards. These standards are dependent on belief systems and may or may not be correct, fair or established on the basis of God's truth. Let's look at the primary standard systems in our life.

Measurement by Self-Standards

Through our life experiences, upbringing and other acquired beliefs, we build an ideal in our own life for the standards we should attain. From the way we're taught to care for our body, our home and our relationships, we filter everything through these standards. Sometimes, these standards are unrealistic or are based on the standards of the world around us and the people in our life.

While dreaming and goal setting are healthy, setting standards that are impossible or difficult to achieve can bring shame into our life. We may place enormously huge expectations on ourselves and therefore feel like a chronic failure when we can't meet those expectations.

Often, we impose the same standards on other people that we impose on ourselves. Therefore, when people don't measure up to what we perceive to be the "right way," we are critical, judgmental or even demeaning. Whether or not we are conscious of it, this standard system drives many of our thoughts, feelings and behaviors.

Measurement by Other People's Standards

The standards of those around us are based on their personal beliefs, life experiences and preferences. We often feel shame when rejected, criticized or put down by others if we don't fit their criteria of what is acceptable. We often don't realize that failing to measure up to another person's particular set of standards doesn't necessarily mean we have done something wrong. Just the same, we can feel good about ourselves when we succeed at measuring up to those standards. We may even perceive ourselves as being better than the system of standards around us demand. Taken to an extreme, some codependents may deliberately seek to hang around others they would consider "less than" in order to lower the standard bar and thus outshine everyone else. Why? It's a mechanism to deal with a prior root of shame. By being the "good one" in the midst of others who have lower standards, we receive a false sense of validation and personal worth.

Measurement by Family System Standards

In the family system, spoken and unspoken rules dictate acceptable standards. These standards can encompass all aspects of our life, roles and love styles. The standards may be extremely dysfunctional, skewed or exceedingly unrealistic. If we've lived by toxic family standards, we'll be bound to feel shame as a result. On the other hand, we might find we are the only responsible person in our family and thus feel one notch above the others. We may become harsh and critical toward others who don't do things quite as well as we do and will be prone to drag that same mentality into our relationships.

Measurement by Cultural Standards

Standards and social acceptance by the culture can be extremely influential in how we live our lives. We are inbred with a desire to be accepted by the larger population. Therefore, if we don't measure up to what the world presents as acceptable, we can carry a sense of shame.

Cultures shift from generation to generation on what is acceptable. For example, we live in a culture that accepts sex outside of marriage. Since the culture accepts it, we could falsely assume that we should accept it as well. On the other hand, we may feel shame for having things in our life that are not socially accepted. These could be anything from the way we wear our hair to the shape of our body. Even more painful, it could be the stigma of an alcoholic father or some sort of illness.

Measurement by Religious Standards

A church or a group of "Christians" can promote a set of standards for conduct that emphasizes outward behaviors—rule following and appearance—more than the heart (what's happening on the inside). They can present a form of God that leaves us thinking we are unacceptable unless we can be what those people say we should be. When we don't live up to those standards, we can be rejected by the group and thus feel we are being rejected by God.

The Effects of Not Measuring Up to Standards

There is great danger in attempting to live up to the standards of self, other people, a dysfunctional family system, the culture or religion. First, all forms of this attempt lead to pride. Furthermore, if we believe these standards are accurate, we actually trade in the truth of God's Word for expectations that are self-imposed or based on other people's views. While we usually have no conscious awareness of this, in essence we say, "However this person thinks of me, sees me, judges me must be true." This can also drive our codependence in a variety of ways like these:

- **External referencing.** Because we are driven by a fear of rejection, failure or lack of acceptance, we will seek to understand, evaluate and figure out the standards of people around us in order to comply. We will learn to "read" the needs of people as our personal baseline for life. Essentially, the systems of others dictate our own thoughts, feelings, actions and behaviors. While those standards may be influenced by an outside party, eventually they become self-imposed as well.
- **Rule-orientation.** To overcome our shame, we may be prone to try to perfectly follow standards. This can lead us to develop religious lifestyles, focusing on rules and regulations more than on people. We not only put ourselves under harsh standards, but we also often allow little room for failure and grace in our relationships.

The Accurate Source of Measuring

As challenging as it can be, we must learn we can't judge ourselves in accordance with the standards of self or others (whether we can or cannot measure up to them). Rather, we need to judge ourselves by the standards of Christ. "But they are only comparing themselves with each other, using themselves as the standard of measurement. How ignorant!" (2 Corinthians 10:12).

The Word of God is also clear that the world is the last place we should turn to as an accurate source for measuring ourselves. In fact, Romans 12: 2 says the opposite: "Don't copy the behavior and customs of this world, but let God transform you into a new person by changing the way you think. Then you will learn to know God's will for you, which is good and pleasing and perfect." Furthermore, the Bible actually warns us against viewing Him religiouslyand in terms of rules.

So why do you keep on following the rules of the world, such as, "Don't handle! Don't taste! Don't touch!"? Such rules are mere human teachings about things that deteriorate as we use them. These rules may seem wise because they require strong devotion, pious self-denial, and severe bodily discipline. But they provide no help in conquering a person's evil desires. (Colossians 2:21–23)

In evaluating how we experience shame by attempting to measure up to standards, we need to understand an extremely important concept: God measures us through the perfect standard of Jesus Christ when we come into a relationship with Him. Our ability to comply with God's system and standards doesn't depend on our own effort but on our relationship with Christ. In 2 Corinthians 5:21, Paul says, "For God made Christ, who never sinned, to be the offering for our sin, so that we could be made right with God through Christ." Through this transaction, we are perfectly acceptable to God, no matter what we've done. Since God's standard encompasses every single expectation, need, desire, action and thought, it overrides all other systems and standards. In other words, God's standard is the basis of truth. If you've not heard that theology before, really give it some thought.

Meditation points: How do I think God measures my worthiness? Do I ever consider that when God sees me, He sees the standard of Jesus Christ perfectly met through me? Is that enough, or do I still crave acceptance by outside people and sources?

_____

_____

_____

While embracing this concept mentally may be easy, allowing it to be imprinted on our heart can be challenging. This exercise requires that in all situations we don't look to simply follow the rules of the given situation but focus on the standard of God. We have to learn to say, "Who is the real voice of authority in my life in this situation?" Or "Where did I develop that standard? Is it accurate?" In some cases, we certainly do need to comply with the situation or standard. But in dysfunctional systems, we need to allow the Holy Spirit to be our Influencer, determining the decisions we need to take. When your unworthiness and inability to measure up attack your mind, say this: "My sufficiency is in Christ." Claim 2 Corinthians 3:5: "It is not that we think we are qualified to do anything on our own. Our qualification comes from God."

A Prayer to Break Unhealthy Standards

Father,

I ask for Your wisdom to know how You would have me see, hear and respond to situations, especially _____ (name the situation). Show me Your heart and give me Your hands so I don't run people over by my harsh and unfair judgments or walk in the shame of never feeling good enough. Place in me the spirit of grace and give me the delight and pleasure of resting in the truth that I already measure up to Your standard as your child. As I receive that, Lord, give me the ability to share that grace with those around me— walking by the standard of Your love.

In Jesus's name, amen.

Application Points:

Explain how you use standards in your life to measure your worth.

_____

_____

_____

Do you feel you don't measure up to someone else's standards right now? How about in your past?

_____

_____

_____

What have you done in trying to overcome the sense that you weren't good enough?

_____

_____

_____

Shame Enters by Not Dealing with Our Sin Biblically

We can feel the guilt and shame of what we did or the ways we don't measure up as evidence that something within us is inherently wrong. Sometimes the guilt doesn't even belong to us; it is still a residue of what others did to us. But we can often hang onto sin issues, feeling the need to continually be punished for the ways we haven't lived up to a standard. As we will learn in the next chapter, as children of God we've already been forgiven. The blood of Jesus took all our sins—past, present and future—and paid the price to have them removed from our "debt" bank. But sadly, we can continue to live in the reality of that sin rather than the reality of God's grace and forgiveness.

Several things can prevent us from being able to experience freedom from our past violations. Condemnation, guilt and shame are tactics used by the Enemy to prevent us from seeking God's remedy and the power of His Holy Spirit.

- Guilt: a sense that we violated something or someone either by what we did or did not do.
- Shame: a sense of unworthiness whereby we feel we are unacceptable to God and others.
- Condemnation: a sense of being damned. It stands in complete opposition to salvation.

If we experience guilt, shame or condemnation, there may be real issues we need to deal with. (If there is a chance that you honestly might not know Jesus Christ as your Lord and Savior, we invite you read the appendix, "Do I know Jesus?"). However, as children of God, we can stand on the promise that we've already been washed clean in His blood.

The Enemy tries to produce in us a sense of God's judgment, rather than God's love and grace. He will point out how unworthy we may be and try to bring us to a place where we hide from God in fear. There is a tremendous difference between the Enemy's guilt and shame tactics and the conviction of the Holy Spirit when we really do have issues that need to be dealt with. Let's take a closer look:

Table 6: God's Conviction versus Guilt/Shame

God's Conviction	Guilt/Shame
Woos us in loving rebuke.	Tears us down and points out what a failure we are.
Focuses on the solution.	Focuses on the problem.
Reminds us of our true identity despite the things we do.	Wants us to think our behavior defines our core value.
Encourages us to draw closer to God, realizing our need for His grace and mercy.	Encourages us to move away from God, thinking He is angry with us.
Offers forgiveness for our wrongdoing if we humbly and willingly admit our sin.	Holds us in the bondage of shame where we feel unable to receive forgiveness.

We will biblically deal with each of our sinful acts in the next chapter. For now, simply attempt to identify where your own acts of sin have left you feeling bound and condemned.

Application Points:
Do you recognize the power of guilt and shame in your life? In what instances do you often pay attention to it?

_____

_____

_____

Do you feel forgiven? Why or why not?

_____

_____

_____

Shame Enters Through Acts of Violation Committed Against Us

Most codependents have experienced some form of abuse. Abuse occurs when someone enters an area in our lives without permission in a way that violates or hurts us. Some abuse can also occur when people neglect to fulfill a responsibility in our relationship with them.

Anytime an act is committed against us that is a violation, shame can be introduced into our lives. If we could see it in the spiritual realm, it might look like bloody hands being wiped all over us. The very nature of an act of violation against us is to produce the feeling that we are dirty.

No matter what our attempts, we can't rid ourselves of this sense of dirt. It is a by-product of the act itself. We may have tried to cover it with something that looked outwardly good, but despite our efforts, the shame continues to deliver toxic messages. If we can't directly do anything to rid ourselves of shame, does that mean we are obliged to remain a victim of abuse forever? Thank God, the answer is NO! There is a cleansing remedy and a process to get rid of shame. In chapters 8 and 9 we'll deal directly with learning how to apply the blood of Jesus Christ as the cleansing power to eradicate both the shame imposed on us through our own behaviors and the shame imposed on us by others. But first we are going to review some of the realities of how abuse and acts of violation can manifest as shame in our life. If necessary, be sure to add on your inventory sheet any new revelations or insights you receive about personal violations.

Types of Abuse

Physical abuse. When someone hits, touches or hurts our physical body, our natural and God-given boundaries are violated. Our body belongs to us personally and other people don't have the right to touch us without permission. A shame message in physical abuse says, "You deserve this" or "I have a right to hurt you." In fact, we never deserve physical abuse. It is an evil act generated by the perpetrator, not the receiver.

Sexual abuse. Anytime we are touched by a person inappropriately in a sexual way without our consent, it could be considered sexual abuse. Not all sexual abuse comes in the form of actual intercourse. A child may be asked to touch the genitals of a perpetrator. Or a teenage girl has her chest touched in an unwelcome manner. Sexual abuse is unbelievably damaging because it enters our deepest, most sacred and most intimate place—a place so precious it was reserved only for the covenant of marriage. Violations in this area shatter that sense of preciousness and sanctity. More than any other abusive act, it will deeply affect the ability to bond and trust in future relationships. Even when we willingly participate in sexual acts outside the context of marriage, we are participating in the sexual abuse of our own body (see 1 Corinthians 6:18).

Mental abuse. When someone attempts to enter our minds to manipulate what we think in order to hurt us, we can experience mental abuse. For example, an abusive husband may not only physically hurt his wife but may also give her a list of reasons why he did so. "See what you made me do? You need to learn to shut your mouth." The skewed and toxic message makes the victim seem to be the instigator, thus justifying the perpetrator's actions.

Emotional abuse. Emotional abuse feeds off vulnerabilities and weaknesses. It can use fear, shame, guilt or rejection to gain power over us. Often people don't even realize they are hurting us with words. That isn't necessarily abuse. Actual abuse occurs when someone sets out to cause us emotional pain through words or actions. For example, a woman feels angry with her teenage daughter for her careless and sloppy living habits. She begins to belittle her and tells her, "No man will ever want you. Look at what a slob you are." The mom used those words as emotional weapons to try to change her daughter's behavior. This is cruel and unfair and could be considered emotional abuse.

Abuse by neglect of legitimate needs. We can be abused by not having physical or emotional needs met. When a parent withdraws a privilege as a form of discipline, it is intended to impose consequences. When a parent withdraws necessities including love, attention or nurturing or fails to meet other legitimate needs, as discussed in chapter 6, actual abuse is occurring. Often this form of abuse is not intentional but a projection of the internal issues of that parent. Nonetheless, it can be abusive in nature.

Spiritual abuse. Parents and other authority figures can use the Bible to frighten and scare children (or adults). Spiritual abuse uses the name of God to exercise control over others. While God is powerful, He never attempts to force us to do anything. Furthermore, God doesn't shame us. He convicts us and desires to set us free. A spiritually abusive person wants us to feel bad. They might say things such as "God sees that and is angry with you." Or "God could never love you when you behave that way." Sometimes spiritual abuse is far more subtle. There can be implied messages that God loves only a certain kind of person who is doing a certain type of thing.

Cycles of Abuse: Perpetrator and Victims

Two types of people participate in acts of violation: a perpetrator and a victim. Let's learn more about each of these roles.

Understanding a Perpetrator

First, an abuser or perpetrator is an unhealthy person. While we can see abusive people as "less than human," we must understand that everyone who lives in a fleshly body is subject to being led astray by the Enemy in various ways. The Bible reminds us, "For we are not fighting against flesh-and-blood enemies, but against evil rulers and authorities of the unseen world, against mighty powers in this dark world, and against evil spirits in the heavenly places" (Ephesians 6:12). As human beings, we are being influenced by the spirit realm around us. People influenced by biblical truth will manifest behaviors in keeping with that truth. People influenced by evil spirits will manifest other behaviors. God's objective for our lives is to give us life; Satan's objectives are to kill and steal and destroy (see John 10:10). God uses people as vessels. Satan uses people as vessels. Understanding this perspective is critical as we face the violations of a perpetrator because it helps us identify the true Enemy.

Who is a perpetrator then? A perpetrator is a carrier of shame. Instead of biblically dealing with shame, the perpetrator acts out an emotional pain or demonic influence. Sadly, the behaviors they inflict on others often (but not always) stem from shame imposed on them through someone else's sin. This means that sin is contagious in the sense that when they were exposed to it, it made them subject to repeating it. Our culture may blame genes for the emotional and behavior challenges we face as human beings, but in the spiritual realm, the shame of sin is passed along from one person to the next. For example, a sexual predator, as repulsive and horrible as that behavior might be, is often someone who at some point was the victim of this same act. Certainly, that doesn't excuse the behavior, but it does provide insight and a warning about the serious nature of dealing with toxic shame.

What would make a person cross the line to become a perpetrator? As we will continue to learn, people learn to cope and deal with life in different ways. Before we make claims or say, "I would never be a perpetrator," we should realize we can be perpetrators in small and subtle ways. We might use "guilt trips" to control how people treat us. It sounds harmless enough, but it infringes on the free will of others.

For the darker and more evil forms of abuse, the person who becomes a perpetrator has developed a hardened heart. They have listened to the Enemy rather than to God's principles and now act out their anger, shame, fear or powerlessness by hurting others.

While we are allowed to hate the perpetrators' acts, it's important to remember that he or she needs God's grace as much as any other member of society. Even more humbling is to realize that every one of us could have been, or could still become, a perpetrator in some way.

The Victim

The person on the receiving end of abusive behaviors is the victim. The victim is prone to be captured by the message the actual abuse sends. Essentially, in being the recipient of an act of abuse, a tainted and skewed perspective of God, self and others can develop. Let's look at some of the ways victims can wrongly learn to adapt to violations and the sense of being a victim.

Belief abuse is deserved. Some victims get so broken down they actually feel entirely responsible for the abuse. They don't even offer up defenses other than efforts to not do things that might prompt the abuse. No matter how hard they try, when the abuse continues, it sends a message to them that says, "I did something to deserve this."

The cycle of enablement. Victims often feel the need to defend the person who committed the very acts of abuse that hurt them. The victim will essentially believe the abuser couldn't help it. They may also justify the acts because they believe the abuser is "hurting" or because they want to earn the abuser's love. This skewed form of protection actually encourages the abuse to continue. That doesn't make it the victim's fault, but it does mean they are participating by enabling it.

The "I am a victim" mentality. Some victims who do not deal with their issues appropriately will develop dysfunctional relationship skills where they tend to always be in a "victim" situation. They will not be able to see themselves or others accurately and will participate in behaviors that either encourage bad behavior or falsely set people up to be perpetrators. As difficult as it can be to comprehend, this sort of victim feels safe in this role and therefore recreates it in other scenarios.

For example, Vicky had a history of emotional and mental abuse. Eventually, she married a man who physically abused her as well. Vicky grew accustomed to this dynamic, and as horrible as it was, she developed a poisoned way of seeing life as constantly being the victim. Most people were unaware of Vicky's situation because she didn't ask for help. Instead, she often volunteered to help people in the church, at work or through personal relationships. While her intentions seemed good, she was actually looking for the appreciation and validation she didn't receive at home.

Vicky didn't always receive the response she wanted when she offered to be of service to others. At times, she "turned" on the very people she appeared to want to help. She would slander and put those people down, citing a list of violations and wrongs they had committed against her. Usually, these people were stunned by her accusations, which were twisted and filled with faulty perceptions. Vicky didn't understand the problems she was causing because in her own warped thinking, it seemed to be everyone else's fault.

It's likely that most of us have known some sort of "Vicky" who lived from the perspective that life was always unfair and unjust to them. We ourselves might even be a Vicky. The tragedy is that Vickys really do become victims. The Enemy has fooled and trapped them into believing that a victim mentality is an appropriate and fair response to the issues they face in life. But as we will learn, remaining a victim is not a right but a lie from the pit of hell.

Application Points:
Describe specific areas of abuse that apply to you.

_____
_____
_____

Do you see yourself as a victim? As a perpetrator?

_____
_____
_____

Are you caught in a victim mentality? Why or why not?

_____
_____
_____

A Prayer to Understand the Shame of Violations
Father God,

As I look at the violations in my life, at times I have minimized them. Other times, I felt like a victim of circumstances. I may have even been mad or angry with You as a result. Please help me to understand the reality of the shame and the messages that shame imposed

on me, and prepare my heart as I seek a remedy.
In Jesus's name, amen.

8

Receiving the Gift of Forgiveness

Workbook Keys

- How Does Jesus Deal with our Sin?
- How Can We Receive Forgiveness?
- What Prevents Us?

By now, we've already acknowledged that shame is a tool of the Enemy in the believer's life that robs us of the freedom and power God intended us to have. If our lives are filled with shame, we are in desperate need of an authentic and long-term remedy. All our coping skills and survival strategies were attempts to overcome shame. Little did we know that those efforts offered no possible means of a solution and, in fact, worsened the problem.

We could think of each sin we carry within us as a chain that we are bound to. Those chains keep us living with a sense of guilt, compelling us to drag ourselves through life heavy hearted and filled with pain. We could also think of the acts of violation committed against us as an actual wound inside our heart. We have been "medicating" that wound or using our own methods of resolving the pain. In combination, it's easy to see how shame can literally destroy our lives.

As we move toward applying the actual solution and removing the shame, the first remedy is the ability to receive forgiveness for our sins. While it sounds simple enough, many of us don't realize how difficult it might be. We are usually prone to thinking either that we don't need it at all or that we can't receive anything for free, so we must work for it or earn it.

When it comes to receiving God's forgiveness, there is an actual method and set of criteria. Anything outside those bounds will hold us in bondage and never offer us the power to overcome the shame within. But before we learn more about those specifics, let's learn how Jesus made it possible for us to be forgiven.

How Jesus Dealt with Sin

The Bible tells us that Jesus Christ identified with our grief and personal sin, including all the acts that were committed against us and the things we, ourselves, did wrong. He felt the piercing reality of our transgressions since they were placed directly onto His own body. "Yet it was our weaknesses he carried; it was our sorrows that weighed him down. . . . But he was pierced for our rebellion, crushed for our sins. He was beaten so we could be whole. He was whipped so we could be healed" (Isaiah 53:4–5).

When Jesus Christ hung on the cross, He was exposed to an inconceivable act of shame. He was spit upon, laughed at, cast aside and murdered. Yet He never did anything wrong! If anyone had the right to claim being the victim, it was Jesus.

Instead, everything Jesus did was mission oriented from a loving heart. As hell itself came against Him, He never strayed from His objective of absorbing the penalty of sin and its shameful effects that destroyed mankind (see 2 Corinthians 5:21). As He faced the ugliness and hatred of the human heart, He never responded bitterly. It was no surprise to Him what human beings living apart from God were capable of doing. He didn't receive the shame imposed on Him by others as truth statements about His own character. He simply remained steadfast to the central mission—to forgive and restore the human race. In fact, while His enemies pounded Him, He was preparing the means for their redemption.

What Jesus understood is something we struggle with. He knew that all evil behaviors are generated by the work of Satan and that the only way to overcome the horrible reality of the sinful human heart is to conquer it through love and forgiveness. Love and forgiveness were in fact the weapons used by God to destroy the power of Satan. By offering this love to people, Jesus Christ took on the punishment that the sinful act itself deserved. Jesus didn't make people His enemies. He had only one true Enemy—Satan and his army of demons.

In our own lives, this same dynamic applies. Since God provided us a redemptive pathway back to Him, He asks that we receive it rather than live under sin's condemnation. He also calls us to forgive others, understanding that people who commit acts of violation are in need of redemption too. When we gain access to the real power behind forgiveness, we discover it is the doorway to a new beginning, offering us the way to be set free from every sin issue. Forgiveness gives us the opportunity to be emotionally and spiritually healed. It can undo and repair the damage done and restore what was lost.

However, as readily as the life-giving power of the blood of Jesus is available, some of us find it difficult to access its power. This is because we often run into a variety of barriers, including these:

- We are angry with God and blame Him for allowing things into our lives.

- We believe we don't need forgiveness since we aren't that bad or it's "everyone else's fault."
- We are unable to receive forgiveness for our own wrongdoing.

Anger at God

How can a loving God allow horrible things in our lives? This question keeps many people from pursuing Him. In essence, some people are bitter toward God, as if He were the one who deliberately willed those things to happen. As we learned in chapter 5, God's being all-powerful doesn't make Him directly responsible for the behaviors and the evil in the world. Anything that is not perfect in this world is a by-product of the reality of a fallen world and fallen mankind. God is the author of free will. He allows people the freedom to make choices, even if they are wrong. We can be victims of things that are unfair. We can have painful childhoods. God knows this. And we can rest assured, it hurts Him too. At the same time, God is in control and will use all things together for good (see Romans 8:28).

If you are angry with God, it's most important that you identify that anger and ask Him to reveal His characteristics and methods of operation. Ask Him to help you understand, despite your circumstances, how He loves you.

Application Points:

Write out a list of the ways you feel angry or disappointed with God.

_____
_____
_____

Write a letter to God describing how these things have made you question His love for you.

_____
_____
_____

Say a prayer asking Him to help you with your anger.

Father God,

I admit that I'm angry or disappointed by You. I don't understand why You allowed me to suffer. I don't understand why You allowed these circumstances in my life. At the same time, I know You are a God of love, grace and redemption. This means that my struggle with anger is something I need to deal with, and it's based on a lie about Your character. Please reveal in Your Word and in my own relationship with You how You love me and desire to restore and resolve the wounds in my life. Please take my willing heart as the first step toward

learning how to love You more and feel less anger toward You.
In Jesus's name, amen.

When We Feel Unworthy to Receive Forgiveness

As we discussed in the previous chapter, we can be bound by a sense of guilt, shame and condemnation that seems to justify why we can't be forgiven. For example, Marilyn knew all about God's love and forgiveness as a child growing up. She just didn't know how to personally receive it. After she had an abortion, Marilyn was plagued by guilt and shame. She honestly decided she didn't deserve to be forgiven. She vowed to live the rest of her life suffering for her horrible mistake. Marilyn saw children and felt the pang of her decision. She distanced herself from God, believing He was as angry and disgusted with her as she was with herself.

A friend of Marilyn's invited her to a Bible study that taught about God's redemption. This friend was aware of Marilyn's spiritual struggle. When a lady at the study shared about an abortion, the words penetrated into Marilyn's soul. This woman explained how she honestly knew she didn't deserve to be forgiven but one day in her grief, Jesus "showed up." She came to understand that the very essence of forgiveness is that it is unmerited. She visualized a gift and realized that although her choice was so horrible, the gift simply needed to be received and opened. This woman then went through an entire process of grieving and releasing the lost baby to God. But the healing was only possible after she received forgiveness.

For the first time, Marilyn realized she could be forgiven. She reached out to get the support she needed and eventually received that same forgiveness and healing.

God's forgiveness is a free gift based on His grace (see Ephesians 2:8–9). Receiving this gift with nothing attached goes directly against our codependence. We are faced with a choice when we feel unworthy of forgiveness. Either the blood of Jesus Christ is sufficient for us, or it's not. The belief we choose to live by determines our future.

How foolish that we could reject a gift that God already bought for us, one that took such precious resources to purchase, simply because *we aren't worthy*. The truth is, we aren't worthy—but the *blood of Jesus is*! Declare that blood over your life. Call upon that blood to cover you and cleanse you, removing things you can't remove on your own.

Receiving Forgiveness

How can we receive forgiveness for our sins? Here's the basic process of how to receive God's gift of forgiveness:

Confess. Because we may have the impression that God is looking to us to be perfect, we may tend to want to bring Him the good, rather than the bad."Actually, God wants us to admit the sins and defects we carry. "If we claim we have no sin, we are only fooling ourselves and not living in the truth" (1 John 1:8). We don't just say, "Oh, yes, I realize that sin is there." God requires that we actually speak and tell Him specifically what occurred. "But if we confess our sins to him, he is faithful and just to forgive us our sins and to cleanse us from all wickedness" (1 John 1:9). In other words, don't cover it up and don't offer your efforts—come to Him as you are, admitting what's not right.

Repent. Repentance indicates a turn in direction. It's not just an outward change in our behavior. In fact, if we get legalistic and focus only on our outward appearance, we'll miss the entire point. Real repentance comes when our heart and mind are able to recognize the truth of God rather than the lies we've believed. We see things from His perspective and realize how we didn't measure up and where we went wrong. If we did anything, or believed anything, that opposed the Word of God, we will need to repent. Acts 3:19–20 says, "Now repent of your sins and turn to God, so that your sins may be wiped away. Then times of refreshment will come from the presence of the Lord." What a wonderful promise that as we repent, not only will God forgive our sins but He'll also bring us the refreshment of His presence!

Receive God's forgiveness. Receiving is the most difficult step in this process for the codependent. God's forgiveness is always a gift. He requires some things on our part, but the forgiveness itself is free. We may continually push aside forgiveness to invoke our own form of punishment. We may even feel this is a noble and responsible thing to do, but how this grieves God's heart! On the cross, Jesus paid the price of our sin. Therefore, when we reject His forgiveness, we essentially reject the finished work He did on our behalf. If you struggle with this, pray this prayer:

A Prayer When We Don't Feel Worthy
Father God,

I don't feel worthy of forgiveness for some of the things I have done. I know Your forgiveness is free, but the things I've done don't seem to fit the criteria. Yet I must face the truth that You hung, bled and died on that cross on my behalf. Why would I deny You that right? Help me, Lord. Fill me with Your truth. Create in me a clean heart and remove everything in me that is not of You.
In Jesus's name, amen.

Believing We Don't Need Forgiveness

When facing our inventory of sin, if we find ourselves saying, "I'm not that bad compared with _____," there is a major barrier in our lives that will inhibit our further growth and freedom. Simply put, we won't receive a remedy if we can't see that a problem exists.

Many times as codependents, we can fool ourselves into believing that our own efforts and sense of goodness override any sinful acts we have committed. But this is so untrue. We can also use a personal justification system that says, "When I'm better than everyone else around me, I'm not really a sinner." This is extraordinarily false because in God's eyes, sin is sin.

We all have sin issues. We all fall short. It's a normal part of being human. Furthermore, we can't do much about it apart from a true transformation in our heart. Acts of morality can be done by anyone. Human beings, by nature, are capable of doing good things. But the only acts that please God are those done through Him, through the life of His Spirit residing within. "We are all infected and impure with sin. When we display our righteous deeds, they are nothing but filthy rags" (Isaiah 64:6). As innocent and harmless as it appears, when we live before God with a checklist of how we are good, we are living by a sense of our own righteousness. We cannot be forgiven in this condition. If you struggle with the inability to see your sin, pray this prayer:

A Prayer to Break Self-Righteousness
Father God,

I have lived my life believing I was a good person and that my goodness made me acceptable to You. It's hard for me to think that I have been believing something that actually contradicts and opposes You. I renounce the lies I have believed about my own sense of righteousness and ask that You please break me to the point where I can see myself accurately. I know You love me enough to rescue me from this destructive mentality. Please forgive me and change me. I thank You in advance.
In Jesus's name, amen.

Application Point:
To help you apply this personally to your own sin issues, use this process:

Make a truth statement about the act.
When I committed _____ (name the behavior or violation), Jesus already knew I would do it. That act was horrible and wrong, and I am deeply sorry for it. However, Jesus already felt, suffered and paid the penalty for that act. God's Word tells me if I confess and repent of my sins, He will give me the gift of

forgiveness. I choose to receive that gift.

Pray

Dear Father,

    I acknowledge that I sinned against _____ or You. It was wrong. I truly feel sorry and wish I could take it back. But Lord, I'm asking You to remove that sin from me and help that person I sinned against. I pray that they would be able to forgive me and release me from that debt. I renounce this sin in the name of Jesus Christ, and don't want it to ever return in my life. Show me in time if I need to make amends or simply release the situation to You. I thank you that despite whether they are able to forgive me, You will forgive me. I thank you that the power of your blood is truly sufficient to deal with my sin. Thank you in advance.

In Jesus's name, amen.

Other Steps to Initiate Forgiveness and Healing

1. Look at the items on your list of the ways you violated someone. If necessary, write a letter to that person describing how you hurt them and saying that you are sorry. Ask them to forgive you.

2. If you struggle with receiving forgiveness, write a letter to God asking Him to help you. Confess and repent of the sin and ask for the gift of forgiveness. Once this has occurred, keep that letter as a reminder that God has forgiven you, just as He has promised.

3. Find a trusted friend, mentor, counselor or sponsor, if possible, and confess the things to him or her (see James 5:16).

Identifying False Guilt

    While we may have legitimate sin issues in our life that Satan plays on, sometimes we experience false guilt. False guilt is based entirely on a lie. It tells us we are to blame for something that has nothing to do with us. When we begin to "own" that guilt, we become confused, burdened and plagued. This guilt may drive erratic behaviors to try to overcome it.

    For example, Craig grew up in an environment where he felt responsible for and guilt driven by the needs of his parents. His mom only had to pull "the string," and Craig knew he needed to comply. She used statements such as "I thought you would want to help me with this, but I guess you have more important things to do with your time."

    In adulthood, Craig operated the same way. He analyzed the statements of others and owned whatever guilt message he may have picked up. He did anything and everything for people out of this sense of guilt, believing it was his job to accommodate them. Often they weren't asking or expecting anything from him; he was acting out of his own skewed and distorted thinking.

When we accept false guilt, we can also feel the need to constantly excuse and explain ourselves. It's as if we are responding to accusations all the time, often over things no one directly mentioned to us. Remember, the Enemy is the accuser, and often this sense of guilt is a direct attack in the spiritual realm. Regardless of the origin, when we perceive people to be judging us, we can respond in ways like these:

- Become extremely defensive and assume people are accusing us of wrongdoing
- Point out other people's faults or wrongdoing to move people down to a level "below" us so we feel more acceptable
- Point to our "righteousness" in an attempt to prove ourselves

The problem with these defensive measures is that often, not only is the guilt not for us to own but now we create new problems through our wrong reactions. That's why identifying false guilt is so important. False guilt takes away our peace and our sense of *righteousness in Christ Jesus*. Romans 8:1–2 says, "So now there is no condemnation for those who belong to Christ Jesus. And because you belong to him, the power of the life-giving Spirit has freed you from the power of sin that leads to death."

If we struggle with feeling guilty all the time, it's important to pinpoint and identify the messages in our head. We also must learn to speak back to those messages in rational ways. For example, if we are feeling guilty for not helping a friend in need because of a prior commitment, we might say, "I wasn't available, and that doesn't make me a bad friend. God knew ahead of time that I wasn't available, and He must have something else planned for her."

When we hear guilt messages, we must know they are somehow sent from Satan. We can recognize the voice of God when it speaks in accordance with the truth of God's Word. God will, however, use conviction, so we can't discount our conscience when we are doing something that opposes the things of God. If we are feeling the guilt of another person's behavior because we feel somehow responsible, we need to pray for the wisdom to learn to separate our own behavior from theirs. If we do need to own something, we should, but we cannot own other people's wrongdoing.

Just remember, God is a Savior. He isn't interested in standing up in heaven with His finger pointed at us—so anything that comes from that way of thinking isn't of God. Instead, everything God does in our lives, including His conviction, is to lead us toward freedom. And how liberating it is to know that in God we never have to be defensive. We only need to offer ourselves up with honesty and vulnerability.

While our natural inclination might always be to defend ourselves, we must learn to stand in the shelter and protection of God's Word and declare, "I am what God says I am." As we learn to believe that statement, guilt will no longer hold any power over our life.

Application Points:

Do you own things that aren't your fault? Why? Do you feel motivated to do things for others because you think it's what they want and you don't want to disappoint them or let them down? Give one example. Explain.

_____
_____
_____

Do you feel the need to vindicate yourself? Are you defensive, thinking people are judging you? Explain.

_____
_____
_____

Do you ever find yourself putting other people down—those who you are afraid might be judging you or rejecting you?

_____
_____
_____

Facing Failure

Most codependents find it difficult to face self-failure. Failure isn't the same as sin. As human beings, we constantly fail and make mistakes. It is normal and necessary to fail in order to learn and grow. Even the moral failure of sin can still be a learning tool in our life if we see it in the proper perspective.

For example, a baby learns to walk by continually falling and getting back up. Over time, the baby learns how to balance and make steps that lead to less and less failure. Through this trial and error, the baby is strengthened. Imagine if a baby stopped trying once he or she fell. Or worse, imagine a parent scolding the child the first time he or she fell! Of course, that sounds ridiculous. But God sees us as His little children, and He understands that we are trying to take the "steps of life." He's not screaming at us—He's encouraging us to keep trying!

Some of the most accomplished people in the world will say that failure is a necessary ingredient in working toward success. For the codependent, we think mistakes mean the end of success. We go to great measures to avoid them, and then when they happen, it can seem catastrophic.

In truth, God gives us plenty of room to make mistakes. He uses mistakes to teach and train us. Even if people do reject us as failures, God will never reject us (see Hebrews 13:5). Furthermore, we can find shelter under His grace while we are in the process of learning. And in that grace, we are sufficient (2 Corinthians 12:9).

Application Points:
Describe how you feel when you make a mistake.

_____

_____

_____

_____

Do you feel you don't have the right to experience failure like others? Why? Do you allow others to fail, or do their failures make you exceedingly hurt or angry?

_____

_____

_____

The Power of Forgiveness

If you have applied the remedy of God's grace and forgiveness over the sin issues of your life, you are prepared to move on toward freedom. Receiving forgiveness opens the doorway toward all future growth and healing. It also leads to an indescribable feeling of gratitude. How do you know if you've truly received God's forgiveness ?

- You will thank Him. You will truly understand that without His forgiveness you would be hopelessly lost.
- You will desire to move closer to Him in a relationship, not run from Him. The shame of our sin made us hide from God; forgiveness draws us close to Him.
- You will know in your heart that you are completely accepted. You will no longer feel as though He is in any way rejecting you.

If you have not gotten there yet, do not be discouraged, but rather diligently seek Him through faith. God's entire redemptive purposes in your life rest in your ability to receive His forgiveness.

A Prayer for Forgiveness

Father,

I have heard that I need Your forgiveness over and over. But sometimes "feeling" I'm forgiven is a struggle. I pray that every barrier and obstacle that might keep me from fully embracing Your forgiveness—including my self-righteousness or condemnation—be removed from my heart. Please help me. I thank you in advance that Your forgiveness is my freedom.

In Jesus's name, amen.

9

Offering the Gift of Forgiveness

Workbook Keys

- WHY MUST WE FORGIVE?
- WHAT PREVENTS US FROM FORGIVING?
- WHAT ARE THE BENEFITS OF FORGIVING?

The biggest miracle we will ever experience is receiving God's forgiveness and entering into a relationship with Him based on His grace, not our efforts. From there, the Christian life calls us to do things we couldn't otherwise do. In our codependent mindset, we have often believed that God was on the sidelines watching us attempt to fix, resolve and overcome the problems we face, despite how miserably our efforts fail. How inaccurate! Instead, He invites us to walk alongside Him, where He supernaturally enables us to live this life. We can keep running ahead of Him, feeling exhausted by our own efforts. Or we can accept His invitation and learn the peace of resting in Him, where we move through Him into deeper levels of freedom (see John 15:5).

As we continue on this journey, we come upon tasks and challenges that go beyond our human strength. These challenges are actually opportunities for us to learn how to access God's power rather than rely on our own strength. One of the most difficult things God requires of us is to forgive others who have hurt us. It is a responsibility we are given as Christians, yet one that challenges our humanness at every level. We need God's power working in us to do this for us.

In the next chapter we will learn specifically about the purpose behind the need to forgive others, as well as the freedom it offers to us personally. We will also be given the opportunity to offer forgiveness for the very wounds that caused us much pain and suffering.

Hating Behavior, Not People

As we approach forgiveness, it is reassuring to acknowledge that the wrongs people committed against us were not okay. As Jesus Christ Himself stands in heaven and views that sin, He is not minimizing its harmful and horrible effects. In fact, He painfully endured it. When we look at the list of ways people have sinned against us, we have the right to hate those lists. Trying to go through life forgetting and getting over it will not change the effect those sinful behaviors have had on us or the gaping wounds they inflicted on our heart. But it goes deeper than that. The effects of those violations sent a message. If those messages influenced us, they essentially have gained ownership in our life. We need to not only get rid of the sin itself, but we also need to permanently remove the messages imposed on us.

Why Must We Forgive?

God requires we forgive those who hurt us. In chapter 7 we learned that when someone violated us, they wiped their bloody hands on us and left us feeling dirty by the shame of the act done to us. This shame continued to infect our life through messages and a sense of feeling dirty. It's helpful to understand that forgiveness is not just about letting that person off the hook or pretending the act didn't matter. Instead, forgiveness is a powerful remedy against the very damage that the sin imposed—it has the power to set us free from the harm it caused.

Just as the blood of Jesus Christ was shed on our behalf to overcome the power of sin and death in our life, we can apply that same remedy against the violations that occurred to us. Indeed, forgiveness will conquer the violation. When we learn to forgive people (but not the behaviors), the blood of Jesus is placed on the wound that the sinful act brought about. It doesn't mean we are immediately and entirely set free from the damaging consequences of that sin. For example, if someone stole from us, we may have to live with that reality forever. But through the act of forgiveness, the dirtiness of the shame itself is removed, thus making it possible for the wound to be healed.

Application Points:

Do you harbor resentments toward people you find difficult to forgive?

_____

_____

_____

Describe how the blood of Jesus Christ has the power to set you free from that act. Do you truly believe that? Why or why not?

_____

When We Don't Want to Forgive

Forgiveness is a choice of the will, not necessarily something we emotionally desire. We may not want to forgive, but that doesn't mean it isn't the right thing to do. Unforgiveness and bitterness are some of the results of not biblically dealing with violations and unmet needs. It is human nature to want justice and to seek revenge for violations committed against us, rather than to forgive. In fact, nothing in our human nature will desire to forgive people.

In truth, God makes it very clear to us that to live in His will, we must forgive those who hurt us. "If you forgive those who sin against you, your heavenly Father will forgive you. But if you refuse to forgive others, your Father will not forgive your sins" (Matthew 6:14–15). Based on this scripture, it's clear that our own relationship with the Lord is affected if we are unable to forgive others. Furthermore, when we choose unforgiveness, we stay bound by the dirt of that violation. That means we won't be able to heal.

Forgiving God's Way

When we get in touch with the heart of God, we discover that His methods of operation are entirely different from our own ways (see Isaiah 55:8–9). In fact, God tells us in His Word that we are to actually get revenge on our enemies by showing them love and forgiving them. As we previously learned, God calls us to a lifestyle of love and forgiveness because that is God's lifestyle. "Get rid of all bitterness, rage, anger, harsh words, and slander, as well as all types of evil behavior. Instead, be kind to each other, tenderhearted, forgiving one another, just as God through Christ has forgiven you" (Ephesians 4:31–32).

Does this mean we allow people to hurt us? Does this mean that a person can just violate us and we are to willingly accept it? *Absolutely not*. In fact, there are times when people commit wrongs against us in such a way that there needs to be a consequence. That is something altogether different and will be dealt with in chapter 11 when we learn about boundaries.

God clearly tells us this in 1 Peter 3:9: "Don't repay evil for evil. Don't retaliate with insults when people insult you. Instead, pay them back with a blessing. That is what God has called you to do, and he will bless you for it."

The truth is that when we choose to deal with our pain independently of God's prescribed methods, there will be a consequence. Not only will we have to deal with the shame that sin imposed upon us, but we'll also have to live life outside God's blessing. But when we choose to respond to violations through love, we will be blessed.

A Bitter Spirit

If we remain bitter over a particular event or person, we can eventually develop a spirit of bitterness. It becomes an entirely polluted way of looking at life through chronically negative perspectives. Many codependents develop a resentment "bank." As they overly help others, they simultaneously experience a sense of victimization. While emphasizing their own acts of service, they continue to build up the bank of resentment that says, "Look at what I do for you."

For example, Paul had some deep traumas in his childhood upbringing that he never dealt with. As an adult, he learned to be a compensator in his relationships. He saw himself as the person who met people's needs and focused on ways to fix their problems. He did it so naturally that he wasn't even aware of this behavior in his character make-up. He was inclined to give people advice and usually sought validation in return. Because so many of his behaviors toward people seemed to show a genuine concern for them, people would have been surprised to know how the needs of others frustrated and angered him. He felt entirely responsible to meet those needs yet at the same time felt bitter in having to "help" everyone in his relationships.

Paul's compensation skills developed in early childhood when, as the older child, he was expected to take care of the family's needs. The pressure he carried exhausted him and caused a lot of pain and suffering. He was angry with a father who abandoned him and a mother who was unavailable to him between her job and boyfriends. That lack of support and the need to be responsible led him to carry a deep sense of victimization throughout life.

We can visualize everything Paul did for others by seeing him put a coin into a bank of credit. But at the same time, Paul put a coin into his bank of resentments. This cycle of needing payment for all he did led to a feeling of being abandoned and unappreciated.

Eventually, Paul just lived this way and had no joy, peace or fulfillment. His negative spirit poisoned all aspects of his life. What a horrible way to live! As Paul faced himself in recovery, he needed to unwrap those original resentments and traumatic events that led to his overall polluted way of looking at life. He ultimately needed to learn to forgive and to receive forgiveness for the wrongful coping mechanisms he had developed.

Acknowledging that we have a bitter spirit is the first step toward freedom. God asks that we release people and situations to Him for judgment. He only asks that we offer a willingness to forgive others, just as He is willing to forgive us. Before you become too overwhelmed, recognize that forgiveness can take time. It is often a process, not something we can just start "doing." Just because you are going through this workbook doesn't mean you will be immediately ready to forgive. Don't let the Enemy lay condemnation on you. God knows your heart, and if you sincerely desire to forgive a person, or if you struggle with a bitter spirit, God can meet you right where you are. However, if you forthrightly refuse to deal with your bitterness, be prepared to deal with the long-term ramifications.

God doesn't force us to forgive people. We really don't have to do it if we choose not to. But what we can lose is the ability to experience freedom and the supernatural ability to experience God intimately. Remember, no matter how bad the act was, and no matter how undeserving a person might be, your willingness to forgive a person will set *you* free.

Application Points:
Do you recognize an unforgiving spirit in yourself?

_____

_____

_____

Are there bigger violations that you feel do not deserve to be forgiven?

_____

_____

_____

A Prayer about Bitterness
Father God,

I realize that I've taken on a victim mentality because of the things others have done to me. I've become angry, frustrated, and resentful of both the people responsible for those violations and people who weren't responsible at all. Specifically, I pray about _____
_____. I also pray for the way I react, complain and backbite. Father, heal my heart. Show me grace, and then give me the ability to view other people with that same grace.

In Jesus's name, amen.

Applying Forgiveness

We are going to deal first hand with the ramifications of the ways others have hurt us, abused us, neglected us or otherwise violated us. Talking about forgiving people is one thing, but facing those sins on an individual basis—and fully connecting with the emotions, the damage and the consequences—is entirely different. Most of us inappropriately deal with the ways others have hurt us. We don't understand the significance or the effects, so we think it will "just go away."

The purpose of this project is to fully recall and work through each event that occurred. That's why it's important not to get too caught up in the process but recognize that it is more important to evaluate and pray over these violations so we might identify which ones need to be dealt with. Also, it's important to know that God must be the one who directs this process. Before we go any further, let's pray. Here's a suggestion:

A Prayer to Prepare to Forgive

Father God,

I desire to be set free from the damaging consequences of sin in my life. I realize I have been hurt or violated by others. Whether or not they intended to, and no matter how much I love those people, I ask that You give me the courage to face those things that have held me in bondage. Father, You already know what is happening inside my heart. Please, based on Your character of love, grace, power, goodness, kindness and mercy, help me. Meet me right now wherever I am and connect me to your spiritual resources. I praise You and thank you in advance. You are a good God.

In Jesus's name, amen.

Step 1: Process Feelings

As we discussed in chapter 6, the ability to connect emotionally is an important aspect to healing. Based on the inventory list of the acts committed against you, answer the following questions for each item listed.

Recall Past Violations

1. Can I acknowledge that the act was wrong and that as a human being I had certain rights that were violated? (For example, I was abused by my uncle. I did not deserve this.)
2. Can I identify with how that act made me feel?
3. Have I been able to connect emotionally with what happened? Have I ever cried, grieved or expressed hurt as a result?

If you answered no to everything, it's possible you are still protecting the event through some form of denial, whether or not you are doing it intentionally. Truly, only the power of the Holy Spirit can "break through." If you trust Him, ask Him to reveal where you may have been wounded. Remember, you may not be ready to deal with this issue yet, so don't put pressure on yourself. It's okay to move on for now and focus on something else. Just remember to continue to pray for the Lord's guidance and power, not allowing the spirit of denial to take root.

Step 2: Acknowledge the Truth

If you were able to answer yes to the questions above, then you can begin to write and speak truth statements about the act. Find a place where you can be completely alone. Speak the words of this assignment aloud (this is important). You are going to declare this

Forgiveness Worksheet

(Use separate sheet for each person or act)

Name of Violator: _____

Name of Act: _____

1. Can I acknowledge that the act was wrong, and that as a human being, I had certain rights that were violated? (i.e., I was abused by my uncle. I did not deserve this)
2. Can I identify with how that act made me feel?
3. Have I been able to connect emotionally with what happened? Have I ever cried, grieved or hurt as a result?

Declaration against the sin

"It was not okay that this violation occurred. I refuse it and the message it sent into my life.

I felt _____(angry, dirty, sad, etc.)

I saw myself as _____(unworthy, unlovable, rejected)

As a result, I continue to (think, feel, believe) _____ (I'm not worthy, not lovable, etc.)"

Truth statement:

While the act of _____ told me a lie, I choose to accept the truth of God that I am _____ (loved, accepted, precious).

Jesus, I hate this, but I realize I must forgive this person. I can't do this on my own. Take it for me."

to yourself, to God and to the satanic realm.

Declaration Against the Sin

"It was not okay that this violation occurred.

I refuse it and the message it sent into my life.

I felt _____ (angry, dirty, sad, etc.)

I saw myself as _____ (unworthy, unlovable, rejected)

As a result, I continue to (think, feel, believe) _____ (I'm not worthy, not lovable, etc.)"

As you look at your answer for each act, it's important that you acknowledge the lie that you believed. When you realize someone hurt you, at some point you need to make a truth statement against it. For example, the act of sin left you feeling devalued as a person, but in reality you are a valuable and precious child of God—heaven-bound, filled with a future and hope.

Truth statement:

While the act of _____ told me a lie, I choose to accept the truth of God that I am _____ .

Step 3: Forgiveness

The final step in this process is a willingness to forgive the person who committed the act against you. Some important things to remember about this step:

- Forgiveness is a choice of the will, not a feeling.
- Forgiveness opposes our human nature. Therefore, we'll need God's divine power to do it for us.
- Forgiveness begins with a small willingness, not necessarily a strong desire.
- Whatever violation was committed against us, Jesus felt and bore it personally Himself. Therefore, we don't go through this alone. He has gone through it with us already.
- As we deal with forgiving others, we aren't necessarily going to ever be in a relationship with them again. Forgiveness is not reconciliation: we can only be reconciled to those who have realized their part in the situation.
  - o If you don't know where to begin, a simple prayer like this is encouraged: "Jesus, I hate this, but I realize I must forgive this person. I can't do this on my own. Take it for me." Then apply these steps to each significant

person on your inventory sheet who committed an act of violation against you. Start with the most significant people (parents, spouse, ex-spouse, children, and others) and work down.

Application Points:

1. Use a separate worksheet for each violation and fill it out completely (page 169).

2. Write the violator a letter that expresses how they made you feel and then the choice you make to forgive them. (You don't need to give them this letter unless you feel entirely sure God is directing you to do so.)

3. Renounce that sin and its shameful effect in your life in the name of Jesus. A suggestion is listed below:

Father God,

I was really hurt by _____ (name of person), but today I choose to forgive. I ask that You please forgive _____ for sinning against me by _____. I pray that you would meet _____ (name of person) at his/her point of need. I release _____ (name of person) to you. I renounce the sin and every damaging effect and message it has imposed on my life. I pray and earnestly seek full redemption, trusting that what Satan meant for evil, You can use for good. Set me free.

In Jesus's name, amen.

Larry's Story

Larry grew up in a hostile environment. His father had an anger issue that often resulted in physical abuse. This behavior caused everyone in the home to live in fear. While Larry's mother did her best to love and protect her children, the seeds of shame were planted, and the message was sent into Larry's life that he was responsible for his father's anger and that he continually did something to deserve it.

Because Larry didn't address his feelings of powerlessness and unworthiness of love as a child, he took on ways to compensate for those needs in adulthood. As a result, Larry was drawn to women with problems. In some ways, he wanted to fix their problems; in other ways, he didn't want to get too close to them at all. These unhealthy relationships led to a variety of issues. In fact, Larry began to act out in violent and rage-filled behaviors, something he had vowed he would never do. When he did reach out for help he had not yet hurt anyone, but he was terrified he was going down that path.

As part of Larry's recovery, he went through the forgiveness process as stated in this chapter. First, Larry had to recall those events that had been blocked and minimized for a very long time. He also began to identify the messages he had received as a young child that carried over into adulthood: "You're unworthy. You deserve nothing." As Larry began to understand the pain and trauma he faced from his father, he found himself experiencing the feelings he was never able to before. Larry always had a difficult time trusting in God, but because he was so broken, he finally surrendered himself to God.

Eventually, Larry wrote his father a letter and prayed to forgive him. In fact, Larry continued to pray for him every day. While the healing didn't happen immediately, Larry became more and more free as the resentment and anger that ran his life began to dissolve. As he recalled this process, the most freeing thing of all was being allowed to actually hate and hurt over what had occurred. Larry realized that since his mom always minimized everything, he was never before given that opportunity. He eventually forgave his father as a person but didn't have to ever accept those horrible behaviors as being okay. They were not.

Although Larry had forgiven his dad, they had been estranged for over fifteen years. But one day, out of nowhere, Larry's father called him and apologized for all he had done wrong. He had become a Christian and wanted to know if Larry could forgive him for his wrongdoing. Larry had already forgiven his father. Because he dealt with those violations properly, Larry willingly received his father back into his life, thus allowing for reconciliation.

The Gifts of Our Wounds

Larry didn't ever forget what happened. In fact, it became part of his life story. But as those wounds healed, they became a testimony of God's great power and love in his life. In the same way, our wounds will eventually heal as God administers His truth to us and takes away the distortions and lies fed to us. Although God is able to heal those wounds, we won't completely forget the pain. Rather, as we encounter the power of the blood of Jesus Christ and His remarkable love and grace, we will become carriers of hope. We will possess tangible proof, the miracle of what God can do inside the heart of a human who has been injured. We can carry the message of God's love and power to others who are struggling. This means that at the very places and points where Satan attempted to destroy us, God will restore us and use that experience to further His Kingdom.

Meditation points: What's holding you back from forgiving? Do you see the benefit of forgiveness? Why or why not?

Saying Good-Bye: Learning to Grieve What We Lost

While forgiveness allows the opportunity to remove the toxins of an injustice committed against us, we must also deal with those things that stem from neglect. As we learned in the previous chapter, what people didn't do also hurts us. If we don't effectively deal with this, we can go through life trying to replace those unmet needs in illegitimate ways.

Much of the early recovery stage includes grief. We are asked to deal with those losses we weren't able to face before. We will also find current losses in our lives for which we need to grieve. This might be the pain felt due to an absent spouse or the distant relationship of a child.

Like anything we grieve, it may take time. Grief has a purpose and a season, but its goal is to move us through to a point of healing rather than keep us bound to things that continue to destroy our lives.

Grieving a Loss

Your inventory sheets include a list of unmet needs. For this process, also include any painful deaths, abandonment or separation that occurred in significant relationships (past or present). For each thing listed, and for those things that arise in the future, you eventually need to grieve over the loss. The grieving process itself involves a variety of steps.

Steps to Grieving a Loss

- Identify the loss for what it is. We already did this by listing out in black and white the things we currently understand that we lost or never had. Remember, it's important to start with the earliest memory of our unmet needs and work forward to the present. The perceived needs we have in the "here and now" might be skewed. We may expect people to meet needs that actually stem from our unmet childhood needs.
- Legitimize the needs we have listed. We spent most of our life trying to minimize our needs. We must do the opposite. Say something like this: I needed you to _____ (love me, nurture me, protect me), but you didn't. I know you had your own reasons and issues, but it didn't change the fact that I truly needed this from you.
- Connect emotionally to the pain of not having something we needed. We may have had it at one point, and then eventually lost it. This could be the death or separation of someone close to us. It may have been the loss of

childhood. If we are still in denial or trapped behind anger, we may have not yet "felt" the raw emotion. Remember what we learned in chapter 6—we must "feel to heal." Use this exercise about each unmet need you are grieving:

When you _____ I felt

_____.

- Acknowledge where we blamed others. Often when needs aren't met, we begin to blame people and grow bitter and angry. We may blame a sibling for the loss of a parent: "He died because he was so worried about you." We may blame God. Understanding our blame helps us see why we've been hindered from moving on.
- Acknowledge our powerlessness. We must come to a place where we simply recognize that we are powerless over the person and their inability to meet our need. Or that we can do nothing to change the fact that they left us. In that powerlessness, we are ready to surrender it to Jesus (chapter 5).
- Choose (it is a choice) to forgive the person who let you down. Using the same process, we learned in forgiving a person for an act committed against us, we can forgive the person who didn't meet our needs.
- Accept that person (not their behavior) and the circumstances that led to where you are today. Often people who neglected us were unavailable because of their own painful issues. We must understand that when we forgive and accept someone, we stop trying to change that person. We stop trying to get our needs met. Or we stop recreating scenarios to get someone else to meet those needs.
- Say good-bye. If you are grieving the loss of a person, write that person a letter to say good-bye. Explain the pain of separation but the desire to move on without them.
- Ask God to meet our needs. While we are asked to let go of the painful, unmet needs of our past, we must have the perspective and mindset that we have a God who is infinitely higher and bigger than any need at any given time. Ask God to meet your needs through His perspective and to give you the willingness and patience to wait on Him to do so.

"Now all glory to God, who is able, through his mighty power at work within us, to accomplish infinitely more than we might ask or think" (Ephesians 3:20).

A Prayer to Initiate a Grieving Process
Father God,

I am so prone to not wanting to feel pain that even the thought of grieving scares me. I realize there were things in my life that I lost. Sometimes, I just couldn't face it. Other times,

I resorted to anger and blame. I may have even blamed You for allowing this in my life. Lord, You know the barriers in my heart that have prevented me from healing. I ask that You please work in me and do for me what I can't do for myself. I ask, in exchange for my willingness to grieve and let go of losses, that you give me those things I really do need. I trust You, Lord. I know that You are able.

In Jesus's name, amen.

Application Points:

Can you identify where you struggle in the grieving process? Describe.

_____

_____

_____

What is the number one most painful or tragic loss in your life? Have you dealt with it?

_____

_____

_____

Free to be Accepted

The journey toward healing is extraordinary. We may begin this journey bitter and angry toward others for the wrongs they committed against us. We may live our lives based on our perception of not measuring up. We may have felt overwhelmed by our own shame and guilt. But through recovery, we find authentic acceptance. We also discover that wounded areas in our lives become gateways to new beginnings. The negative experiences don't go away, but they do become a part of our overall life-experience. When we embrace forgiveness and benefit from its remedy, we can offer that same remedy to others. This means we are able to accept others too. Imagine this—spending the rest of our lives feeling totally accepted exactly how we are! Imagine not having to worry about the flaws or the failures in our life. How freeing!

Those burdens we've carried certainly were valid. But the process of recovery moves us through those experiences to a new place. The entire process we undertook was meant to take away the damaging effects of sin and shame, those things that attempted to disrupt and infect God's plan and purpose for our life. The Bible says, "The thief's purpose is to steal and kill and destroy. My purpose is to give them a rich and satisfying life" (John 10:10). It also says, "Weeping may last through the night, but joy comes with the morning" (Psalm 30:5).

Rest assured, if you are faithful in your desire to be set free, there is a new day on the horizon. The life of abundance isn't necessarily one that is problem free; it's one that is Spirit-filled. God does not intend that you stay and live in the past. He is waiting to pull you out into safety and set you on a pathway of fulfillment and wholeness. King David described a moment such as this in his life:

> I waited patiently for the Lord to help me, and he turned to me and heard my cry. He lifted me out of the pit of despair, out of the mud and the mire. He set my feet on solid ground and steadied me as I walked along. He has given me a new song to sing, a hymn of praise to our God. Many will see what he has done and be amazed. They will put their trust in the Lord. (Psalm 40:1–3)

Have you been in the pit? Has He freed you? What God did for anyone else, He can do for you.

A Prayer to Declare Acceptance

Father,

I renounce the lies I have believed for so long regarding my lack of self-worth. I renounce the sins and violations that people imposed on me and the shame messages they sent. I renounce the wrongful ways I have acted out in order to cope and survive. I declare Your righteousness over my life. I declare that I am accepted as a child of the living God and that through the blood of Jesus Christ nothing can condemn, shame or cause me to feel guilt again. I am free. I am loved. And I am ready for a new day in Christ Jesus.

In Jesus's name, amen.

10

Embracing Authentic Identity

Workbook Keys

- Understand "Identity Theft"
- Embrace Spiritual Identity
- Define Giftedness
- Seek Vision

As we learn to confront shame, we are given the opportunity to disengage its power. The removal of shame is both a process and a lifestyle. It is a choice we will be asked to make every day for the rest of our lives: Will I live my life based on the shame, fear, the need to "measure up" and the dysfunction in and around me? Or will I live my life on the basis of God's grace, forgiveness, mercy, love and power toward me?

In Matthew 9:17 Jesus explained a profound truth. He said, "And no one puts new wine into old wineskins. For the old skins would burst from the pressure, spilling the wine and ruining the skins. New wine is stored in new wineskins so that both are preserved." The effect of sin and shame in our life and our own efforts to overcome it may have caused us to "burst." Even as Christians, we may have incorporated God's principles into an overall unhealthy belief system—a system infected by sin and shame. We may have thought if we could just add some good things, somehow everything would be all right. But it didn't work.

That's because in the Spirit-filled, authentic Christian life, change must occur at a foundational level where entire mentalities, coping mechanisms and belief systems are brought into alignment with God's truth. When this takes place, an entirely new world unfolds for us. The people and circumstances in our life may not change, but we are able to see them through a new filter—the filter of God's grace.

As this process occurs, there is perhaps nothing as healing and restoring as being able to embrace our authentic identity.

Who Am I?

Identity simply means how we see ourselves. When we were covered in the muddy film of shame, our identity was stolen. We lived our life based on lies—we believed what other people told us. We believed that the measurements and standards of the outside world dominated how we should measure our own worth.

Here are some of the places we try to find our identity:

- **Finding our identity through our family role:** Within our family of origin, we functioned in a role that told us how to love, how to give and how to see ourselves and others. If that family system was unhealthy, our sense of identity might have been based on outrageous lies, or it may have never been developed at all. We may have learned to take care of the needs of other family members and in the process were never able to define our personal likes, preferences, goals, desires, beliefs, etc. Instead, we adapted to whatever others needed or desired.

- **Finding our identity through relationships:** We can become so enmeshed in our relationships that we feel unable to separate ourselves from a particular person. We might only feel secure when this person is around us and continually focus on his or her needs and life issues. Because we don't have healthy boundaries (see chapter 11), we don't distinguish between "you" and "me." Our entire identity gets lost in this person. We can also bring unhealthy people into our life who continually criticize and put us down, and we learn to see ourselves through that filter. When these people are close to us, it can be difficult to overcome.

- **Finding our identity through appearance/sexuality:** We may have learned that our core value is in our physical appearance. We may have received validation when we outwardly made ourselves appear good. We may have taken that to even more of an extreme and used our sexuality to gain power or attention from the opposite sex. Even in marriage we may continue to believe we are only as good as our appearance. If our identity is wrapped tightly in how we look, a bad hair day can leave us feeling insecure and unworthy. More commonly, we may become terrified of the changes age will bring.

- **Finding our identity through material possessions or status:** We may have become attached to our material possessions or social status, using them to measure our personal worth. We can even reason that with enough "stuff," we will find the security and confidence we need in life. For example, a sports car we drive may feed into our overall sense of identity—believing it somehow proves we have worth in itself.

- **Finding our identity through reputation:** We can strive hard to produce an outward reputation based on moral living, kindness, and other outward acts. We can find security in how we are viewed by others, including church members, co-workers, and others. That's not to say it may not align with our character, but often we can become obsessed with this reputation. If we ever entered into situations in life where this reputation appeared smudged, we could be devastated. We might come from dysfunctional family systems where those around us have negative reputations. We use our efforts to create a good reputation to overcome the shameful activities of another family member.

· **Finding our identity through work:**   Work is an important part of our life. We carry a title and set of responsibilities related to the work we do. Some of us find our entire identity through that title. Furthermore, we become so consumed by our work, our entire sense of worth rests in our success or failure. Others of us may have jobs or careers we took out of obligation and need but find no joy whatsoever in the tasks. These jobs may stand in complete contrast with our skills and talents. We feel chronically negative, detached, unsatisfied and unmotivated as a result.

What is the common thread among our family roles, relationships, appearance, material possessions, reputation and work? In truth, they don't *offer* identity—they *steal* identity. By becoming fixated and secure in these areas, we become frightened at the thought of losing or changing anything where our identity stands a chance of being threatened. This means that when relationships fail, when we lose a job, when we develop wrinkles, when we face financial hardship, our entire world can seemingly fall apart.

If these are unhealthy methods of seeking identity, what is the true method by which we begin to "find ourselves?" Surely, it can't mean we stop relationships, live immorally, change our material possessions, let go of our appearance or quit our job! Of course not. Identity involves a much deeper self-talk and self-visualization that may actually take some time to build. In reality, identity isn't based at all on anything outward, including relationships, work, possessions, etc.

Instead, identity is a core issue. It is the very essence of our being—the intricate and detailed things that make us who we are. The only potential we have to truly capture our identity is to ask our Maker and Manufacturer. He designed us before time and space. By seeking His point of view, we are going to find who we are and the purpose for which we were created. Jeremiah 1:5 says, "I knew you before I formed you in your mother's womb. Before you were born I set you apart."
In order to do this, we need to recapture our authentic identity at several levels:

· We find identity at a spiritual level with God, as His spiritual child.
· We find identity at a personal level through our own skills, talents, life calling, and so forth.
· We find identity through what we offer in our relationships.

· We find identity that enables us to carry our unique calling to serve others.

Application Point:
Before we continue, let's try to discover those things that may have been holding our true identity hostage. Who tells you who you are?

Answer the Following:

Do you define yourself by your appearance, reputation or material possessions? How?

_____

_____

_____

Do you define yourself by the work you do or the job you have?

_____

_____

_____

What do you think your spouse or significant other would say about who you are? (if applicable)

_____

_____

_____

What would/did your parents and siblings say about who you are?

_____

_____

_____

What do you think your children say about who you are? (if applicable)

_____

_____

_____

What do your friends say about who you are?

_____

_____

_____

What do people at church and/or your pastor say about who you are?

_____

_____

_____

The Process of Gaining Identity

Everything that has been done in this workbook up to this point has led us to the place where we are finally ready to embrace authentic identity. However, if our identities have been damaged or entirely lost, simply finding them won't happen immediately.

Let's look at the example of Megan, a woman who entered recovery for her codependence. Megan had always believed her childhood upbringing was normal. She thought it was something in her that was flawed. However, as she looked back, she realized her identity had never developed in a healthy way. She had felt undervalued and rejected within her family. Her parents never affirmed or encouraged Megan. In fact, her parents often finished or corrected her attempts to do normal, everyday tasks. This taught Megan she was incompetent. Furthermore, her parents never discussed her grades or achievements in school. Instead, they overly focused on her older sister, who won scholarships and awards for her scholastic prowess. They felt so proud of her older sister that by comparison, Megan had little reason to be recognized. In reality, Megan was very bright and always received As and Bs in school. It wasn't that her parents told her she didn't measure up; they simply never paid attention or offered her affirmation. Megan's parents were completely unaware.

Because Megan had no confidence in her abilities, she inwardly saw herself as a failure. Instead of pursuing college, Megan wound up in relationships with men who consumed her life. Megan didn't realize that her fear of being seen as incompetent or stupid led her to find people she thought wouldn't be a threat to her low self-esteem and identity. She was attracted not only to people who didn't judge her but also to relationships in which she would be required to overly compensate. For a long time, Megan found validation in these relationships because she had never seemed useful or special in her own family. These people truly needed her. But eventually, the addictive cycles of others and her own codependence perpetuated into insanity. Megan's role in unhealthy relationships no longer left her feeling special or validated. In fact, the relationships became toxic.

In her recovery, Megan had to go back and first uncover the messages she received from her family of origin. Megan needed to identify them and forgive her parents and herself for allowing these false truths to influence her in such a profound way. She also had to the deal with the further layers of baggage that resulted. But that didn't automatically set Megan on a healthy course. She needed not only to reject the negative messages but also to receive new messages into her life based on truth. She had to then make a choice to either continue as a victim of her past . . . or as a child of God filled with a future and with hope (see Jeremiah 29:11).

Here's where many misunderstand the process of recovery, or sanctification. Forgiveness is a one-time event, but the consequences may leave enough damage in our soul that we need time to regain what has been lost. Megan lost an entire childhood and early adulthood, believing she had nothing to offer in the world. Because her childhood was intended to be a time when she would have grown and developed skills, talents, interests and ambitions, she was literally "growth stunted" in this area of life. Megan needed not only to renounce shame and find forgiveness but also to initiate the very process that would have naturally occurred through her childhood in a healthy family system. She had to discover her gifts, unique talents, interests, skills and passions in life. Because Megan had grown to become so insecure, she had stopped trying to do much of anything. It would be necessary for her to step out in faith and try new things, discover new interests and essentially learn who she was inside. While she needed to be spiritually grounded, there were also many practical things to learn that would require time, careful planning, goal setting and encouragement.

How could Megan go through this discovery process? She would need a Guide to lead her. As Megan pledged to claim the Word of God as the source of her identity, she began to see herself as God's precious and valuable child. From there, Megan naturally felt inclined to follow after her interests. Because the shame mask was removed and the Holy Spirit had been given access to her life, He was in the process of helping her redefine herself. He was working with her—in ways that only she could understand—to unmask and reveal the desires of her heart. Desires He had given her and gifts and talents He had placed in her.

Megan's self-discovery process became exciting. She began to understand that connecting with her true identity was a privilege and that the person God made her to be was fulfilling. She found interests she never dreamed of pursuing and eventually found healthy, whole relationships.

As was the case for Megan, the struggle for identity first happens as an actual spiritual battle in the mind for the messages and beliefs we choose to receive. Just as a root springs up and produces some sort of fruit, when messages come from God, they eventually produce the wholesome perfection of His will in our life. We honestly don't have to frantically pursue what to "do next." God begins to show us and places things directly into our heart and mind that align with His will for us (see Philippians 2:13).

Who God Says We Are

God clearly gives us an identity in His Word. Our true identity comes as we see ourselves through the truth that we are called, loved, chosen, redeemed and empowered by the Lord. There are precious truths we can embrace that will guarantee us the ability to be transformed, healed, delivered and set free to be the person God intended us to be.

But simply reading a piece of Scripture doesn't mean that transformation will occur. We must receive God's promises and truth into our hearts. How does this occur? True change occurs at a belief level (see Romans 12:2). Let's look:

- We must first have faith in order for the seed of that promise to have the "soil" where it can be planted into our hearts (see Hebrews 11:1).
- We must speak that truth into our personal situations, even if we "feel" differently.
- We must hang on to that promise and claim it, even when things don't "appear" to align with what God says (this allows the promise to take root).
- We must wait and see the faithfulness of God translate this promise into a reality. This produces the actual fruit of that promise (see Galatians 6:9).
  (Read Luke 8:4–15)

Claiming God's truth will allow us to see the world through His perspective. It will defend us against the false and potentially threatening ways we formerly used to secure our identity. For example, relying on the love of a person who fails us can shatter our sense of worth and value. But as we learn to secure our anchor on how God loves us, no matter what happens, we find security in this knowledge.

As we change at the very core of our being, we begin to see ourselves as precious. We begin to operate through the Holy Spirit, not our self-will or learned, adaptive behaviors.

Where True Identity Begins: Claiming Our Identity as a Child of God

The entire Bible is a revelation of God's truth. But to help you get started, here are some of the fundamental ways we can become stabilized in our identity and purpose in life.

I Am Rescued, Ransomed, Adopted and Chosen

He led me to a place of safety; he rescued me because he delights in me. (Psalm 18:19)

Do not be afraid, for I have ransomed you. I have called you by name; you are mine. (Isaiah 43:1)

God decided in advance to adopt us into his own family by bringing us to himself through Jesus Christ. (Ephesians 1:5)

You didn't choose me. I chose you. I appointed you to go and produce lasting fruit, so that the Father will give you whatever you ask for, using my name. (John 15:16)

And having chosen them, he called them to come to him. And having called them, he gave them right standing with himself. And having given them right standing, he gave them his glory. (Romans 8:30)

I Am Loved

And I am convinced that nothing can ever separate us from God's love. (Romans 8:38)

Because you are precious to me. You are honored, and I love you. (Isaiah 43:4)

But God showed his great love for us by sending Christ to die for us while we were still sinners. (Romans 5:8)

And may you have the power to understand, as all God's people should, how wide, how long, how high, and how deep his love is. (Ephesians 3:18)

See how very much our Father loves us, for he calls us his children, and that is what we are! (1 John 3:1)

I Am Empowered

Yes, I am the vine; you are the branches. Those who remain in me, and I in them, will produce much fruit. For apart from me you can do nothing. (John 15:5)

It is God who enables us, along with you, to stand firm for Christ. He has commissioned us, and he has identified us as his own. (2 Corinthians 1:21–22)

For I can do everything through Christ, who gives me strength. (Philippians 4:13)

For God has not given us a spirit of fear and timidity, but of power, love, and self-discipline. (2 Timothy 1:7)

The Spirit who lives in you is greater than the spirit who lives in the world. (1 John 4:4)

I Have Significance

"For I know the plans I have for you," says the Lord. "They are plans for good and not for disaster, to give you a future and a hope." (Jeremiah 29:11)

For we are God's masterpiece. He has created us anew in Christ Jesus, so we can do the good things he planned for us long ago. (Ephesians 2:10)

Application Points:

1. Pick out scriptures of your own that apply to your life situation and areas of struggle. These should be promises you need to personally receive into your life.
2. Post the scriptures in a place where you can access them throughout the day, perhaps a bathroom mirror, refrigerator door, etc.
3. Speak the promises aloud whenever possible.
4. Pray for the faith to claim and endure until that promise becomes real to you.
5. Next to the scripture, write dates, or descriptions of how God made that truth real in your life.

Take Back Your Identity

The best gift God gave you is the true vision, plan and purpose He created for you. Imagine—there was a day in heaven when God thought of you. When He determined the color of your eyes, the place where you would live, the people in your family. Now imagine how He looked into your heart and implanted your personality, your preferences, your desires. And then He gave you a free will. So despite how He created you, He left you the room to make choices on your own.

For many of us, life got complicated along the way. Our survival mode caused us to lose focus and become distracted. Spiritually, Satan and his army worked hard to attack us in the very places where we had giftedness, knowing that if God had His way in us, we could be a danger to his empire. Emotionally, we became detached and even disassociated from our true selves, causing that separation between the external and internal.

Now, just as we asked the Lord to reveal and then remove the damaged areas in our life, it's time to become the person God made us to be. The REAL us! When we begin to approach our search for authentic identity, it can appear to be a selfish process. However, when we see it in the proper context, we find it is not self-focused, but God-focused. In fact, God desires us to find and use all our skills and abilities just as He has given them to us (see Matthew 25:14–30).

The formation of a healthy identity is a process of growth, not an immediate event. If you recall the example of Megan, her self-identity had been stunted because of insecurity and her focus on others. Just like Megan, if we never had the opportunity for proper self-discovery, we are essentially asking God to lead us on the journey that we may have skipped in our youth. Grab hold of Him like a child, and ask Him to reveal what makes you, you. Are you ready?

Who Are You? Finding Your Gifts and Calling

Let's look at three primary areas: spiritual gifts, life gifts and personality.

Spiritual Gifts

The Bible is clear that God gives us spiritual gifts. These are supernatural enablers so we may serve God more effectively in the world and in the church through the power of the Holy Spirit. Every Christian has at least one spiritual gift, and many are given more than one.

The various spiritual gifts are listed in Romans 12, Ephesians 4, 1 Corinthians 13–15 and elsewhere. Read those scriptures and learn more.

What's most important to understand about spiritual gifts is that they may, or may not, complement our personality and other talents. Since these are gifts of the Spirit, they are not based on our humanness at all.

We must both understand and receive our spiritual gift for it to be activated. If we are led by our emotions, we may end up reacting to the perceived needs around us and literally miss out on the actual calling we have. It's possible to do many good things and still miss the opportunity to live out God's personal plan for our life.

Passionately seek after your spiritual gift. Ask God to wisely place you in the right church where this gift will be used in accordance with His purposes.

Application Points:

1. Find a spiritual gift test. They are often available on the Internet, and you might also want to ask your pastor for information.
2. Determine your top three spiritual gifts. Then answer the following questions:
   - How do I see myself using these gifts in the church right now?
   - How can I better find a way to offer these gifts to the body of Christ?

Life Gifts

God placed natural resources throughout the universe that over time have been used in a variety of ways to support life as we know it today. Think of the oil in the ground or the minerals deposited in the soil that have unlimited benefits. God knew ahead of time that these very resources would be discovered and used at the proper time and place.

In the same way, you have natural resources that were deposited into your life. These gifts afford much value to you personally but were also designed to contribute to the place, time and purpose God designed for your life.

Unfortunately, many of us haven't come to that place of discovery and may be living completely out of line with our giftedness. Furthermore, the dysfunction of our codependence has literally blinded and crippled us from finding who we really are.

Here are some reasons we aren't using our gifts:

- Our gifts and individual purpose weren't properly seen, valued or understood in the role we played in the family of origin.
- We are aware of our desires and gifts but are afraid of using them. Fear of failure (or success) has literally paralyzed us from moving forward.
- Our gifts and talents got so buried under character defects, they were never allowed the chance to grow and thrive.
- We discarded our gifts as unimportant or insignificant; thus, we spent time trying to operate and function outside of them or tried to acquire new and different gifts that don't necessarily match who we are.

Just like God's natural resources, we may need to spend some time digging and asking Him to reveal those gifts. Typically, these types of life gifts would be used to fulfill our career or vocational objectives or to serve in volunteer organizations and other community functions.

Application Points:

Begin to search for the natural life skills you might possess. Consider taking a vocational, career or skills assessment test to get an idea of your areas of general giftedness and/or interest.

Answer the following:

1. Do I currently have life gifts that I am or am not using?
2. Does my vocation align with my true talents, skills and desires?
3. If not, what action can I take to better understand my skills?
4. How can I begin to implement them into my life and career?

Understand Our Personality

In addition to our skills, gifts and spiritual giftedness, we also have a God-given personality. Our personality denotes the way we speak, move, interact, converse and relate to others. While we can be motivated by faulty beliefs, negative feelings and dysfunctional behaviors (chapter 3), underneath we still have a personality that makes us who we are. Infants demonstrate personality the best. Every baby develops a unique personality even though all babies tend to do similar things. As human beings, we aren't cookie cutters, and by definition, our personalities make us unique.

As we see defects in our character, we must be careful not to want to take away things that are actually just a part of our personality. That means, even if we suffer from codependence, we might continue to be very friendly, helpful and outgoing. This can be confusing at first, but in actuality, we don't really have to seek after our personality. We simply need to learn to accept the person we are at a core level.

As we continue to work to remove those things that aren't of God, our natural personality will continue to develop. We are asked to die to our flesh, but that doesn't mean God is throwing away everything about us.

Also, it's important to know that not everyone views the world the same as we do because they have different personalities. Part of what we embrace in recovery is not only a sense of self but also a respect and honor for other people's God-given right to be who they are.

Application Points:
1. Fill out an online personality assessment (look online for "Christian personality test"), or choose another personality assessment tool such as Myer-Briggs.
2. Write out the name and description of your personality.
3. Do you agree with this assessment? Why or why not?
4. Write your own analysis of your personality.

Reclaiming Our Identity in Relationships

The ruts we've dug in relationships can be difficult to overcome. We get into relationship patterns and wrong ways of thinking. Because of this, we project our emotional issues and defend our actions. We may even fight to function in relationships where we desperately want to be understood and noticed. Relationships can be difficult to mend when two broken people aren't just looking to have personal needs met but are seeing each other through faulty and inappropriate filters.

Just as the Enemy taunts us, in relationships we can both receive shame messages and project shame onto others. Even as we begin to understand our true identity, others may not see or respect it. What can we do? How can we overcome this? In truth, authentic identity has to be embraced by no one other than God and ourselves. It can still hurt when people reject us, but we must learn to take those offenses before the throne of grace. As we discover some people in our life to be dangerous and unhealthy, it will be necessary to set physical and/or emotional boundaries (see chapter 11). We must also be aware of groups of people or certain situations where we are vulnerable to external referencing.

On the other hand, we must seek the fellowship of those who can love us as we are. If we've been hiding and unable to express ourselves authentically, this may be awkward at first. In close relationships, such as marriage, we must understand that this process will take time. Just because we "get it" doesn't mean any other person will understand.

In truth, walking with God requires the ability to take the assaults and attacks waged against us and refuse them. Not only that, but we are actually called to pray for and forgive those people who wage the attacks. We must learn to live life before an audience of One, our Lord—not the group, family members or culture. We will eventually discover that when we please God, we have all power to overcome, and God can reach the people in our lives.

We must also learn to speak over our identity with truth from the One who created us—the Sovereign, all-powerful and infinitely wise God whose acceptance, love and peace surpass all other things we can gain from pleasing people.

God Needs the Real You

The Bible isn't filled with people who are super heroes. They are regular people, people God chose, redeemed and ignited with the Holy Spirit. They are people who messed up, failed and didn't have anything of any great value to offer the world. Yet "God chose things the world considers foolish in order to shame those who think they are wise. And he chose things that are powerless to shame those who are powerful. God chose things despised by the world, things counted as nothing at all, and used them to bring to nothing what the world considers important. As a result, no one can ever boast in the presence of God" (1 Corinthians 1:27–29).

We must come to a place where no matter what we do or who we are, we know we are chosen based on God's grace. If it is offensive for us to think we aren't chosen by all our efforts, degrees and positions, we aren't ready yet. God requires only true surrender—people who are willing to let Him fill them with His truth in the power of His Spirit. "The eyes of the Lord search the whole earth in order to strengthen those whose hearts are fully committed to him (2 Chronicles 16:9).

God needs *you.* Of course He doesn't need you to satisfy His own desires, He needs the person He hand-created you to be, so He can use you in accordance with the gifts and abilities He has already equipped you with. This will allow Him to build His Kingdom in this generation and in the generations to come.

.

Pray for Vision

As you courageously move forward on this journey, it's now time to ask God for a vision of your life. Ask Him to give you a picture of your life, including your calling, your purpose and your relationships. Proverbs 29:18 declares, "When people do not accept divine guidance, they run wild." Other versions of the Bible call that divine guidance a "vision."

While the Word of God provides stabilizing truths, a vision is especially for us and isn't directly stated in the Word of God. The tricky thing is that a real vision comes from God. Although we may already have our own vision of how we want things to be, we must be willing to let God give us a vision. God assures us that His vision will align with our desires:

> For God is working in you, giving you the desire and the power to do what pleases him. (Philippians 2:13)

> I take joy in doing your will, my God, for your instructions are written on my heart. (Psalm 40:8)

> Take delight in the Lord, and he will give you your heart's desires. (Psalm 37:4)

We are given the promise in Scripture that if we surrender ourselves to God, He will align His will with our desires. This means that we won't be forced to just do a bunch of things we don't enjoy, but we will be passionate and fulfilled with God's sense of purpose.

Some Things to Remember About Vision:
- A vision from God is always planted in the truth of God's Word. Therefore, if our vision has anything in opposition to God's Word, we know it's not from Him.
- A vision from God will provide generalities, not necessarily details. We need to wait and let God provide each detail as we need it.
- A vision may be for the future, not right now. In others words, God may place within us a calling or a desire that will take time to complete. This will test our faith, just as Abraham and Sarah were tested.
- God can't deny His own vision and plan for our life. Therefore, we never have to fear that it won't be fulfilled.

How can we determine if we are heading toward God's will in our life as we seek vision? It's actually simple, yet profoundly difficult. We offer and surrender things to Him constantly, asking Him to take away those things that aren't of Him and to keep those things that are.

In God's Eyes, We Are Already "There"

An amazing revelation is to know that God already sees us at our best and already knows the finished result in our life. When God views us, He sees our potential, not our current challenges or hang-ups. When God looks at us, He begins to speak into our life in ways that define us as victorious, strong, righteous and loved. Even if we don't appear remotely close or in line with God's vision for us in the beginning, He is working to make us into the person He already sees us to be.

Application Points:

1. Over the next day, pray for vision.
2. Whatever comes into your head, begin to write it down and continue to pray over it.

A Prayer for Identity and Vision

Father God,

Thank You for claiming me as Your very own child. I stand in assurance of who I am based on Your grace. I renounce and rebuke the lies I have believed, especially _____ _____. My identity isn't founded in anything or anyone else other than the truth of who You say I am. Father, just as I have asked You to release me from the shame in my life, I now ask that You usher in the authentic person you made me to be. Help me to find all that You have for me personally and also what I am to share with others.

Give me a vision so I am not confused about the future. I thank You in advance. In Jesus's name, amen.

11

Building Healthy Boundaries

Workbook Keys

- Define a Boundary
- How do boundaries get distorted?
- How can boundaries be built?
- Describe boundaries and intimacy

Growing in recovery can be wonderful, painful and filled with unexpected twists and turns. As we go down this path, we must expect that negative behaviors and emotional reactions in others and ourselves will arise and cause us to face tough decisions: "What should I do?" "How should I respond?" "Is that acceptable behavior? "If I forgive, must I allow this?"

As we embrace our authentic identity, we learn to value ourselves in God's eyes. We no longer desire to engage in the same unhealthy patterns of behavior that held us in bondage before. Just as we had been in a survival mode, we find that learning to live life in a healthy way can be fun, exciting and fulfilling.

Yet even as our healing begins, those old ways of thinking don't quickly die. And just because we've changed doesn't mean that other people in our life have changed one bit. In fact, we may become more aware than ever of our unhealthy relationships.

How can we find the freedom to be our authentic selves yet at the same time protect ourselves from harmful and destructive relationship dynamics? We will take an in-depth look at the concept of boundaries in order to address our need to develop new forms of responses to relationship challenges based on God's principles.

What Are Boundaries?

Boundaries are visible or invisible fences that define ownership, protect our rights and set rules to determine what's acceptable and what's not acceptable in a given situation. Boundaries say, "I belong to me and you belong to you." Rather than merely separating, boundaries protect what we possess and value, including our own life and body. They enable us to defend ourselves physically, emotionally and spiritually against intrusive or unwanted dangers. But their entire design and purpose is to set the course for mutual respect, consideration, protection and safety in all areas of relationships.

Some of the things boundaries define and protect include:
- Our bodies
- Our emotions
- Our family and loved ones
- Our beliefs
- Our values
- Our identity
- Our time
- Our responsibilities
- Our roles
- Our possessions

God's Boundary System

All of God's principles, laws and promises rest on a perfect set of boundaries established through His Word. These boundaries are specific for each area of our lives. In love, they are established to protect us and give us a safe environment in which to grow in our relationship with God and others.

God doesn't establish boundaries because He needs protection, but He establishes them to offer His guiding principles for our *life*—principles that, in fact, will protect *us*. With His boundaries in place, we learn how to thrive both in our relationship with Him and our relationship with one another.

Development of Boundary Systems

The establishment of boundary systems begins while we're small children. We learn the "rules" to life and the concept of consequences for wrongful behaviors. We are furthermore taught about the role of grace and forgiveness versus punishment when we violate a boundary.

As we learned in chapter 2, the boundaries of a given family are composed of individual family member's belief systems. Depending on how healthy or unhealthy those family members are emotionally and spiritually determines whether the boundary system is established fairly and under safe and healthy biblical guidelines.

For example, Rebecca was raised in a home that had no structure or safe boundaries.

Her parents were both drug addicts, and "anything went" in her home life. Parties, drugs and sex were common things she was exposed to as a child. Her exposure to boundaries didn't teach her morality or right from wrong, much less anything from God's Word. She didn't understand consequences because life was about learning to survive, trying to cope and numbing the pain.

Ryan, on the other hand, was raised in a Christian home filled with love, grace and safe boundaries. He learned he had the freedom to make choices, but wrong choices carried consequences. He also knew the purpose of forgiveness. He was filled with the Word of God and learned it held answers for his life.

It shouldn't be a surprise that Rebecca struggled to develop any type of healthy boundary system in her life as an adult. Her eventual recovery entailed a lengthy process of recognizing false beliefs and negative behaviors and acquiring new belief systems based on God's truth. From there, Rebecca's boundary system began to naturally align with God's truth.

Ryan grew up to become a healthy person; he was instilled with a sense of boundaries that was naturally an inbred part of his make-up. He chose to walk with the Lord and therefore continued to mature spiritually.

Whether or not we have been given healthy boundaries in our family of origin, it's wonderful to realize that no matter how skewed our boundary system may have been, God's Word provides the guidelines, answers and specific boundaries we need to live life. And as we will learn, He not only provides those boundaries but also gives us the desire and ability to adhere to them.

Types of Boundary Systems

We are going look at three primary boundary systems: open, closed and flexible. Understanding how your boundary system operates will help you begin to identify where you might be vulnerable.

Open Boundary System: An open boundary system occurs when outside influences and people determine the way we set and adhere to boundaries. We may actually base our boundaries on other people's needs, demands, issues and desires. Furthermore, with an open boundary system, we may become so enmeshed with other people's thoughts and feelings, we are unable to separate ourselves from them and thus lose our sense of "I" altogether and become "attachments" of other people. Having an open boundary system means we have little protection and are vulnerable to allowing things on the inside that are dangerous or harmful.

To visualize an open boundary system, picture a home with fences broken down and trampled upon. Perhaps the front door and all the windows are open. What does the picture tell? Intruders are allowed inside. The place is vulnerable to outside attack, and strangers may inhabit the home along with the rightful owners.

Closed Boundary System: This system of boundaries is rigid and strict and often is not influenced by anything or anyone from the outside. Families and people with closed boundary systems do not let people close to them, do not share life with others and do not look toward outside influences to determine how they should live. People operating under a closed boundary system live with sheltered, secretive and protective measures. They are often exacting in their approach to life and like to keep things within specific and set confines. Anyone who might disrupt their structure, schedule or system would be seen as a threat.

To visualize a closed boundary system, we could envision a home barricaded with deep, thick walls around its exterior. Windows and doors would be locked, and drapes would be kept tight. What does that picture say? Stay out!

Flexible Boundary System: God created us to have a flexible boundary system. This gives us the ability to protect ourselves from threats, while at the same time allowing people into our life. Flexible boundaries have specific guidelines and consequences for negative behaviors. They aren't just black and white because they are open to the influences of grace and forgiveness. We will be learning in detail about God's boundary system, which is the ultimate example of a flexible boundary system.

To put this system into a biblical context, we could visualize this boundary system as a house with a fence that has a gated access point where people and things can come and go as necessary. The gate has truth as its Guard. To take that even further, that Guard is the Person of Jesus Christ. What does this picture say? That we have certain rights based on truth that we can and should defend. But even more important, we have a wise Protector of our gate!

Application Points:
Which boundary system applies to you? Is that the boundary system you were exposed to in early childhood?

_____

_____

_____

If you have an open boundary system, do you recognize the things and people that you let inside that aren't safe for you? Explain.

_____

_____

_____

If you have a closed boundary system, can you recognize the fear of what others might do to harm you? Explain.

_____

_____

_____

Have you ever considered making Jesus Christ your Gatekeeper? How might that apply in a certain area of your life?

_____

_____

_____

Boundaries, Rights and Responsibilities

As we prepare to set our boundaries in life we are going to first look at two basic areas:

- Our God-given right as human beings
- Our responsibilities in relationships versus God's responsibility and other people's responsibilities

Yes, We Do Have Rights!

One of the saddest misconceptions is that being a Christian means every single right is stripped from us, and we should always meet the needs and demands of others in the name of Christian love. The Christian life indeed requires that we surrender some rights, some comforts, some preferences and some securities as sacrifices for the needs of others. Furthermore, in standing up for God's truth and the foundational belief systems regarding Jesus Christ, we are willing to be persecuted for the cause. Thus, we surrender our right to be treated kindly by anyone who may oppose our belief systems.

But Christianity does not mean that we throw away our individuality and our right to think, feel and act, based on free will. We do, however, surrender ourselves to the Lord; thus, our individuality, thinking, feeling and behaving will eventually align with His character. Early in recovery, we can be confused about how to distinguish between claiming our rights and offering sacrificial love.

To help bring some clarity, listed below are some of the basic rights we can claim as Christians and as human beings:

- We have the right to make our free-will choices, based on facts and the guidance of the Holy Spirit. We do not have to live by what other people need, feel, desire or want from us if it may cause us harm. We then have the choice to do things for others because of God's love and His leading, not because we merely feel forced or obligated.

- We have the right to feel our feelings, even if someone else doesn't like what we feel. If our emotions are sin-based, we bring them to God, asking Him to deal with us. We don't change our feelings merely to please another person. God did not authorize another human being to be in charge of our emotions (nor are we in charge of theirs).

- We have the right to say no to something a person requests from us when it opposes our own God-given conscience or God-given responsibilities. Just because people request things from us doesn't mean we automatically need to comply. We need God's discernment and judgment to do those things God asks us to do, not what we feel pressured to do to please others.

- We have the right to be the person God created us to be, even if it doesn't align with another person's expectations. We belong to God first and foremost. Other people's ideas of how they want us to live our life, including our parents and family members, do not supersede God's vision for us (chapter 10).

- We have the right to not condone or allow sinful behaviors and tendencies, placing protections and consequences as necessary. God doesn't overlook or "wink" at sin. Just as God deals with sin through boundaries and consequences, so can we. We must seek His wisdom in a given situation so we don't overstep those boundaries.

- We have the right to pursue dreams, to find joy, to live in peace and to have balance in our relationships despite what those close to us choose to do. We do not have to stay bound by toxic emotions and feelings of despair. The revelation of God's Word reveals His individualized plan to us repeatedly. To think we should live in emotional pain contradicts God's plan for our life.

It's important to remember that these rights should not in any way infringe on our ability to love others sacrificially and to die to self. Therefore, if we begin to claim our rights to justify anything we want to do, we are misusing them to elevate self. That contradicts God's Word. Discerning where our rights begin, end and can be offered up as submission takes wisdom. We can start by asking these questions:

1. According to the Word of God, do I have this right?
2. Is my right infringing on or violating someone else's same right?

3. Do I claim this right for myself but remain unwilling to give this right to others?

Giving Others Rights

Setting boundaries and establishing mutual basic rights in relationships becomes tricky when we confuse our need to protect our own life with the right to control another person's behavior. While embracing our rights can be a welcome relief, the challenge is that we must allow others the same freedom. In truth, we have no right to try to change how another person thinks, feels or acts. We have no right to get a person to become who we want them to become. Any effort to do so is a major boundary violation.

If we are dealing with unhealthy people, this means we must allow them to make choices that might lead them to do destructive and damaging things in their life. Soon we will learn how to deal with boundary violations, but the key in this section is to simply give people their freedom to choose—whether it be right, or whether it be wrong. People have rights.

Submission versus Claiming Rights

God doesn't call us to be doormats, but He does call us to submission. Submission does not operate by someone else controlling us, or by us feeling obligated or "guilted" into doing something. Submission is a by-product of love. It is built upon the respect and honor due to another person. In essence, when we submit, we give up our own rights and allow someone else to make a decision. This is assuming that we aren't compromising our core rights and belief systems as we just stated.

The most important thing to understand about submission is that it does not seek to manipulate someone to get personal needs met or control an outcome. Instead, as two people come together in love and submission, there should be compatibility, not compromise.

> Is there any encouragement from belonging to Christ? Any comfort from his love? Any fellowship together in the Spirit? Are your hearts tender and compassionate? Then make me truly happy by agreeing wholeheartedly with each other, loving one another, and working together with one mind and purpose. Don't be selfish; don't try to impress others. Be humble, thinking of others as better than yourselves. Don't look out only for your own interests, but take an interest in others, too. (Philippians 2:1–4)

We are able to submit to a person when we love God, ourselves and others properly (chapter 4). If any of these are missing or lacking, submission will quickly become unhealthy and lead to codependence.

Application Points:

Write a list of those rights that you clearly have felt were invalidated in your own life. Why do you think you didn't believe you were entitled to these rights?

_____

_____

_____

Write a list of the ways you invalidate the rights of others. Do you see any similarities?

_____

_____

_____

Do you struggle with understanding true submission? How do you think you fall short?

_____

_____

_____

Responsibility in Relationships

Part of learning how to establish fair and reasonable boundaries is to decide where "I" ends and "you" begins. To break this down, we are going to look at three functions in a relationship: our responsibility, reasonable expectations we can place on others, and God's responsibility.

Our Responsibility: We develop our sense of responsibility in relationships based on our own beliefs and convictions. This means our roles and responsibilities stand independent of how another person behaves in the relationship. As we grow spiritually in God's grace and truth, we learn deeper and deeper what He requires from us at a heart level (not just a list of rules to follow). Growing in codependence recovery requires that we learn to continually focus on our own responsibilities in a given situation, rather than constantly pointing out or focusing on the needs of others.

Reasonable Expectations: Just as we take responsibility for our own behavior, we can have reasonable expectations of the things we desire to receive in relationships. The term "reasonable" is important because often people will fail to meet them, and even more so, we may have expectations that are not fair or realistic. Boundaries are different from expectations. Boundaries protect the things in our life that we value, but expectations are focused upon things we wish to receive from others. Reasonable expectations should be based on biblical truth, not simply our own emotional needs. Discerning how to set these expectations can be difficult and may initially require outside assistance.

If we are in a relationship with someone who is emotionally unavailable, for whatever reason, it's fair to say even reasonable expectations won't be met. Just because we set expectations doesn't mean we have the right to enforce them as the "rule of law." We cannot cross over and make a person do anything simply because we want them to.

God's Responsibility: God always fulfills His responsibility in His relationship with us. ALWAYS. We need to understand that we can have high expectations of Him when they are based on His own promises. Sometimes our expectations of God can be based on our own desires and perceived needs; thus, we feel angry when He appears to fail us.

In our relationship challenges, we will learn that our dependency on God will fill in the gaps where our human relationships at some point will fail us. This is the goal of recovery—to reach the place where we can find that God's resources in our lives truly are sufficient.

Table 7: Responsibility and Expectations

Our Responsibility (to God, self and others)	Reasonable Expectations (from others)	God's Responsibility
We offer ourselves as complete human beings in relationships, not needing someone else to make us whole.	We can expect people to be complete human beings in relationships, not looking to us to make up for deficiencies.	We learn to find sufficiency in Christ—He will make us complete through Him.
We are able to offer forgiveness on a continual basis when others commit wrongdoing against us, offering a relationship pattern of grace.	We can expect people to offer forgiveness and grace where we fall short.	We know that all forgiveness comes from God. Where we fail each other, we find grace through God.
We are responsible for the changes we need to make in our life. We are not responsible for others.	We can allow people to be responsible for the changes they need to make in their life. They are not responsible for ours.	God convicts us of those things that need to change and then gives us the power to change.

Our Responsibility (to God, self and others)	Reasonable Expectations (from others)	God's Responsibility
We take responsibility for our own emotions and don't make others responsible for our moods, good or bad.	We can expect people to take responsibility for their own emotions, not holding us accountable for their moods, good or bad.	We know only God can help us identify our emotions and the root causes behind them.
We can offer our ideas, beliefs and wishes in the relationship no matter how different they might be from other people's. We respect their differing views but don't allow them to compromise our core beliefs.	We can expect people to offer their ideas, beliefs and wishes and respect our differing views.	We ask God to take our ideas, beliefs and wishes and align them with His will.
We love others the best way we know how, understanding it won't be perfect.	We can expect people to love us the best way they know how, understanding it won't be perfect.	We know that only God loves us perfectly, and we find our deepest need for love met by Him.
When problems occur, we take responsibility for our part and do not resort to blame.	When problems occur, they take responsibility for their part and do not resort to blaming us.	We ask God to resolve the issues in our life, and we seek the Word of God for answers.
We commit to be faithful and honest to others.	They commit to be faithful and honest with us.	God is faithful by nature. It is impossible for Him to go against His own character of faithfulness; therefore, we can always count on Him.

When Others Fail Us

So what happens when we fulfill our responsibilities, but other people in our relationships don't fulfill theirs? If we are the recipients of a violation, we can set boundaries to protect that violation from recurring, but we can't change the other person's heart. Rather than attempting to balance an imbalanced relationship, we must be willing to simply let those gaps occur and ask God to fill in the missing pieces. If the relationship is extremely unhealthy or harmful, we may also need to withdraw from the relationship (permanently or temporarily).

Not only will we find that God can meet our needs when we do this, but when we don't manipulate the situation and simply focus on keeping our "own side of the street clean," God can also deal with the other person. In fact, it is often our own efforts to fix the situation that accelerates the problem.

Learning how to set boundaries in this way, allowing ourselves, others and God to be held accountable for their own responsibilities, requires the discipline of letting go and letting God. If we begin to ask God to give us the ability to both understand and change our hearts in this area, it will lead to profound new levels of freedom. It will allow us to gain some sanity as we are able to focus on the things we can change and realize there are some things we cannot change. When we learn to depend on God as our ultimate source, we no longer allow people to emotionally manipulate us, nor do we attempt to manipulate them. Furthermore, we come to understand that we are no longer reliant on what the other person has to offer, understanding that we have all our needs met through God. Just because others are irresponsible, unhappy, unhealthy or unloving doesn't mean we need to be. We don't need to compromise our life in any way just because people fail us.

Applying Solutions to Boundary Violations

Can you imagine how many boundary violations God deals with in a day? The number must be staggering! But it should be a welcome relief to know that God has a method of dealing with our boundary violations that is based on His love and grace for us, not a desire to punish us. To understand the basic operation of God's boundary system, we are going to extract some truths we find in the parable of the prodigal son. (If you aren't familiar with this passage, please take the time right now to read Luke 15:11–32.)

Some of the things we want to key in on in this parable are as follows :

- The Father doesn't hold his son down, tell him no or try to stop him from leaving. (This denotes how God gives us a free will. He doesn't radically and forcefully control our decision making.)
- The Father doesn't chase after the son, even though at some point he probably realizes something is wrong. (This denotes God's willingness to allow consequences to take effect without directly intervening.)

- The son leads a wild and foolish lifestyle, eventually spending all the money. Out of desperation, the son is left to eat pig food to survive. (Yes, pig food! This denotes how bad God will allow those consequences to get.)
- Things dramatically turn around as the son comes to his senses and realizes what a terrible mistake he made. He also remembers that his father is a reasonable man who owns a fortune. He decides he'd be better off becoming his father's worker than living with the pigs. (This denotes the power of painful consequences that lead to the state of brokenness.)
- When the son returns home, his father greets him with open arms, kisses him and throws a party on his son's behalf. While his son intended to be treated only as a slave, he is instead embraced with forgiveness, love and restoration—and given all rights as a son.

As we can see, the way God deals with boundary violations is by allowing consequences to produce enough pain to lead to repentance and ultimately reconciliation. Interestingly enough, the prodigal son's brother—who had stayed home and seemingly did everything right—found it appalling that the wayward son received this level of attention. In fact, he felt entitled to the reward himself.

Like so many of us, it's difficult to conceive that the heart of God isn't moved by our simply doing everything legalistically and in rule-following format. In fact, New Testament Christianity is based on the principle that God is a heart-changer, not just a rule-maker who expects us to comply through our own effort (see Romans 2:29). This means that when we fall short we are reliant on God's grace and forgiveness toward us, not on our own efforts to undo the damage our sin caused.

As we approach the development of boundaries in our own life, we must keep this perspective in mind. God hates sin and deals with it accordingly when it pops up. He never excuses it, winks at it, or minimizes it. Rather, He lets us reap the consequences of our own choices. This is what makes God's love "tough" at times. But as we are humbled and sorry for our behaviors, God forgives us. In fact, God's ultimate objective at all times is to forgive and restore us from the sin in us . . . and the sin that's been done to us.

The principles we just learned from the parable of the prodigal son can help us build a framework to establish healthy boundaries in our relationships. These include the following:

- Defining what is or is not acceptable (based on my moral, beliefs, etc.) in my own behaviors and in the behaviors of those around me.
- Prescribing or allowing consequences and allowing those consequences to take root, no matter the ramifications (not bailing out or cushioning those

consequences from happening to others).

- Learning that the ultimate goal of a consequence is sorrow and contrition so we can offer grace to the person who violated the boundary. (We learn to not punish negative behaviors but to deal with them biblically. We love the person but don't accept the sin.)
- Learning that when no contrition occurs and a person continues to disrespect our boundaries, we are allowed (and should lovingly) continue to prescribe the consequences. (Remember that we aren't attempting to control or change another person's behavior; we are protecting ourselves from the misbehavior of another person who is directly affecting us.)
- Forgiving a person needs to happen regardless of whether the person violating a boundary is truly sorry. However, reconciliation only occurs when the person who is breaking the boundary is repentant and desires forgiveness.

To apply these principles, we are going to look at an example of a married couple. Sheila and Todd married directly out of high school. They were best friends and drinking pals who shared simple but common goals and interests. After marriage, however, Todd began to drink more and more, which began to cause him to withdraw from the relationship. At first, Sheila didn't recognize the problem because "partying" seemed normal, but eventually he was drinking all the time. She didn't know to handle his drinking and went to extreme efforts to make him quit. She began to hover and manage his life. She demanded to know how he spent his time and fought with him over his lack of interest in their relationship.

The more Sheila fought to control, the more Todd shut down and pushed away from the relationship. He drank more. She did things to try to spark the romance and draw him back into the relationship, but because he continued to drink, she felt rejected and thus attempted to control him more. The cycle continued.

Sheila didn't understand the nature of Todd's addiction and found herself exhausted by her efforts to manage the home, the finances, the relationship and everything else in between. The final straw occurred when Todd received a driving under the influence citation and spent the evening in jail. She felt so devastated and hopeless she thought the relationship should end. By then, she had begun attending church and had become a Christian. After consulting with the recovery pastor regarding Todd, she was offered a better alternative than simply ending their marriage right then.

The pastor explained to Sheila the reality of addiction and how Todd actually needed help. The pastor also helped her see that, as horrible as Todd's behaviors were, she had become an enabler to his addiction. Because her boundaries were lacking, she had never held him accountable for his behavior. Instead, she tried to control him and make up for the things he couldn't give in the relationship.

Together, Sheila and her pastor discussed ways she could develop some boundaries. With his help, they wrote a plan that listed both the boundary and the consequence of his addictive behavior. Through a family intervention, friends and family expressed to Todd their love and concern. He was given a choice to get help for his drinking problem or face some serious consequences: essentially getting "cut off" from those he loved.

While he resisted it at first, Sheila didn't back down on the consequences. It hurt her deeply, but she required that Todd move out of their family home. She began to use prayer as her biggest weapon to fight Todd's addiction and pleaded with God to intervene on Todd's behalf. It took several more months of Todd's drinking for him to realize he didn't want to live that way. Just like in the parable of the prodigal son, the circumstances became so severe he was ready and willing to get help.

Sheila gave Todd a second chance based on the specific boundary that he first get help. But most of all, for this process to work, she had to decide that she could genuinely forgive Todd and give him the space and time to go through his healing process. She also had to explore why she had such poor boundaries. Sheila's boundary violations weren't just that she allowed Todd's addiction but also that she felt she had the authority to control his behaviors. Furthermore, she needed to understand why she wound up in this unhealthy lifestyle in the first place.

She traced many of her tendencies back to her family of origin. Besides forgiving Todd, she also needed to forgive her parents and herself for allowing such insanity into her life. Sheila's newfound boundaries allowed Todd to suffer negative consequences for his behavior. But her ability to forgive him ultimately led to the restoration of their relationship. Because she gave Todd grace and understanding, he was able to focus on himself and the reasons why he'd learned to medicate his emotions.

Like Sheila, we have a right to establish boundaries in our home. However, we have an obligation to make sure those boundaries are realistic and fair and founded in love, not control. Most important, we must be willing and ready to follow through on the consequence; otherwise, the "fence" (boundary) gets trampled and is no longer valid.

In the case of addiction, the family member must learn to love the person while standing against and opposing the addictive behavior at all costs. While we can't make someone quit, we can take away any and all cushioning that would enable the addict to remain in addictive behavior. Like in the parable of the prodigal son, only when the pain of the consequences brings the addict to a breaking point is there even the potential for change to occur.

The difficult part of this scenario is that in letting a person go, we have to brace ourselves for the reality that they might make a choice that leads to a negative outcome. In these situations, we must pray that God would grant us the grace to handle that outcome. We can continue to pray that He would divinely intervene in the addict's life.

Before we allow ourselves to get overwhelmed by this process, remember the fundamental principle of following God's boundaries: He deals with us at a heart level when we are indwelled with His Spirit. Therefore, if we make seeking God our priority in life, our ability to make and adhere to boundaries will naturally follow our pursuit for recovery. And we must remember God's motives—they always push toward love and grace toward us and the people in our lives who struggle with negative behaviors.

Application Points:

How can we begin to set boundaries in a difficult relationship? Here's a process that can be used in learning how to define and set healthy boundaries in relationships:

Identify Where Boundaries Should Be Built

- Identify where you may compromise or allow wrongful behaviors in your life because you don't want to upset or lose a person.
- Write a list of those behaviors along with the name of the person. State it something like this:
    - I cannot allow _____ (name behavior) in my life.
    - If _____ (name the person) engages in that behavior in my life, I need to impose a consequence to protect me from the harmful effect it may impose on my life.
- Apply the consequence. If this person continually breaks this boundary without sorrow or change, I am willing to follow through on a consequence, including:
    - _____

In setting boundaries, we need to pray and seek the wisdom of the Lord. If we are led by our emotions, we will not make wise decisions and can hurt relationships even more. In other words, if we are simply reacting in anger to punish someone, that isn't a boundary at all.

Evaluate Your Heart Motive

- Is my desire for the person to make a change of behavior valid? Is the current behavior in clear violation of a healthy, safe relationship? Is it just my personal preference or emotional needs?
- Do I understand it's not my responsibility to control that person's behavior, but I can refuse to allow it in my life? Yes or No.
- Why can't I allow this behavior into my life? What will happen if I continue to allow it? What will happen if I set a boundary that refuses this behavior?

Remember, a boundary isn't used to exercise control over other people's behavior; it's used to protect our own lives, values, etc.

Note: Physical abuse is always a game changer and may require the immediate physical departure from the relationship if imminent danger is clear. That's not to say the person inflicting the abuse won't be able to get help, but the risk of being hurt may require physical separation. Please seek help immediately if you are in a physically or severely abusive situation.

Boundaries and Reconciliation

What do we do if someone has grossly abused or mistreated us in a relationship? Are forgiveness and setting new boundaries enough? Should the relationship continue? We must not confuse forgiveness and boundaries with reconciliation. Whether we have violated a person or they have violated us, reconciliation is about a healing process that occurs when both parties participate. If a wall of separation has been resurrected in a relationship because of wrongdoings or painful dynamics, we can decide whether we wish to walk toward restoration of that relationship. Sometimes unhealthy relationships may need to be forgiven but not restored. God's heart and desire will always be to reconcile broken family relationships and to restore marriages, so it would be entirely wrong for us to walk out on those commitments. However, we may need help in discerning the exact approach to adopt in a given situation. In the end, all we can do is own our personal responsibility, pray and leave the outcome to God, trusting in His perfect plan.

Boundaries and Intimacy

While it can seem as though living a life based on varying degrees of boundaries could cause separation, nothing is further from the truth. In reality, when two people learn healthy boundaries, they establish a safe environment characterized by mutual respect. It is in this environment that the relationship can thrive and grow, creating the atmosphere for true intimacy.

What is intimacy? Intimacy is the ability to see into another person without the fear of being rejected. It is a form of closeness based on vulnerability and honesty. It allows people to see us at "raw" levels, where we can reveal the deeper things that make us who we are.

We can only have intimate relationships as we develop a healthy sense of self-identity. If we simply merged with the person in the relationship, that wouldn't be intimacy; it would be codependence, leading to a loss of identity altogether. In intimacy we retain who we are and allow others to retain who they are. It is in seeing, accepting and forgiving that we draw close in these relationships.

How can we be certain that intimacy can be achieved in this manner? In truth, God deals with us intimately. He asks that we be transparent, open and honest before Him. In return, He receives us as we are, forgives us for our wrongs and accepts and loves us unconditionally. As we learn to trust Him more, we give ourselves fully and passionately to the relationship. Fulfillment is found through our intimate relationship with God and then our ability to be intimate with those close to us.

If you are recovering from a painful relationship, intimacy should not be the goal in and of itself. Rather, the goal should be to get your life and your own boundaries aligned with God. As we learned in some of the prior examples, when this alignment occurred, it set an environment that was conducive to intimacy.

A Prayer for Reconciliation and Intimacy

Father,

As I see my boundary failures, I'm overwhelmed with where to begin. In one sense, I need to "own" myself again. But in another sense, I actually am setting the stage to love people more and love them more intimately. How these two realities collide is difficult for me to comprehend, yet I know this is exactly how You operate with me. God, I ask You to change my heart, and I ask You to intervene in my loved one's life so we can first experience intimacy with You and ultimately experience intimacy with each other. Thank you that You are a God who created me to be in relationships that are filled with fulfillment and passion. I pray that I would be able to experience that in fullness.

In Jesus's name, amen.

12

Balancing Priorities & Principles

Workbook Keys

- EXPLAIN THE DIFFERENCE BETWEEN SPIRITUAL AND PRACTICAL PRINCIPLES
- DEFINE PRIORITIES
- HOW CAN WE BALANCE CHANGE?

We've been on a journey. A journey denotes that there is a beginning point and an ending point. We may have begun this journey worn out and worn down, looking for answers as to why life wasn't working. We may have found some things we expected, but more than likely, we found many things we didn't expect.

In truth, recovery can be painful. Now that we have encountered the reality of the issues we need to face, it can be extremely overwhelming to realize that the journey doesn't end here; it's really only beginning. Recovery is a lifelong process. It requires rigorous honesty, fearless self-confrontation, daily surrender to God and a willingness to take up our cross and follow Christ Jesus. But what exactly is the end result of this process? If we are courageous enough to follow God's ways, we will embark on experiencing the fulfillment we've been seeking all along: a true, abiding inner peace and understanding of the love of God. When we experience intimacy with God, we will be able to be the exact person we were created to be. Even if our human relationships do at some point fail us, we will discover we still have the capacity to experience the highest form of love possible—the agape love of God.

This workbook is one of many tools that can aid and assist us along the process of healing. But take heed, it is simply a guidepost to provide direction. By itself, it will do little unless we are able to apply the principles to our life. It's one thing to feel different or to see life from a different perspective. The real test is how we take those things we learn and apply them in day-to-day situations.

As human beings, by nature we want short cuts. We want to get the end result without going through the pain and discipline required along the way. But the things in life that yield

212/ *The Christian Codependence Recovery Workbook*

the most benefit can require difficulty and suffering. It's amazing how much time and effort we were willing to invest in the needs and problems of others. That type of pain left us exhausted and hopeless. If we can take that same amount of effort we used negatively and apply it to a solution-oriented lifestyle based on God's healing principles, we are bound to see dramatic results.

Balancing Spiritual and Practical

There are two sides to the process of recovery. The first is spiritual: it rests in the unseen things and the battle we are engaged in for our entire system of living, including our beliefs, thoughts, feelings and behaviors. To grow and become strong spiritually, we need to develop a lifestyle of spiritual discipline. In truth, this all comes down to nurturing an intimate relationship with God. It means being saturated in His truth and finding the fellowship of others who personally know and have experienced God's love. It does not mean legalistically attempting to "do" the Christian life.

The other side to authentic recovery is the practical. Since we live in a physical world and deal with physical circumstances, we need to apply biblical spiritual principles to tangible life events. If we spiritualize our lives to the point that we are absorbed by the concepts but don't know how to apply them, we can feel frustrated. We can even use spiritual sounding "stuff" to hide behind, thus causing a separation between our internal and external personas.

The transformation process occurs as God changes us spiritually at a heart level and makes our understanding of things a reality in our practical day-to-day situations. We cannot compartmentalize the Christian life. Things such as our jobs or family life are not independent of our spiritual life. In fact, our lives in their entirety fall under one of two systems: a system of self-effort or a system of Christ-dependency. The outcome of this and all the small and intricate details between rest in our ability to learn life through God's truth.

Where We Are Headed

Jesus taught a parable of two men: a priest and a despised tax collector. If we were to re-tell this in today's culture, the story could take place between a church leader and someone the world may consider a loser. Here's how it goes:

"The Pharisee stood by himself and prayed this prayer: 'I thank you, God, that I am not a sinner like everyone else. For I don't cheat, I don't sin, and I don't commit adultery. I'm certainly not like that tax collector! I fast twice a week, and I give you a tenth of my income.'

"But the tax collector stood at a distance and dared not even lift his eyes to heaven as he prayed. Instead, he beat his chest in sorrow, saying, 'O God, be merciful to me, for I am a sinner.' I tell you, this sinner, not the Pharisee, returned home justified before God. For those who exalt themselves will be humbled, and those who humble themselves will be exalted." (Luke 18:11–14)

We so often look at the "religious leader" type person and think that the model for our life is the person who has it perfectly altogether. We measure our progress in recovery by how we are attaining God's checklist. Yet, in truth, God isn't interested in that at all. In fact, He says that those who think they've "got it," haven't "got it" at all!

God desires our humble admission of our weaknesses. We are justified, which means we are made right with God as we admit where we fall short. In this transaction, we are given access to the Holy Spirit. The Holy Spirit causes our lives to change through the inward reality of Christ living in us.

So how can we actually measure our progress in recovery and in the Christian life in general? It's safe to say that simply setting boundaries, learning new rules and even walking in obedience while refraining from evil won't cut it. The measurement of a changed life is someone who abides by the principles that reveal the heart of God: walking by grace, thankfulness and love. As more and more of our life comes under the truth of God's Word and these principles, we yield more and more fruit.

Setting Priorities

Life is all about priorities. We have only so much time in a day to accomplish things, we have only so much room in our hearts to carry things, and we have only so much energy to focus on things that need to be done. That's why the infrastructure of our priorities will determine the manifestation of all the practical functions of our life. If we are driven and compelled to please people, our activities and the balance of our lives will manifest accordingly.

Relationship Priorities

In codependence, our relationship priorities got skewed. We took upon ourselves the needs of others, based on compulsion, shame and guilt. We believed we needed to focus on others. But these misplaced priorities led to numerous problems.

Rather than change each and every thing in our life that isn't working in the physical circumstances, we need to learn to start each day learning to live by God's priorities:

- **We must seek an intimate relationship with Jesus Christ first and foremost, above everything and anything.** This will be the entire goal of our days and the entire purpose of our lives. We simply need to learn to come to Him as we are and be in His presence.

- **We must open our heart to allow God's truth to enter into our life.** That means our heart must be able to receive the gifts He gives, and we must get rid of our prideful tendencies. Under the "knife" of God's truth, we become willing to let God teach, convict and change us (see Hebrews 4:12).

- **We learn to serve and love people in the way God asks us to serve and love.** We no longer feel obliged to react to others, but we allow God to lead us in ways where we can biblically respond in situations. This shows itself as real love, love derived from God's own heart.

Applying God's Principles in Relationships

As we take everything we've learned up to this point, how can we apply it to our relationships? Relationship changes won't necessarily happen right away. One of the most dramatic lessons we have learned is that we can't change other people. But just the same, we have the ability to be changed ourselves as we submit ourselves to God. He then transforms us through His love and grace and teaches us His relationship principles. These same principles are a recipe for success in how to operate in relationships in our own life. Here are some of the principles:

1. **Love:** The basis of God's relationship with us is based on unconditional, agape love (see 1 Corinthians 13). We learn to give away this same love to others. We don't love people because they are necessarily lovable. We love them because God first loved us.

2. **Holiness:** The basis of God's relationship with us is His holiness. He would never condone or allow sinful behaviors. We can learn to hate negative behaviors in our relationships with others and realize we don't need to allow them into our life. We do have the choice of saying no.

3. **Freedom:** The basis of God's relationship with us is free will. He doesn't ever operate by control until a willing surrender on our end has occurred. In our own life, we honor the free will of others and avoid our tendency to control their behavior. We give them the right to act and behave in the way they choose. If their choices could harm us personally, we can set boundaries that protect us and impose consequences (chapter 11).

4. **Grace and mercy:** The basis of God's relationship with us is grace and mercy. Grace is getting the things we don't deserve. Mercy is not getting the punishment we do deserve. As we receive these amazing gifts from heaven, we offer them in our relationships.

5. **Discipline:** God loves us enough to discipline us when we do things that take

us away from His best. His discipline is evidence of His love (see Hebrews 12:6). We apply discipline to our relationships where we stand in a position of authority (such as a parent) by using this same form of loving discipline.

6. **Forgiveness and reconciliation:** God reconciles us to Himself through forgiveness. Forgiveness is the bridge that continually gives us access to enjoying God's fellowship, peace and love. Our relationships are reconciled and restored through that same forgiveness. Sometimes we need to forgive ourselves. Sometimes we need to forgive others.

7. **Becoming our best:** God seeks to build us into a vision He has for our life; this means everything He offers in our relationship is to nurture us to become like Jesus and to fulfill His purpose in our life. In the same way, we must learn to offer others the freedom to become the people God intended them to be. We don't interfere or attempt to make people into our own idea of what we think they should be.

8. **Intimacy:** The highest desire of God's heart is that we find intimacy with Him. This is a closeness where we see Him and He sees us. We allow Him complete access to our life in this condition. The highest desire in our close relationships is this same intimacy. When we learn to be authentic, vulnerable and honest, we have the potential to grow close to others who reciprocate and honor that intimacy.

Working these principles into our daily lives by first experiencing them with God and then transferring them into our relationships with others may take some time. It's a maturity and a growth process. But by understanding these principles and encountering God at a heart level, we have the opportunity to apply these same principles to everyone.

Please note: *A House that Grace Built* goes through relationships in detail as the second phase of recovery.

A Prayer to Apply God's Relationship Principles
Father God,

Indeed, this list overwhelms me! I am amazed by how You love me, respect me and care for me in our relationship. I don't even know how to receive it entirely, much less offer it to others. I pray that as I abide in You, I will become more and more like You. And that in that likeness, I would know how to give these same gifts to others through the primary gift of love You have given me. I thank You for who You are.

In Jesus's name, amen.

Application Points:
Write out the principles you struggle with the most.

_____
_____
_____
_____
_____

1. Pray over that principle each day and ask God to transform you at a heart level.
2. Watch and pay attention to situations where you can apply that principle in your relationship with others.

Practical Priorities

As codependents who overcompensated, we felt drained by the pressures and expectations placed upon us. So much of our focus was spent on doing things that we weren't even intended to do. We took on everyone else's priorities and neglected our own. As we face the new day of our recovery, we need to take on our ordinary daily schedules and commitments, as well as our long-term goals, and allow God to sift through them. How can we know where to begin? How can we determine what we should keep or what we might need to release?

First, we need God's wisdom, which is why our relationship with Him must remain at the forefront of our to-do list. Through His perspective, we need to wisely manage our time, resources and gifts. In making decisions about the use of our time and energy, we can consider and implement the following:

- Why are you doing this? Evaluate your motives.
- Has Jesus asked, called you or moved you to do this? How do you know?
- Who or what emotion is motivating this? Is it a negative feeling such as guilt, shame or fear?
- Who will be pleased if you do this? God, yourself or someone else?
- Would doing this prevent you from carrying out any other of your responsibilities? What might it interfere with?
- If you are taking on multiple things at one time, which responsibility has priority? Why?

If we ask these questions and find our motives are wrong, we need to continue to pray for clarity. For example, if we see someone in need but at the same time have a responsibility to fulfill, we need to be able to make a decision about which thing God would have us do.

We may have continually been prone to neglect our own responsibilities to help others. However, in a given situation, God might be asking that we actually do help someone else. We need God to guide us. In codependence recovery, we don't stop loving people; we simply switch our motives from self-serving to Christ-centered.

A Prayer for Priorities

Father God,

I realize that sometimes I am being governed by the needs and urgency of the moment rather than being led by the Spirit. Please help me understand what You would have me do in each situation. I feel unable to separate my priorities and responsibilities. I pray that as I step forth in faith, You would guide and direct me from this day forward. In Jesus's name, amen.

Application Points:

1. Write a list of your current responsibilities. Pray over them and ask God to reveal those responsibilities that don't belong to you.
2. Over the next week, keep notes of when you take on responsibilities outside your own. Ask God this: "Am I supposed to be doing this?"
3. Take note of when you distinctly replace your own responsibility with that of someone else's. Why did that happen?
4. In time, learn to set boundaries and say no to things that would overlap or interfere with your commitments.

A Balancing Act

If we look at all the concepts we have learned and the patterns of behaviors that were evaluated, we see two extremes: God's way and our own dysfunctional survival strategies. Our tendency would be to attempt to externally change our behavior and move to the opposite extreme of whatever negative behavior was revealed. That sounds like a logical thing to do, but in fact, in our own strength it could be very damaging. Without that heart change, we may externally do the opposite, but the unhealthy root is still driving that behavior.

When the Holy Spirit enters our lives in an experiential sense, He gives us the ability to take the many facets of our life and perfectly balance and align them in accordance with truth. In fact, it is only when the presence of the Holy Spirit enters us that we can recognize the difference. He deals with the root and applies the remedy, causing our behavioral reaction to be balanced.

Here are some examples of how we can be imbalanced in our approach to recovery:

- We can realize that we are needy in relationships and therefore cut ourselves off from relationships altogether and begin to isolate ourselves.
- We can see that we find security in our job performance and stop trying altogether, causing us to become lazy and irresponsible.
- We can see how we've been enabling a person and completely cut them off on the spot without further explanation.

Imbalance appears in many other ways. In order to deal with the core drive of our codependent roots, it's hard to know where to begin. Here are some primary root issues we can apply in the area of balance.

Balance truth with love. If we just focus on the truth of what we have learned, we could become harsh and critical with others and ourselves. Truth is a marvelous gift—it ultimately sets us free. However, if we use truth as the standard by which to evaluate others and ourselves, we have negated the need to balance truth with love. In fact, in 1 Corinthians 13:1–2 we are reminded that all gifts we possess, including knowledge and understanding, are meaningless if we don't have love. God truly does operate in truth as the method by which we are set free. But that truth is engulfed in His love and acceptance.

Balance our ability to see flaws with our ability to give and receive grace. When God begins to reveal the areas in our life that need to change, that doesn't mean He expects us to change everything on the spot. For example, we may have learned that we use controlling measures in relationships. God may show us this tendency continually in our daily experience. He uses the exposure of this behavior to allow us to confess, repent and ask Him to change us, knowing that this stubborn character defect won't necessarily "just stop."

As we continually confess and ask God to change us, we gradually move away from our controlling tendencies and learn to adopt a system of freedom in relationships. Learning to embrace grace means that we can be assured of God's patience and love in our struggle to change. When we receive grace into our life, we'll be able to offer it to others.

Balance tolerance of people with the intolerance of sin. Through healthy boundaries, we gradually begin to learn how to reject and discourage sinful behaviors, yet love people where they are. If people are sinning or committing acts of violation, we can set whatever boundaries we need to protect ourselves from those effects. Sometimes those boundaries will have nothing to do with the person but will empower us to respond differently to negative situations.

If we suddenly have the revelation that we have allowed negative behaviors, we could be prone to begin to "throw people out" entirely. We could even become rude and judgmental in our approach, sickened by how we had previously encouraged that bad behavior.

While we can defend or protect ourselves from spiritually and emotionally unhealthy people and sinful lifestyles, we must remember that they too need deliverance. Our focus should always be on prayer for them. As we grow in Christ, our heart should be loving and compassionate, despite a person's behavior. That doesn't mean their behavior will be allowed into our life, but we will see it through another perspective.

Balance our need to detach with the ability to be intimate. We may need to detach ourselves from unhealthy bonds that were created in our relationships. These bonds were based on our sinful, need-based system of "love." Detachment may occur for a season, but that doesn't mean we need to separate or isolate ourselves from others. Instead, detachment means we are removing the harmful ways we were bonded in relationships. These bonds were actually based on our codependence, not genuine love.

Once we detach from the unhealthy, we can prepare our hearts for healthy attachments that will ultimately give us the ability to be intimate. The process of recovery prepares our hearts to properly give and receive love.

A Prayer for Balance

Father God,

As I learn these new principles and understand how I may have been unhealthy in my relationships, give me the grace to change slowly and in accordance with Your Spirit working within me. I can't do it all right away. I can't fix it all instantly. Help me to learn balance!

In Jesus's name, amen.

Summarizing It All

Living the life God intended us to live is one filled with purpose, significance, passion, relationships and most of all, love. Recovery is a separation process where we own what's ours, don't own what isn't ours and are provided with the God-given ability to know the difference (cf. the "Serenity Prayer"). More than anything, it's believing in a God who is infinitely higher and wiser than we are.

As painful as it can be, the very places where we were hurt end up being the places where God can use us the most. This means our codependence is not a curse, but under God's healing and restoration, it will be a blessing.

All praise to God, the Father of our Lord Jesus Christ. God is our merciful Father and the source of all comfort. He comforts us in all our troubles so that we can comfort others. When they are troubled, we will be able to give them the same comfort God has given us. For the more we suffer for Christ, the more God will shower us with his comfort through Christ. Even when we are weighed down with troubles, it is for your comfort and salvation! For when we ourselves are comforted, we will certainly comfort you. Then you can patiently endure the same things we suffer. We are confident that as you share in our sufferings, you will also share in the comfort God gives us. (2 Corinthians 1:3–7)

How amazing to grasp this truth—that the more we have suffered, the more we

God's Love Letter to You

There is one purpose to this entire workbook and this journey—to know your Father and your Savior intimately. The "quiz" at the end of this workbook is to help you measure your heart against this radical love He has for you right now.

Fill in the details:

Dear _____ (your name),

I realize that sometimes you feel you don't measure up. I realize especially because of _____ (name a current struggle) you have had a difficult time. I want you to know that I love you. I want you to know that no matter what you do or don't do, it won't ever change my love for you.

I see the way you've tried. I know the efforts and the struggles you felt obligated to accomplish. But don't you understand that you don't have to try or work for me? I want you—not your jobs, or your efforts, or your striving. I want to take your burdens and carry them for you. Especially those things that are consuming you right now: (name some major struggles you've had) _____

_____

_____

_____

What I see is what you haven't been able to see. I see the real you. I see those tiny, intrinsic details that make you who you are, especially (name distinctions about yourself)

My child, I made you. I knit you together in your mother's womb. How many times did my heart break when you didn't accurately see yourself. But now, I ask you to come out of hiding. Live, do and become what I made you to be. I especially want to see you fulfill those dreams and visions I gave to you: (list your dreams)

_____

_____

_____

_____

_____

I know that in your relationship with _____ (name a difficult relationship) you still feel challenged. Stop wrestling, and give it over to me. Don't you know how much you have to offer? Remember, you have a responsibility in that situation, but beyond that, you can't change or fix it. You know what you've been trying to do to make that relationship work (name those ways you tried to compensate in relationships) _____

_____

_____

_____

When you wrote those lists of the ways you have been hurt and the things that you had done wrong, I already knew the damage they caused you. I cried with you. You may not understand it, but since I experienced all the sin in your life already, I could identify more than you can comprehend. In fact, we experienced it together. But see, I know that the blood I shed on your behalf is sufficient. You just need to accept it as gift. If I forced it on you, it wouldn't be a gift at all. Apply that gift to those wounds. Forgive yourself and others, and especially receive My forgiveness: (name the wounds)

_____

_____

_____

If only you could see your future! Will you let Me guide you into it? I want to remove those behavioral patterns that are destructive so you can be everything I created you to be. Those survival mechanisms aren't necessary, especially (name some of the ways you learned to survive) _____

_____

Instead, I'm asking that you simply trust me. Let me be your Protector, Healer, Defender and Lover. As you pursue your life goals, your calling, your dreams and your relationships, don't look at me as though I'm a list you need to measure yourself by. I'm your Creator, and I love you and desire a relationship with you more than you could ever comprehend. I have a plan and purpose for you. It is through me you will find the desires of your heart. Reach high and don't quit. You are worthy based on your relationship with Me, and nothing in heaven or on earth will ever, ever change that.

Love,
Your everlasting Heavenly Father

Application Point

Write a letter to God with your honest understanding and assessment of these issues:

- How He loves you
- How He sees you
- The plan He has for you
- How you desire to serve Him
- How you love Him
- What you are "stuck" on and need help with

Appendix A
Do You Personally Know Jesus Christ?

Wherever you are and whatever brought you to read this book, understand that everything it contains has promises that can belong to you. Perhaps you've searched and wondered about the purpose of life and tried to satisfy that inner emptiness and need for significance from outside sources. Religion may have hurt you, and people may have let you down.

But today you can make a new claim that stands independent of anything that has occurred externally in your life. Jesus Christ already knows you. He already purchased and carried the weight of your shame—past, present and future. He knows the ways people have hurt you, and He knows the things that you have done wrong. Wherever you are right now, Jesus is a real Person who loves you and is willing to meet you at your point of need. He has the solution to your needs.

How can you have that personal relationship?
1. Acknowledge that your sin has separated you from God and you need a Savior.
2. Acknowledge that Jesus Christ is the Son of God and came to earth as a man (see John 1:14; 1 John 3:5).
3. Confess the past life of sin—living for self and not obeying God. "If we confess our sins, he is faithful and just and will forgive us our sins and purify us from all unrighteousness" (1 John 1:9).
4. Repent of that sin, which means "change direction" (see 2 Corinthians 7:10–11).
5. Trust Jesus Christ as your Savior and Lord.
    > "That if you confess with your mouth, "Jesus is Lord," and believe in your heart that God raised him from the dead, you will be saved. For it is with your heart that you believe and are justified, and it is with your mouth that you confess and are saved. As the Scripture says, "Anyone who trusts in him will never be disgraced" (Romans 10:9-11).
6. Ask Jesus to take ownership of your life.

Here's a Prayer to Help You:
Father in Heaven,
    I am broken and lost. I have tried to live life on my own and I've failed miserably. I need You. I believe that Jesus Christ is Your Son and came into this world to die for me. Please forgive me for my sins and fill me with Your Spirit. I repent of my sin and want to begin a new life following you. I ask You, Jesus, to come into my heart and be my Lord and Savior. I surrender my life into Your hands.
In Jesus's name, amen.

∞ Leader's Guide

A resource for leading a group through codependence recovery is important and much needed in the church and recovery arena. Your role as a group leader is to lay the foundation of the process covered in this material and direct the people in your group as they individually pursue personal healing. You are providing infrastructure, prayer and guidance but allowing God to do what only He can do—get inside and deal with hearts!

Group Formats

This process works best in a small group with not more than ten participants. If you have more, consider having one part of the session for teaching and then breaking into smaller group discussions. Two hours is a good time frame for the workshops, adjusting as needed. Anything more than two hours may be overwhelming.

Make prayer a priority, devoting as much time as necessary at the beginning and end of a group session. This process will be most effective when led by a person who has been through it and can offer a personal testimony.

In forming a new group, it's most important to establish an emotionally and spiritually safe environment. As a recovery leader, your job will be to help create that environment and establish any group rules that could aid and protect the participants. Please use your own discretion, but here are some common example rules:

- Do not use profanity.
- Keep shares to "I"—do not focus on another person's issues.
- Do not engage in cross talk or interrupt when someone is sharing.
- If a person needs to express emotion, let them. Don't interrupt what the Holy Spirit is doing.
- Do not make negative complaints about the process that might affect others—speak to a group leader instead.

Breaking Up the Workbook into Smaller Doses

This workshop can be completed in twelve weeks if you complete one chapter each week. However, some chapters can be overwhelming and accomplish more spread over two weeks (or even more) instead of one. Also, the application points—the heart of the entire process—are sometimes neglected when only a week is allowed for each chapter.

It's important that you get comfortable with each chapter and the application points that will be assigned. We'll be reviewing each chapter in this leader guide, and you can decide for yourself how to break it down in a format that will work best in your particular circumstances.

Setting Expectations

Before beginning, explain to the group that this process must be led by the Holy Spirit to be effective. This is not merely an intellectual or educational workshop. It is an inner healing process. Each application point must be worked through to see results. Stress that the results are not about the process itself. They are about encountering God intimately and allowing Him access to the innermost places of our heart.

About the Participant's Needs

This workshop doesn't replace the need to get professional help or to see a pastor or counselor. Please have an emergency plan in place in case you become aware of situations that pose imminent threat to a person's safety or health. Remember that this process could bring up painful memories, so be sure to have referrals to offer at any point if the needs are beyond your group's capabilities.

Chapter 1: Facing Codependence

The purpose of chapter 1 is to help participants get a baseline understanding of codependence through both an emotional and spiritual perspective. Codependence is often understood to be the relationship dynamic between an alcoholic and a family member. However, in truth, codependence expands into a much broader definition. There is an entire system that gets resurrected that has misconstrued and misunderstood authentic love. The relationship issues that erupt in a person's life are typically rooted in much deeper things. Typically, the current relationship crisis is long-time symptom of foundational toxic beliefs about self, others and God.

In leading a group, it's important for participant(s) to see the patterns in their own lives. Keep in mind that in the beginning they will be overwhelmed and possibly even angry and confused. That's why as you work with the group, it's a good idea to lay out recovery and healing objectives and point them toward the solution principles from the very beginning. The only reason they are asking for help is that the pain of their lifestyle has become so difficult they want to do something about it. Where the pain has become intense enough, you can begin to instill hope as the main motivator to continue.

Application Homework

Writing a life story. Writing out the story is a must—it is foundational to the rest of the process. The story should focus on the painful events and memories more than the positive events simply because this process is for healing wounds. To be effective, the story should begin from the earliest memories and travel all the way to the current circumstances.

Why do this? Much of codependence revolves around the inability to speak, feel or express personal thoughts and opinions. Often people who struggle with codependence repress and hide their feelings and needs to the point they don't even know how to explain their inward reality. Therefore, in this process we must begin to sort through life experiences with a filter of truth. Some people struggle tremendously with this project because it lacks structure. They will want to know "exactly" how to write their stories. As a leader, please understand that the purpose of this project is to simply "break up the soil" to sift, sort and deal with each thing expressed. Therefore, the only purpose is for each man or woman to benefit from seeing his or her story in black and white. Some people will ask to skip this project. I suggest encouraging them to try their best and just write out what they can recollect, focusing on how they felt more than simply presenting facts. This is only the first project in a series of projects that will help in this way.

About codependence questions. These are basic questions about identifying with symtpoms of codependence. You may use these as discussion points in groups.

Chapter 2: Family Systems

The family system is the most influential place where we learn how to love, how to be responsible and how to give and receive in relationships. It's also where we often form our initial sense of identity and learn specifically how to function in our gender roles. If participants have been exposed to dysfunction and even chaos during their beginnings, they likely have a distorted perception of God's intent for the family system.

This chapter involves a basic sifting process to understand how families function and to correlate that with God's truth. While we may not be able to offer immediate remedies for a family crisis, we can offer the truth of God's family system. As children of God, that family system can supersede anything negative or toxic that has occurred and can heal and transform us despite changes in any of our earthly circumstances. How so? We learn to depend on our perfect Father and perfect Spouse to make up for what is lacking. Based on that relationship, we will find the wisdom to deal with the relationship challenges.

This chapter can be extremely overwhelming and painful. It's an area where participants are often the most fragile and hurt. Be sensitive to people's past dysfunction but firm in the truth of God's solution, even though it may not be popular. We need to be loving—but remember that the truth will set people free, not keep them in bondage.

At this point, we want to help them simply align their situation with God's plan, not fix or correct anything at a behavioral level. When people want to make immediate changes, such as divorce, you should strongly recommend they continue through the process first to gain God's entire perspective. Encouraging a divorce is outside the bounds of a group leader. Even a Christian counselor must deal delicately with this area, believing in the power of a redemptive God yet validating extreme forms of dysfunction. Continue to remind the participants that this process is to help them see what's going on inside themselves.

Group Note

Chapter 2 is long and packed with important information about God's heart and purpose for the family. It is recommended that you break this chapter into more than one week.

Application Homework

Answering questions about mother/wife and father/husband. Emphasize the importance of this application assignment. It begins a discovery process that may lead to some important insight.

Family questions. You may use these as discussion point in groups.

A Note about Families with Addiction

We have an additional resource available for participants who have an addictive dynamic in their family system. We don't recommend combining it with this workbook unless there is a crisis situation. The book is called Christian Families in Recovery: A Guide to Addiction, Recovery and Intervention Using God's Tools of Redemption written by Robert and Stephanie Tucker. Learn more at www.christianfamiliesinrecovery.com or purchase a copy through Amazon.com. You may even want to consider adding this resource before you start a codependence workshop in the future for specific participants who may be dealing with.

Chapter 3: Emotional Strongholds

This chapter offers a basic assessment process of the functions within the soul: thinking, feeling and doing. Most people with codependence have many emotional troubles. Some have emotionally checked out and are desensitized altogether. Others are consumed with anger.

While helpful, the chapter is not intended to treat each emotion on the spot as some sort of biblical magic potion. Rather, it provides a basic understanding of the roots that drive our emotions to help gain sanity over them in a given situation. It's most important for people to begin to learn that emotions stem directly from thoughts, which stem directly from beliefs. Also, keep in mind that all thoughts and beliefs have a motivating influence in the spiritual realm. Thus, they originate from heaven or hell. As thoughts are captured, understood and secured by truth, dramatic changes occur that will stabilize emotions.

Now keep in mind that at this point, people are operating on an old system of thinking and feeling. Therefore, they should not expect dramatic results immediately. We are going to continually challenge belief systems throughout this workshop. As we do so, we hope participants will come more in tune with their true emotions and the reasons behind them.

Group Note

Participants may ask questions about medication and psychological diagnosis. As a Christian counselor, I personally feel medication should usually be used temporarily (with some exceptions), with the long-term goal of complete abstinence. I also believe that the symptoms of mental disorders are real, but the difference between the Christian approach versus the secular approach is that we are seeking a spiritual remedy. With that said, only a psychiatrist or doctor should direct a person off medication. Please use discretion in this area! Never, ever advise someone to stop taking medication—that could put them in an extremely dangerous situation!

Application Homework

Inventory emotions. Encourage the participants to have a notebook to begin writing their emotional inventories daily—including anger, fear, shame and loneliness (refer to the application point under each emotion).

"I think, I feel, I act." This application project is a very helpful tool to begin understanding emotions and seeking to remove the irrational from the equation. I have honestly witnessed people change immediately from this project alone. They won't find emotional healing right away, but emotions will suddenly not feel so out of control. Participants often say they continue using this tool after completion of the workshop.

Chapter 4: Love Systems

ℰↄ

Chapter 4 provides a brief definition of God's love, followed by the countless ways it is misunderstood or misappropriated in our own lives. Like the previous chapters, this chapter is intended to be used as a sifting and sorting process to understand what's dysfunctional and harmful and what God actually intended love to be.

Almost everyone who struggles with codependence has a warped love system based on performance and efforts. In fact, that could be one way to define to codependence. It's amazing how we can go through life with these faulty belief systems and be completely unaware of how harmful they may be. That's why examples are used in this chapter to seek to expose some of the general misconceptions.

People who haven't had a true encounter with God's love may have a difficult time grasping these concepts at this point. This is where knowledge must give way to experience. Participants can understand God's love only through an actual one-on-one encounter with Him. If participants have not experienced that yet, it doesn't mean that they are not a Christian, but it does mean they have not yet partaken of the fullness of God's peace and love.

Above all else, prayer is the most important ingredient for finding guidance. Only the Holy Spirit can allow the walls to be torn down and the outpouring of God's love to manifest in a person's life. If there are "plugs" in participants' systems, the following chapters will begin to systematically address that.

Group Note

This chapter is very detailed but covers extremely important concepts that cut at the very heart of codependence. It is recommended that it be broken into at least two weeks.

Application Homework

Assessing God's love. This is critical in laying a foundation for addressing distortions in love. It's amazing what people discover when they begin writing assessment this down. Remember, the two parts to deliverance are finding the problem and applying the remedy.

God's love meditation points. These are small descriptions of God's love and how it can can become misunderstood and polluted in our lives.

Loving improperly meditation points. These are entire systems we build in our lives when we try to love without the resources of God.

Giving and receiving meditation point. The entire mechanism of giving and receiving in a codependent's relationship is often distorted.

Writing a personal love system. After evaluating this material, the participants are asked to identify their own love system and how it is playing out in their life today.

Chapter 5: Ceasing Control: the Pathway to Surrender.

ॐ

Understanding surrender is perhaps the most challenging and confrontational issue in our life. The participants are asked to assess their own system of operation in dealing with control issues. They need to begin understanding and assessing how they have been controlled and controlled others . . . and how they depend on others and create dependencies. Then the ultimate challenge is to prepare to let go of the reigns and ask God to take control.

Surrender is the point where all change and healing will begin. It's possible a person can read this chapter and not be impacted by it or see the need for true surrender. Many people will claim complete surrender even though it hasn't actually occurred. If participants are in denial, it's okay to allow them to proceed to the next chapter, where they are asked to confront a variety of situations. Continue to remember your primary role is to guide and to pray.

Above all else, this chapter clearly draws this line: am I trusting in self, another person or God? The answer will determine the outcome from here on out.

Group Note

This chapter is long and contains important concepts about control and surrender. If possible, extend this chapter to two weeks.

Application Homework

Trusting God questions. I am amazed by the impact this set of questions often has on people. This is a good area of discussion for groups. Most people discover they don't trust God fully.

Identifying control and dependency questions. After participants see their tendency not to trust in God, these questions seek to explore who or what they are trusting in. This revelation can be quite important.

Assessing control issues questions. A codependent's ability to recognize control is the beginning to being able to change. This sets the stage for learning how to surrender to God and be able to identify the contamination that takes place when we do not.

End of chapter questions. These are questions that go right to the heart. These would be recommended for group discussion.

Chapter 6: Breaking Free From Denial

℘

While the previous chapters have been diagnostic, in this chapter everything begins to be brought together. It exposes denial and help participants understand why seeing the impact of life events is very important, yet very difficult. The entire point of this chapter is to prepare the participants to write inventory lists. Questions may arise about exactly what to write and how to write it. Some people will be afraid they won't get it "just right" and feel they might miss out if they do it wrong. Others may minimize it so much, they can barely come up with anything.

As a group leader, you can begin to see what's going on inside someone's heart as they face this assignment. Someone who is in touch and connected with the issues in their life may approach this with tenacity. Other people who are still out of touch, disconnected or hiding in denial may have a difficult time. They may even begin to question the purpose behind it.

Remind the participants this must be above anything a Holy Spirit led project, not a human project. What matters is that they bring God into it and ask Him to show them the things that need to be exposed. Also, remind them that if they can't get to something right now, it's okay. God knows and He will choose to reveal it to them when they are ready. ENCOURAGE THEM THAT THIS CHAPTER IS ABOUT WHAT'S IN THEIR HEART—AND THAT MATTERS MORE THAN THE FORMAL PROCESS!

Group Note

While the chapter itself is short, the process it contains and the inventory sheets will draw many questions. Consider this in your planning.

Application Homework

Inventory tables. Each table has a specific purpose. Review the directions of each inventory sheet.

"Violations." This is all about the ways others hurt them—it should deal with all resentments they harbor for the violator.

"Sinful/Immoral." This is about listing their own sin issues. This inventory sheet should be unrestricted and comprehensive. It doesn't need to include minor issues, but anything major should be written in this section.

"Unmet Needs/Losses." This should focus on neglect and loss in childhood and adulthood. The immediate circumstances should be included too. For example, if there is an absent husband in the equation, that loss needs to be addressed. Also, encourage participants to list lost dreams and hopes.

"Love Skills." Some people have a difficult time understanding the purpose behind this chart. For now, they should list how they have engaged in relationships in unhealthy ways.

"Traumatic Events." Major episodes such as death or divorce can have a dramatic effect on a person's life. This needs to be recognized and dealt with more dramatically.

Other Notes

When people get overwhelmed, I sometimes recommend that they format their lists as a time line. This helps them see the progression of these important events. I also recommend that they fill out lists one relationship at a time, beginning with the earliest memories. For example, begin with mom and dad and then work through each relationship issue from there.

_____

Chapter 7: Exposing Shame

Now that lists have been written and the laundry lists have been revealed, they may appear to be a big pile of junk that the participants want to dispose of quickly. The purpose of understanding these lists is two-fold:

- By confronting the realities of these issues, the participants can begin to understand how dangerous and deadly sin and shame are in their own life so they don't continue to minimize or deny.
- As they see the realities of shame, we can prepare the person's heart to receive the remedy.

The Enemy's power over our life lies in shame. It's his secret weapon: he knows that when shame is operating, it will destroy us from the inside out. God's grace and forgiveness have the complete opposite effect. They inwardly expose and dispose of the shame, thus allowing us to be connected to God, self and others. Grace begins to heal and restore us.

There aren't even words to describe the importance of recognizing not just shame itself but also the message shame imposes. Challenge your participants to trust in God in facing shame, knowing it has no power as it is brought in His marvelous light.

Group Notes

Understanding the impact of shame is critical. This chapter deals with three areas, and I recommend you take your time working through all three rather than rush the process. The area of abuse and the cycle of abuse can be an entire group discussion.

Please don't be alarmed if participation drops in this workshop. That's because this subject is uncomfortable. Don't allow that to confuse the purpose of the chapter—even though uncomfortable, this exposure is the access point of their eventual freedom. Trust God to deal with the individual needs being expressed in the group.

Application Homework

Please note: This chapter is not heavy in homework. The participants can use this time to continue to work on their inventory lists, changing or updating as the Holy Spirit reveals more.

Identifying shame questions. After writing the lists, here the participants are asked to reveal their own sense of shame.

Measuring up to standards questions. These ask the participants to key in on where they personally struggle in this area.

Guilt questions. The participants are asked to get in touch with their feelings of guilt and unforgiveness.

Abuse and victim questions. It's important that the participants write out other ways they have discovered abuse in their life and add those to the violations sheet. They should also recognize if they are subject to being a chronic victim.

Chapter 8: Receiving the Gift of Forgiveness

&

The gifts of repentance and brokenness prepare our hearts to understand how desperately we need to be forgiven. Whether a person has arrived at this point is beyond our ability to control as a group leader. However, we may be able to recognize a heart that is broken from sin, thus desiring to repent, and one that is still filled with self-efforts and pride. Our only part in seeing this is that we continue to pray for that person.

Sometimes people will continue to blame others. Remind them this chapter is only about their own sin issues and you'll deal with how they've been hurt in the next chapter. You may deal with others who feel they are unworthy of forgiveness. Remind them that the blood of Jesus was shed on their behalf, whether or not they choose to accept it.

The goal throughout this process is to help the participants see their primary blockage from receiving forgiveness. At one point, this transaction takes place between the participant and God, and we could actually interfere if we continue to overly push the point. Practice prayer above anything else in these situations.

Group Notes

This chapter introduces solution and has some important application points. The application points could take much longer than the workshop allows. This is a process the participants can continue to use on an ongoing basis.

Application Homework

Anger at God questions. Please note that often God is the target for blame and anger when a participant is a victim of painful situations. This is an extremely dangerous belief system but very common--sometimes consciously and other times subconsciously. Chapter 3 taught us that anger is actually an expression of other pain. Therefore, anger toward God is usually rooted in hurt. God knows this.

If anger toward God is discovered, sharing those feelings in the form of a letter to God is important. It's not that God needs to be forgiven but rather that the participants become aware of that anger and begin to process through it. The participants ultimately need to repent but at this point simply need to get in touch with the feeling itself. Then God can show up!

Truths statements. Truth statements are ways we begin to acknowledge and "own" things that we may have been trying to cover over or forget. It's important to use this process on those issues that still hurt—the pain the participants still feel toward something is an indicator that it hasn't been properly dealt with.

Initiate healing. Letter writing is an important project for healing. In fact, it is the most recommended tool of any in the forgiveness process. The letters don't necessarily have to be given or discussed with any of recipients (besides God).

Writing letters of forgiveness to others. Using the list of their own sins, the participants should focus on those issues that really sting when they look at them. If an issue doesn't feel bothersome, it may have been dealt with already or it's not ready to come up yet. Don't recommend that they give people these letters; they need time, clarity and perspective before discerning God's will accurately. Rather, this letter writing is merely for emotionally processing.

Write a letter to God. This letter should be open and honest, stating those issues that have been heavy. It will also be a reminder that when we ask God to forgive us, He will. Therefore, that letter can remain the "evidence" from here on out.

Confess and share. It is recommended that participants share only with someone who is spiritually mature and would understand the nature of this process. Sharing with the wrong person would be catastrophic to healing. Sharing with the right person is powerful and begins to remove the power the shame has had. In my groups, I spend one week doing one-on-ones with people to allow them the opportunity to share their lists.

Dealing with guilt questions. False guilt can mask itself as the voice of God—when actually it's the voice of Satan. Being able to identify and eliminate this can lead to significant and life-long change.

Dealing with failure questions. It's important to see if failure has driven codependence issues and to understand that failure is a part of growth.

Chapter 9: Offering the Gift of Forgiveness

ॐ

Usually, a "forgiven" person is a "forgiving" person. If the dots begin to connect, the people who have just dealt with their own sin issues begin to understand how undeserved forgiveness was for them and are more prepared to begin to forgive others.

People get hung up on forgiving in a variety of ways. They are often filled with bitterness and feel that forgiveness is not deserved. At other times, they have discounted and minimized another person's sin against them so much, they actually lived their life as if that sin were okay.

This chapter is for the participants to get in touch with the reality of how another person's sin affected them. Letter writing is an extremely effective tool when someone gets "stuck" along this process. But letter writing also helps participants to emotionally connect and ultimately grieve a variety of losses.

This chapter brings the most potential for breakthroughs because the root of bitterness is so powerful. If a person truly encounters the power behind this chapter, it will be life changing. Forgiveness opens the doorway to being able to embrace God's authentic design for a person's life—a doorway that was previously blocked.

Group Notes

This chapter is very homework heavy. It's a process they will continue to work on for a lifetime! I would encourage you to split this chapter up as time permits and review the homework assignment as needed.

Application Homework

Resentment questions. The participants should revisit their violation page and include any other resentments that may have come up. It might be beneficial to keep a separate resentment list of people who need to be forgiven in the process.

Unforgiving spirit questions. It's important for the participants to identify if the contamination of unforgiveness is rooted in their heart. It's not a small thing—it's toxic.

Applying Forgiveness

Process feelings. These questions should help the participant see if their heart is prepared to deal with the violator/violation. It's important to note that this process alone could take time.

Acknowledge the truth. This is once again making truth statements and bringing the act into the light. From there, the sinful deed itself can be renounced. THIS IS CRITICAL! We are clearly drawing a distinct line that what happened wasn't right or acceptable. Sin is awful—that doesn't change. People who start to minimize sin ("it wasn't that bad") actually open a door of allowance that can lead to even more pain and devastation. The ultimate truth statement is what God has to say to the participant.

Forgiveness. Letter writing is once again recommended as a critical method for dealing with pain and unforgiveness. This letter doesn't need to be given to anyone unless God directs. It's important that the participants get very specific about both the nature of the sin and the pain it inflicted. This is difficult. But in that confession, God can move in a miraculous way. The prayer of renunciation is foundational to this process.

Grieving a Loss. Participants will likely have at least a few major losses that should be pursued in this process, but it may take time. In fact, all recovery will revolve around a form of grieving. This should be dealt with on an individual basis. The steps to grieving are fairly clear and writing a letter of good-bye to the person or dream that was lost is important.

A Special Note for Group Leaders

I strongly encourage you to spend one session in group prayer before you go to chapter 10. I describe this process as a funeral because all the junk we just revealed is ready to be buried. I also emphasize spiritual warfare, which involves exposing the true Enemy—Satan.

People should bring their lists to the prayer session and be ready to be released from them. The prayer itself can vary as God moves you. We recommend *Steps to Freedom in Christ* by Neil Anderson for examples of powerful prayers.

I use the prayer to acknowledge the spiritual needs and the spiritual warfare taking place. I also use it to emphasize the hurts in our heart and the need for us to both give and receive forgiveness. I pray against the tactics of the Enemy and claim multiple truths about God. I pray that all doors and avenues where Satan had access would be closed in the name of Jesus and especially renounce the sin. I also declare God's love, providence, protection and security from here on out. You may also continue to pray for each other, laying hands on someone who might need to be especially encouraged. The prayer session isn't called for in the workbook, but when doing this in a group setting, I wouldn't go without it!

Chapter 10: Embracing Authentic Identity

After participants have gone through such a dramatic process, they usually enthusiastically welcome this chapter! It basically says, "We may have gotten screwed up, but let's make it work from here on out! God made us for a reason, and He defines our worth and purpose!"

When participants finally begin to see themselves as precious children of God who are loved deeply, they can be grounded and transformed immediately. If they have gone through life identifying themselves as unworthy, unlovable and undeserving, finding the label marked valuable, precious, loved and significant is truly an amazing gift.

But identity is more than just the spiritual. It also involves some of the practical ways every human being is gifted. It's important for people who have lost themselves to their codependence mentalities their entire life to take this process very seriously and recognize it will be lifelong.

If the participants can learn to see their identity and potential through God's eyes, the way they see life can be altered altogether. Not only is the corrupt removed but also the precious truths of God can take root, grow and prosper in their heart. That allows them the freedom to be the person God intended them to be all along.

Group Notes

Several application points in this lesson could be extended to a workshop format. Depending on your group's interest and involvement, you may want to consider doing some of the gifting tests right in your own group. This chapter is about hope and life!

Application Homework

Identity questions. These target those specific areas where the participant is vulnerable to losing identity. It's important to see this in black and white.

Claiming Scripture. While there isn't a step-by-step process a person can do to get Scripture into the heart, this offers some suggestions. The process itself must be initiated through faith and the power of the indwelling of the Holy Spirit. When participants learn to use these practical applications, God has an opportunity to move in a mighty way. God's truths are real—it's just a matter of aligning our heads and hearts to them.

Spiritual gifts questions. Spiritual inventory tests are available on the Internet. I recommend that you find a test and provide it for your group. Then go over each spiritual gift. The issue then becomes how God desires to use their gifts in ministry and beyond.

Vocational questions. I am amazed how many people stay in vocations completely separated from their skills, giftedness and passion. Discovering this can be key to embarking on a spiritual journey to find true calling and purpose.

Personality questions. Learning a bit about personality is helpful, although it could be an entire book in itself! I would suggest keeping this simple in your group. You can search for online Christian personality tests that offer general summaries or use the Myers Briggs personality assessment. There isn't necessarily any solution in discovering our personality. It's more a matter of learning to accept and understand that personality is sometimes how God made us and not something we need to change.

Vision questions. I believe that in recovery we need a vision to carry us through the changes and challenges that lie ahead. Early in my own recovery, I had a vision for this ministry and wrote it down. It seemed ridiculous. People laughed at it! Then, year after year, God orchestrated circumstances that would begin to bring that vision to fruition. The faithfulness of God is astounding! Encourage people (and yourself) that if your vision doesn't happen right now, simply keep praying and ask God for direction.

Chapter 11: Building Healthy Boundaries

Almost every person who enters recovery wants to learn about boundaries immediately. That seems like the most tangible method of getting a grip over the insanity of codependence. But in truth, learning healthy boundaries can't solve all the dysfunction that led to an unhealthy boundary system in the first place. This makes boundaries a "symptom" rather than a "cause" of codependence. As the root issues are resolved, boundaries have a way of naturally becoming healthy.

As we establish our identity on the solid foundation of Jesus Christ and learn to understand our preciousness, we become less vulnerable to letting people run over us. As God deals with our heart, we also come to discover the ways we violate boundaries through our controlling tendencies.

Ultimately, we learn the method God uses to deal with boundary violation and apply it to our own circumstances. Learning to respect God, self and others is entirely possible but not necessarily easy to do in the practical circumstances. Therefore, assure participants that boundaries are a direct by-product of recovery and growth. They need to give it time!

This chapter challenges participants to both assess and understand their own boundary systems and learn how to protect their lives through them. Learning to see God, others and ourselves accurately, as well as understanding our own rights and responsibilities as Christians, is a critical lesson to learn.

Group Notes

This chapter is quite long and intensive but extremely valuable. I would remind participants that they will need to continue using this process long after this workshop ends! In reality, we have to make daily decisions regarding boundaries.

Application Homework

Define boundary systems. It's important for participants to see whether they are more prone to let intrusive things into their life . . . or to overly protect themselves and keep everything out. Most codependents have at least initially had an open boundary system.

Understanding our rights. These questions are key in understanding rights. It's normally an area that has been skewed through codependence.

Write a boundary. There isn't a magic science to this, but this is a general suggestion to begin to see the basic mechanism of a boundary.

Chapter 12: Balancing Principles & Priorities

As people go through the process of healing, a variety of emotions and issues may be exposed. It's important to encourage participants to understand that the process of recovery is lifelong. The mindset of the codependent especially is to fix it all "right away." This is impossible. Rather, it's the process of walking by grace . . . seeing the things that need to be changed . . . and relying on God's grace to transform us moment by moment. This is a marathon, not a sprint.

The biggest gift of recovery is moving from a system of self-effort to a system controlled by the Spirit. Making that change allows everything else to align. We realize as we reach this point that this life is impossible without a total reliance on and an intimate relationship with our Lord.

The relationship challenges we face may still be real, but learning to place God first sets things in proper perspective, teaching us to depend on Him, not people, to get our deepest needs met. Above all else, we come to understand that encountering God is the goal—the biggest ambition and fulfillment of our life because it is the purpose of our life.

Group Notes

Don't overlook some golden nuggets of practical application points in this chapter. Because this is the last chapter, it's easy to rush over them. I suggest that you offer the participants time to review the application projects in this lesson and plan time to discuss what they have learned.

Application Homework

Relationship principle questions. Identifying where the participants are struggling is important, but it's not surprising if they struggle with them all! It's okay—there's always a beginning point to any journey.

Priorities questions. I don't have words to describe how important this set of application points is to the codependent. Writing down daily activities and priorities in journal format will help them gain perspective on what they are doing and what is motivating them. Then the big area of growth occurs when they can actually learn to say no to things that aren't being initiated by God.

God's love letter. Participants should fill in the blanks with those issues that have been most revealed in this process. Once complete, reading this prayer aloud can be effective, but the most important goal here is for them to truly feel God's tenderness, love and involvement in their life—deep inside their heart, not just in their head.

Letter to God. Again, letter writing is such an effective tool. Pouring out our heart to God is a giant step in drawing close to Him in relationship.

Testimonies

If time permits, allow each participate an opportunity to share their own testimony. It will be helpful and encouraging for everyone in the group (and you!) to hear how God worked in their heart.

A House that Grace Built

I'm thrilled to be able to offer a second book that helps us learn that we are called to live a lifestyle of God-dependency. This book was made available in August of 2012. It includes a 350-page book and a 200-page workbook. It's a step-by-step process on dealing with relational issues that have arisen and learning how to love, be intimate and connect as God ordained. If you are interested in learning about this, please contact me personally. I recommend training for anyone leading that group and will offer such training on a regular basis.

Common Questions

What if my church doesn't accept the term "codependency?" Sometimes, church people don't receive anything that sounds remotely secular. The term "codependence" can often fit in this category. As the author, I understand this and struggled with it myself at one point. Personally, I don't defend or try to sell the terminology. At the same time, when you are trying to form a group, you may want title it "relationship issues" or something similar. It should be obvious that this process is far from a secular approach. It's also important to help people understand that these issues apply to almost every person who has ever lived, breathed and walked! The truth is . . . we are all codependent!

What if my group wants to keep meeting after the class is complete? After running a workshop, you may want to form an ongoing group for those people who have graduated. This could be an hour-long support group format that allows people to stay connected and discuss growth. You can also recommend local support groups like these:

- Celebrate Recovery
- Al-anon
- Codependency Anonymous

- Overcomers Anonymous
- Local church recovery groups

How do I help people dealing with active addiction? Very often, people in this group have a spouse, friend, child or other relative under the influence of drugs and alcohol. Sometimes as they gain all this information, God reveals new ways of handling that relationship. More resources may be needed for that person dealing with this. We have a new resource available for this specific dynamic called *Christian Families in Recovery*. Visit www.spiritofliferecovery.com to learn more. Also, find a list of recovery-oriented people in your church who can assist you. New Life Spirit Recovery is a resource center—you can call us for advice and we can refer as needed (714.841.1906).

What if the participant becomes angry or hostile toward this process? If you experience someone who is offended by the material, allow some time for him or her to process. Offer to pray and encourage the best you can. After doing what you can, you can suggest that maybe the timing isn't right. Usually people are angered not by what they hear but because of the issues in their heart that hurt. They normally want help but are afraid they might be excluded. It amazes me what the power of the rejection root can do in a person's life! They can close off the very things that will help them and allow in the things that will bring harm! I want to encourage you to be a seeker of compassion. Be understanding, gentle and kind, even when someone has attitudes and difficulties. They may not be expressing it, but they want to know if this teaching is real and if it can help their own situation.

A reminder of copyright and usage of the materials for group leaders:

Leading a group with this material requires that you adhere to some basic copyright laws. We request that you please use this process as it was written, and not add to or take away the author's intentions. You can certainly customize notes, examples, testimonies and experience, but we ask that you maintain the integrity of the original format. Furthermore, we ask that you please do not extract materials to use stand alone that removes it from the initial context of this workbook. This would include teaching the materials concepts but removing the title of the book. This is considered an infringement on copyright laws. We simply request that if you lead and/or teach this material you do so because you are in agreement with what it contains, and would like to share it and lead the group as the author developed. We trust that God will deeply honor your obedience and desire to serve God's people! Thank you so much for your cooperation!

Other Resources

Treatment and Counseling

Codependence Resources

Online on-demand, live events, on-site and online counseling and training information pertaining to Christian Families in Recovery.

www.spiritofliferecovery.com

www.christiancodependence.org

Professional Substance Addiction Treatment and Counseling

New Life Spirit Recovery

www.newlifespiritrecovery.com

866.543.3361

Professional Codependence Treatment and Counseling

New Life Spirit Recovery

18652 Florida Street, Suite 200

Huntington Beach, CA 92648

www.newlifespiritrecovery.com

866.543.3361

For Referrals to Local Counseling Services:

American Association of Christian Counselors

P.O. Box 739

Forest, VA 24551

800.526.8673

www.aacc.net

Meetings & Groups

Celebrate Recovery

Search locally

www.celebraterecovery.com

Al-Anon

Search locally
www.al-anon.alateen.org

Adult Children of Alcoholics
Search locally
adultchildren.org

Codependents Anonymous
Search locally via website
www.coda.org

Websites

Abortion Recovery
www.abortionrecovery.org

Codependent Resources
www.christiancodependence.org
www.spiritofliferecovery.com

Christian Families in Recovery
www.spiritofliferecovery.com

Focus on the Family
Parenting and information on the family
www.focusonthefamily.com

Focus Ministries
Help for domestic abuse
www.focusministries1.org

Books

A House that Grace Built: Moving Beyond Codependence to Embrace God's Design for Love, Relationships and Wholeness
by Stephanie Tucker

Christian Families in Recovery

by Robert and Stephanie Tucker
Experiencing Father's Embrace
by Jack Frost

Spiritual Slavery to Spiritual Sonship
by Jack Frost

Families Where Grace is in Place
by Jeff VanVonderen

Freedom from Addiction
by Neil Anderson

Steps to Freedom in Christ
by Neil Anderson

A Hunger for Healing
by J. Keith Miller

Love Must Be Tough
by James Dobson

Next Level Parenting
by Rich Rogers

The Love Dare
by Alex and Stephen Kendrich

Have questions?
Call our free resource line at 866.543.3361

PART II:
"A House that Grace Built"
by Stephanie tucker

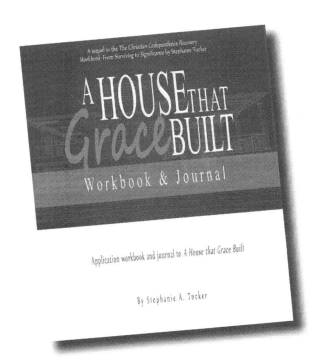

As we are brought back into alignment with God, He wants to teach us how live this life through Him. And what a different way to live indeed! The lifestyle of grace and redemption helps us embrace God's heart and His plans for our relationships!

He gives what we lack.
He restores what was broken.
He completes what He began.

Join the Journey

WWW.CHRISTIANCODEPENDENCE.COM

CHRIST-CENTERED RECOVERY

CHRISTIAN CODEPENDENCE RESOURCES AT SPIRIT OF LIFE RECOVERY

www.spiritofliferecovery.com
www.christiancodependence.org

PROFESSIONAL TREATMENT OPTIONS AT NEW LIFE SPIRIT RECOVERY

New Life Spirit Recovery offers comprehensive and affordable substance abuse and codependent treatment programs with housing accommodations

- State-certified programs
- Co-occurring disorders
- Intensive one-on-one counseling
- Christ-centered groups and classes
- Beautiful housing available
- Located minutes from the beaches of Huntington Beach, CA

**To learn more, please visit
www.newlifespiritrecovery.com**

CALL OUR RESOURCE HOTLINE
1.866.543.3361

Made in the USA
Middletown, DE
15 July 2017